Garden State Gangland

Garden State Gangland

The Rise of the Mob in New Jersey

Scott M. Deitche

ROWMAN & LITTLEFIELD
Lanham • Boulder • New York • London

Published by Rowman & Littlefield
A wholly owned subsidiary of The Rowman & Littlefield Publishing Group, Inc.
4501 Forbes Boulevard, Suite 200, Lanham, Maryland 20706
www.rowman.com

Unit A, Whitacre Mews, 26-34 Stannary Street, London SE11 4AB

British Library Cataloguing in Publication Information Available

Library of Congress Cataloging-in-Publication Data

Names: Deitche, Scott M., author.
Title: Garden state gangland : the rise of the mob in New Jersey / Scott M. Deitche.
Description: Lanham : Rowman & Littlefield, [2017] | Includes bibliographical references and index.
Identifiers: LCCN 2017019023 (print) | LCCN 2017033238 (ebook) | ISBN 9781442267305 (Electronic) | ISBN 9781442267299 (cloth : alk. paper)
Subjects: LCSH: Organized crime—New Jersey—History. | Mafia—New Jersey—History. | Crime—New Jersey—History.
Classification: LCC HV6452.N5 (ebook) | LCC HV6452.N5 D45 2017 (print) | DDC 364.10609749—dc23 LC record available at https://lccn.loc.gov/2017019023

Printed in the United States of America

Contents

Contents

Acknowledgments

I first thank my wife for all her love, support, and, especially, patience through the writing of this and all of my books.

I thank my family for their continued support. Thanks as always to my literary agent, Gina Panettieri, who is always there with advice, guidance, and the ability to make things happen. Thanks to Kathryn, Will, and all the staff at Rowman & Littlefield for their hard work in bringing the book to print.

For help with references, sources, and stories I thank Scott Burnstein, Christian Cipollini, Ed Leiber, Myron Sugerman, Joe Ricciardi, Oscar Goodman, T. J. English, George Anastasia, Tom Hunt, Dominic Woods, David Uslan, Michael Uslan, Mike Russell, John Alite, Sean Richard, Lou DiVita, Ron Fino, Sandy Lansky, G. Robert Blakey, Bob Delaney, the staff at the New Jersey State Commission of Investigation (Kathy Hennessy Riley, Lee Seglem, and Mike Hoey), Lennert van 't Riet, Diane Norek Harrison, David Amoruso, Kenny K., Gary Rappaport, The Black Hand Forum and Real Deal Forum (especially B.), Avi Bash for the use of his photos, Lorcan Otway at the Museum of the American Gangster in New York, Newark Museum archivist and librarian William A. Peniston, Paul Guzzo, Glenn G. Geisheimer at Old Newark, Professor Michael Green, the staff at the Mob Museum in Las Vegas (especially Jonathan Ullman, Geoff Schumacher, Ashley Misko, and Ashley Erickson), and all my other "sources."

Special thanks to Richard Warner for sharing with me his trove of materials on D'Amico and Troia. And another big shout-out to Fred Martens, who allowed me access to his unparalleled library of books and materials.

For anyone I forgot, I'll catch you on the next book!

Introduction

Perth Amboy, New Jersey, is located at the confluence of the Raritan and Arthur Kill River in central New Jersey, just across the Outerbridge Crossing from Staten Island. Once an industrial powerhouse, Amboy became a rust-belt city but was able to hold on to enough of its blue-collar workers to keep it from sliding into total decay and population loss. In the 1950s, when the factories were still running, the city's population of forty-one thousand included thousands of hard laborers, working hard every day for a paycheck that paid the bills and little more.

They gathered in the local taverns and watering holes, like the Bridge Plaza Bar, after work to swap stories, drink a few beers, and maybe place a bet. Large-scale dice games and bookmaking drop-offs were scattered throughout the city. Bookmaking was happening in diverse businesses like Sciortino's Market, the Elks Club, George's Shoe Repair Store, and the Midway Restaurant. There was some oversight by organized crime. Joseph "Whitey" Danzo, local labor leader, and an associate of the Elizabeth-based DeCavalcante crime family, oversaw gambling operations across Middlesex County. Gamblers like Jack Brennan and Pat Russo covered parts of Perth Amboy, and raids were not uncommon, like one in October of 1963 that netted over a dozen gambling figures.

John Lester Deitche was known to friends and family (including his grandson, the author) as Jay. He was an ironworker. Though a member of Local 399 in Camden, he worked out of Local 373 in Perth Amboy, where he also lived. Working on municipal projects and office buildings across the New York/New Jersey metro area, Jay's work was tiring and physically demanding. After-work happy hours with coworkers was as common then as now.

Jay brought home the same pay as his coworkers laying out rebar. But unlike his coworkers Jay always seemed to be a little ahead. When his buddies pulled a few crumpled dollars out of their wallets to pay for drinks after work, Jay pulled out a fat money clip. At social events, while his friends wore threadbare suits that had been patched up repeatedly, he wore tailor-cut suits with encrusted tie clips. For a guy netting two hundred dollars a week, he had quite a collection of five hundred dollar suits.

Truth be known, for the better part of thirty years, Jay Deitche was a bookmaker. A World War II veteran, Deitche started bookmaking after returning home from Europe. He took bets at the bar on the ground floor of the Palace Hotel on Madison Avenue in Perth Amboy, the same hotel where he would stay when his wife, Dorothy, kicked him out for his philandering. His other betting-shop locations were the Lido Gardens Chinese restaurant and Lehighs Tavern, both in downtown Perth Amboy. When Jay was not at home, Dorothy and their son, Peter, would take any bets that came via phone. The operation had run that way for years, winding through the network of old-man bars and corner watering holes that dotted the city.

Jay also ventured southward, across the Victory Bridge that spanned the Raritan River, to South Amboy. When the bulk of his customer base started shifting that way, Jay followed. His main place of business in the early 1970s was the Gay 90s bar in South Amboy. The Gay 90s was located on First Street, in the downtown core. The bottom floor was the bar, with two apartments upstairs. The bar was a popular neighborhood hangout, a member of the local Tavern Association. It was famous for its thin-crust tomato pies. It had the usual bar amenities like a pool table and a piano player who sat behind the bar belting out the latest sing-alongs for the sloshed crowd. To the underage drinkers who frequented the bar, Jay was known as "Raccoon Eyes."

In late 1972, unbeknownst to Jay, the New Jersey State Police were looking into the bookmaking activities going on at the bar, specifically targeting the bartender, whom they believed to be the ringleader. They sent in some undercover agents to stake the place out and gather intelligence. One of the undercover officers was a woman who managed to turn some heads, including Jay's. Though he spent his life married to Dorothy, his eyes—and hands—wandered often. Once, during World War II, he had his sergeant's bars stripped off after making a pass and grabbing the bare leg of one of the Andrews Sisters before a USO performance.

Jay sauntered over to the undercover agent and started chatting away, letting slip what a big deal he was in town and how he was a major bookmaker. She was very interested and pressed him for more information. Jay willingly talked away. It turned out that, in addition to gathering intel, she was also equipped with a recording device she had hoped to use on the bartender. Instead she found a new target.

Jay went in for the sale, asking if she wanted to make some bets on a couple football games. She willingly gave him a few dollars, and he accepted. They talked for a few more minutes, and then she excused herself. She walked outside and waited, along with a couple of fellow law-enforcement personnel. After a while, Jay walked outside, toward his car. The police arrested him and took him to the station, where he was charged with bookmaking.

After the arrest, Jay scaled back on his betting operation while awaiting trial. Although the state attorney was prosecuting gamblers at a record pace, Jay may have been able to make a deal had he been willing to turn on his fellow bookies (which he wasn't going to do) or if he had a competent criminal attorney representing him. Jay did not want to the neighbors to think he was a criminal, so, instead of hiring a criminal defense attorney, he hired a real estate attorney who lived up the street from him.

As expected, with a real estate lawyer representing him, things didn't turn out all too well for Jay at the trial. Unable to come up with any sort of reasonable defense, Jay was found guilty. He went home to prepare for his sentencing hearing.

On the day of his sentencing hearing, Dorothy stayed at home, expecting that Jay would get off with just a slap on the wrist. It was his first brush with the law, after all. She made a big dinner while Peter took his father to court.

At the hearing Jay and his real estate attorney stood in front of the judge, who addressed Jay.

"I sentence you to a year and a day in prison and a thousand dollar fine."

Jay cupped his hands to his ear and leaned forward, offering, in a meek voice, "I'm sorry, I can't hear too good since the war."

The judge leaned forward and shouted, "A year and a day and a thousand dollar fine!" Down came the gavel.

On January 22, 1973, Jay reported to Trenton State Prison to start serving his sentence. A few months later he was transferred to Bayside State Prison in Leesburg, New Jersey, a minimum-security facility. Due to good behavior, he was paroled on June 19, 1973. He swore his days as a bookmaker were over, as he didn't want his grandson to think of him as a criminal.

Authorities never worked far enough up the ladder to see who the ultimate contacts were. In the grand scheme of things Jay Deitche was a small fish in the vast underworld. But there were Jay Deitches in every seedy old-man bar across Jersey. They were the workhorses, the ground-level face of the mob figures who controlled vast swaths of industry, unions, and the underworld in New Jersey for most of the twentieth century.

Chapter One

The Newark Family

To trace the start of traditional organized crime (the mob, the syndicate, the Mafia) in New Jersey, you could begin in a few cities around the state where new immigrant groups at the turn of the twentieth century fell victim to extortion gangs and police indifference. It was in these tight-knit immigrant neighborhoods where the strands and threads of organized-crime groups began. But if there was one focal point, one birthplace where originated the larger, more influential crime figures who would shape both the underworld and overall history of the state through much of the twentieth century, it would be Newark.

Newark, to many, is defined by the airport, the factories, the fuel refineries, and the acres of shipping containers lined up in a patchwork of faded colors and logos. In short, the image of the crowded, postindustrial New Jersey landscape is literally defined and reinforced by the flight into and out of Newark. As one of the dominant nexuses of air, rail, and port shipping in the country, the city's economic vitality is often overshadowed by a certain lack of aesthetics. But beneath the veneer lies a city with a rich and varied history that traces back to the Puritans.

By the early 1900s Newark was the largest city in New Jersey, a title that it continues to hold today despite population losses in the middle part of the twentieth century. In the early twentieth century, buoyed by expanding industries and its emergence as the epicenter of transportation in the region, Newark attracted domestic immigrants from across the United States as well as foreign immigrants making their way through Ellis Island. They settled in immigrant neighborhoods like the First Ward, which was primarily Italian, and the Third Ward, the Jewish section of town. In these densely packed neighborhoods, with new citizens wary and suspicious of the police, criminals saw easy pickings. By preying on their own community, they could make money with little fear of law-enforcement retribution. As a newspaper editor in 1909 stated, "The leeches for the most part prey on their own countrymen."[1] Even through the mid and later decades of the 1900s Newark was a fertile ground for wiseguys, the neighborhoods acting as catalysts, churning out young wiseguys out of neighborhoods, like Vailsburg. "Listen, I grew up in that life. It was as normal as rain. Okay? It was everywhere; there were seven crime families in my neighborhood [Vailsburg] as a kid growing up, as well as my father who had spent a great deal of his life in prison, and other relatives. These were my role models."[2]

One of the earliest type of gangs—though not an "official" organized-crime group—that plagued Italian immigrant communities was the Black Hand. The moniker referred to the practice of placing a print of a black hand on a letter to the family of a kidnapping victim, demanding money for the person's return, often a store owner or other wealthier member of the community. Other missives bearing the black hand would simply be letters of extortion, exhorting their targets to pay up or suffer the consequences. The Black Hand was not a monolithic organized-crime enterprise but, rather, loosely affiliated groups of criminals looking for a quick payday, and kidnapping an immigrant whose family would be fearful of going to the police was for many street-level criminals an easy way to make money.

The letters that Black Hand gangsters sent their targets often fell along the same lines. One such letter was received by a wealthy Italian immigrant in the town of Bound Brook, about thirty miles southwest of Newark, in 1904. It is here translated from the original Italian.

> We have spent much time and have been bothered a great deal about the matter, and have decided to take twenty-five persons for example. We will begin with you. You have no children who will benefit us. You make $25 to $30 a week and in the period of two years you have accumulated $1500.
>
> You must now donate us $200 and you have to bring that amount of money to the first bridge in Somerville at 11:30, Saturday, New Year's Eve.
>
> There you will find a boy sitting on the rail of the bridge. When you stop he will come up to the front of you. After you give him the money you will be safe. If you do not give him that sum of money and you run away we will follow you all over, wherever you may go, and you will be killed.
>
> After you will be other people that will have to pay their amount. We are 1,000 people who live that way and we can't starve to death with our families. Therefore send the money or be killed. Say nothing to nobody, it will be worse for you. Killed, killed, killed. Sig. Black Hand.[3]

The earliest Black Hand gangs operated in nearby New York and among early Italian immigrant neighborhoods in the early 1900s. In New Jersey the activities spanned small towns through the north and central parts of the state, like Bridgewater and Bound Brook, but many of the Black Hand crimes were aimed at merchants and businessmen in the Italian enclave of Newark's First Ward.[4]

The activities of the gangs did not go unnoticed to the population at large. The residents themselves spread word of the Black Hand extortionists through neighborhood tales and calls in local newspapers to stand up to the gangs. And along with cries of justice for the neighborhoods under siege of the Black Hand was a call for restraint in the face of anti-immigrant, especially anti-Italian, sentiment that was growing along with the outrage. The April 16, 1909, issue of the *Asbury Park Press* wrote, "The vast majority of Italians that come to America are hardworking, law abiding, desirable immigrants. These decent nine-tenths are the ones most interested in stopping the importation of the degenerate one-tenth. . . . The Italians themselves are the sufferers. They are the ones chiefly entitled to sympathy and protection. Therefore the last thing that should be permitted to result from this atrocity is any trace of race prejudice. The crusade is against criminals, not against any nationality."[5]

There was also the understanding that the Black Hand activities in the early 1900s may have been connected not only to Italy's Mafia and Camorra (an organized-crime group based out of Naples) but also to the presence of those underworld syndicates in the United States. "Just how much connection there is between the operations of the Black Hand in America and the nefarious doings of the Camorra, the Mafia and other secret criminal societies in Italy the best informed police will not or cannot say."[6]

Some in law enforcement did see the connection as the Mafia and Camorra were becoming a presence in America. Though the Black Hand was not a structured criminal enterprise and often more accurately described as a method of criminal activity rather than an organization, it was out of these gangs that some of the early Mafia figures emerged, and extortion activities brought them income for their climb up the underworld ladder. In many ways these gangs served as internships for career criminals who learned their trade with other like-minded gangsters. Some of the earliest true Mafia bosses and soldiers started their criminal careers as young men in these street gangs.

Even though the initial suspicion of the Italian community in dealing with law enforcement kept may victims of Black Hand crime from going to police, there were some major steps forward in assisting them with the help of local Italian immigrants who joined the police force.

The criminal activities that plagued the Italian immigrant community in the First Ward brought attention from a local advocate, Detective Thomas Adubato, the first Italian detective in Newark. The imposing officer, who "stood well over six feet tall and sported a thick handlebar mustache,"[7] made it his mission to take on the Black Hand gangs. His contemporaries in the Newark PD considered him "by far the best detective in homicide cases Newark has known in years."[8] Adubato himself was no stranger to confrontation and did not hesitate to use force when necessary. While investigating a case in a saloon in 1909 the saloonkeeper drew a revolver and shot at Adubato five times, hitting the detective in the arm. In turn, the detective drew his revolver and shot the man dead.

On August 16, 1918, Adubato, home in bed, sick, was visited by fellow officers. A local gangster had shot and killed another man in Newark, and the police officers wanted some advice. Instead Adubato got dressed and joined them. He caught the trail of the suspect and followed him to a tenement on the Lower East Side in New York City. Adubato recruited a fellow New York officer to accompany him into the building to arrest the suspect. Adubato "burst in the door and was about to enter the rooms when a volley of shots rang out."[9] The suspect shot both Adubato and the New York officer. Despite being hit by bullets, Adubato carried the injured New York officer down five flights of stairs, got the officer into the patrol car, and drove to safety. Unfortunately, Adubato's wounds proved to be too much for the detective, and he died a few hours later at Bellevue Hospital.[10]

By the late 1910s the underworld in Newark was a mix of various gangs, mostly street-level. Over the next decade, some of the gangs would merge and grow, while others drifted away. Black Hand activities started to wane after the federal government began cracking down on the mailing of Black Hand letters and punishments for the crimes associated with the threats increased. So, too, as Italians became more comfortable with their new homeland, the fear of going to the police started to abate somewhat, though extortion maintained its place in the mob's hierarchy of criminal rackets for decades to come.

Some of the gangs were led by future gambling-syndicate and Mafia leaders. There was a Neapolitan gang in the First Ward and a group in the Jewish Third Ward, and there were independent gangs in the Ironbound. But there were also two nascent Sicilian Mafia groups in the area that were bringing in the organization of the Old World syndicates. One of the early New Jersey Mafia families was based out of Elizabeth and the other a homegrown Newark entity.

The Elizabeth crew rose to become New Jersey's only homegrown Mafia family, while the Newark group split apart, sending recruits to Mafia families across the New York/New Jersey metropolitan area. It is this latter family that has largely been a mystery to researchers and historians working to piece together the history of the Mafia in the United States. With scraps of information gleaned from after-the-fact accounts, a picture begins to emerge of this enigmatic crime syndicate. There is very little known for sure about the Newark Mafia family, but one of the early heads of that organization was a Newark businessman, Gaspare D'Amico. Born in Villabate, Palermo, in 1886, D'Amico left Palermo for America in April of 1910, aboard the SS *Re d'Italia*, an ocean liner that had been launched in 1906 and accommodated over two thousand passengers. He arrived in New York City on April 19, 1910, and was processed through Ellis Island. By the 1920s, D'Amico ran the D'Amico Macaroni Company on Drift Street in the First Ward. He lived just north of the neighborhood in a well-appointed apartment building.

While D'Amico's hold on the Newark crime family appeared to be strong, there were rumblings of a challenge from a newcomer to the area, Vincent Troia. He was an interesting mob character. Born in Italy, Troia lived in both Rockford, Illinois, and Madison, Wisconsin, where he was involved in a number of rackets, especially bootlegging. He is listed in some FBI reports as an early member of the Madison crime family, while some researchers peg him as an early boss of the Springfield, Illinois, crime family, where he lived for a short time. Then there is his involvement in the Rockford area, which developed its own independent crime family. Other sources note that Troia was close to Salvatore Maranzano, one of the early heads of the Mafia in New York City, who ascended to power following the assassination of Joe "the Boss" Masseria in Coney Island on April 15, 1931.

Troia was indicted in Rockford in the mid-1930s for the illicit production of liquor, but by that time he had moved to Newark. The reasons for his relocation are not known. It's not clear whether he was brought there by other Mafia figures, like Maranzano, or he went of his own accord to avoid law-enforcement pressure in Illinois. What is known is that once he was in Newark, Troia quickly moved into illegal gambling and the local numbers rackets. FBI files indicate he was the "operator of the Two Eagles Italian Lottery, one of four such lotteries operating in the City of Newark."[11] He moved to the Roseville neighborhood, just west of Branch Brook Park.

Troia began to make moves against D'Amico with the intent of taking control of the Newark family. Here too, it's unclear whether he had the backing of one of the New York families or he was acting alone. He did have a small crew of men under him, so he was not operating in a vacuum, and his emergence on the scene certainly did not go unnoticed by D'Amico. And D'Amico was certainly hearing chatter that Troia was gunning for him. But the wily D'Amico decided to make the first move, to head off a major war.

On the morning of August 22, 1935, Vincent Troia and one of his men, Frank Longo, were at a candy store at 317 South Sixth Street in Newark. Longo was from Springfield, Illinois—where, recall, Troia also had lived for a short time—and had moved to the nearby town of Bloomfield, New Jersey. Four other men, including Jerome Bevinetto and Antonio Sunsara, who had been left in charge of the candy store while the owner was visiting Italy, and Vincent's stepson, Joseph Troia, were playing cards at a table in the middle of the one-story building. It was believed that the location was one of the headquarters for Troia's lottery operations.

Just before 11 a.m. a black sedan pulled up on the curb outside the store, which sat at the northwest corner of Sixth Street and Fifteenth Avenue, just west of downtown. Three men got out. According to reports, "one man held two revolvers, two others one each. They stood in the doorway and sprayed twenty shots into the small store."[12] Vincent Troia was hit in the upper back and killed instantly, as was Longo. Joseph Troia and the other card players were hit at the table; two of them managed to crawl away.

The gunmen got back into the black sedan—which was registered to a man in Union City, New Jersey, who had reported it stolen back in March— and sped away. Police later recovered the car not too far from the scene with the murder weapons still inside. People who lived around the candy store were out in force to see what the commotion was all about. As the newspaper described it, the neighborhood, "inhabited principally by Italians, was thrown into an uproar."[13]

Back at the candy store, the initial thought was that it had been an argument over the card game, as the place was a mess of cards all over the floor. But police also found lottery slips and quickly took a view that this had been a gangland killing. Police held the two survivors, Nicholas "Big Nick" Calliachi and Charles Barraco, as material witnesses, hoping to glean any information they could as to why the shooting had occurred. Authorities also stepped across state lines to arrest Leonardo Cippoli, a Brooklyn resident about whom police received a tip. After witnesses failed to place him at the scene, he was released.

At the hospital Joseph Troia was falling in and out of consciousness, awakening long enough to see two detectives glowering over him. They repeatedly asked Joseph who the assailants were, but he refused to give them any information and fell back under. Within a few days, Joseph Troia succumbed to his injuries. Police were no closer to finding the killer.

It's unclear who ordered the hit on Troia, but it's likely that D'Amico took the opportunity to strike first against Troia's incursions. Some sources suggest that Troia had slapped D'Amico in front of his men, enraging the leader. Or it could have been internal wrangling over lottery operations in the Troia faction. Immediately after the shooting, police believed that "the men were shot by gunmen hired by proprietors of a rival lottery."[14] That could have, of course, included D'Amico and his men.

Regardless of the reason for the Troia shooting, with his rival out of the way, D'Amico retained leadership of the Newark family. But that time at the top would not last long. Around 11:30 a.m. on February 22, 1937, Gaspare and his father, Domenico, were packing macaroni on the ground floor of their factory. A few employees were working on the second floor, but most of the staff had the day off. A lone hit man, armed with a revolver, walked into the factory—without anyone giving him a second glance—and started shooting. Gunshots erupted through the factory, hitting Gaspare and his father. The employees upstairs came running down, while the gunman dropped his revolver and took off in a waiting car. Gaspare and his father lay on the ground bleeding.

Domenico was shot in the chest and leg, while Gaspare was hit in the abdomen and leg. Ambulances arrived and took the elder D'Amico to City Hospital and Gaspare to St. Michael's. The newspapers described his father's condition as critical immediately after the shooting, and the elder D'Amico did succumb to his wounds.[15] Gaspare recovered but was shaken by what had transpired.

After the shooting it was clear to Gaspare that his days in Newark were numbered, so he left the city and the crime family.[16] Theories about the attempted assassination of D'Amico center on a falling-out he had with Joe Profaci, once his biggest supporter in the underworld. With D'Amico out of the picture, the Commission—the Mafia's governing body—reportedly disbanded the Newark family, spreading the members around the New York families.

The demise of the Newark Mafia family also allowed the expansion of another small family operating less than ten miles to the south of Newark, in the city of Elizabeth. This industrial town was less than a third of the size of Newark but had a small Mafia family already operating there, which would come to be known in later years as the DeCavalcante family. Lore, and some mobsters, says that it is one of the oldest operating mob families in the country, but its formative years are murky, as are its ties to the Newark family.

A name that has been floated by some researchers over the years as the original boss of the family was Newark-based mobster Stefano Badami. Originally from Sicily, by the 1920s Badami was an influential member of the Newark family, though his official role is up for debate. Regardless, after the disbanding of the Newark family following D'Amico's hasty retreat from Newark, Badami was alleged to have stepped in to oversee the Elizabeth faction. But the available evidence doesn't necessarily back this up.

Per records, Badami never lived in Elizabeth. In 1942 Badami lived in Orange, a town to the west of Newark. And while the proximity of the two cities doesn't necessarily mean that Badami could have run the family from a distance (as latter bosses did), the early years of the Elizabeth family were very neighborhood-centric and comprised primarily of immigrants from the Ribera area of Sicily, which Badami was not (he was from Corleone, Sicily). There is also the absence of Badami's name in wiretaps from the 1960s of Elizabeth crime family members, where they discuss the history of the crime family.

More compelling evidence comes from famed Mafia turncoat Joe Valachi. In his 1963 testimony to the McClellan Commission, Valachi talks about the formative years of the Mafia in the New York City area, including New Jersey. Valachi refers to Badami (mistyped in the commission transcripts as

Padami) as "Don Steven" and asserts that he was actually the boss of the Newark family by 1930 and that Sam Monaco was his underboss. Monaco was described by police at the time as a "high type racketeer and alcohol trader."[17]

While Badami stayed out of the limelight for the most part, Sam Monaco was gaining a higher profile in the underworld, mainly due to his loyalty to the new powerhouse in the New York Mafia, Salvatore Maranzano. After solidifying his powerful role in the early New York Mafia following the murder of Joe "The Boss" Masseria in April of 1931, Maranzano utilized a cadre of up-and-coming young mobsters to position himself for a long reign at the top of the mob. But his arrogance and hunger for power led to his downfall, less than five months after Masseria.

Salvatore Maranzano was killed at 2 p.m. on the afternoon of September 10, 1931, at the New York Central Building at 230 Park Avenue in New York City. The self-appointed boss of bosses was visited by four gangsters recruited by Lucky Luciano and Meyer Lansky. The hit men were dressed as police. Maranzano was unaware the police were gangsters and let them into his back office. As he walked them back in, they shot and stabbed him, leaving the mob boss to die on the floor.

In the immediate aftermath of the Maranzano killing, an urban legend was born. Termed the Night of the Sicilian Vespers, it postulated that dozens of old-school mafiosi were killed at the hands of the younger, Americanized mobsters under the wing of Lucky Luciano. In reality there is little evidence to suggest that a large-scale mob purge occurred. However, there were some Maranzano loyalists who fell as a result of Luciano's move against Maranzano.

Just four days after the brazen killing of Salvatore Maranzano, two bodies were discovered in the Passaic River near Harrison, New Jersey, just up from the river's mouth in Newark Bay. The first body was identified as Sam Monaco, Badami's underboss. When police fished Monaco's body out of Newark Bay, they found his head and jaws beaten in, his body tied with a clothesline, weighted down by four sash weights. Harrison police also discovered the body of another New Jersey mobster, Louis "Babe Ruth" Russo. His body also showed the same signs of head trauma, though he was weighted down by a large rock. Russo had lived in Passaic, New Jersey. Russo's main source of income had been shaking down other racketeers, a particularly dangerous profession.

Police managed to piece together the movements of the two men. A few days prior, on the afternoon of September 10, just after hearing about the murder of Maranzano, both Monaco and Russo had taken off together from Newark in Monaco's car. A few hours later, Monaco's car was found on West Forty-Seventh Street in Manhattan around the corner from Maranzano's headquarters.

Initial reports tied the Monaco and Russo murders to the November 3, 1930, slaying of Dominic "the Ape" Passelli, a Newark gangster with a long list of enemies. But another theory suggests that Russo and Monaco were Maranzano loyalists and were killed as part of the Maranzano slaying, to pull power away from the established boss and his faction, into Luciano's sphere of influence. Bringing things back around, twenty-four years later, Sam Monaco's brother Frank was held as a material witness in a gangland killing of his brother's old partner in the dress business and one-time Newark crime-family member. The victim of the murder was Stefano Badami.

While it's very likely that Stefano Badami was not the first, or even any, boss of the Elizabeth crime family, establishing who exactly was the first boss, it's necessary to set the scene for the neighborhood from which the crime group emerged. For decades, immigrants from the small village of Ribera, in the province of Agrigento, had been arriving in Elizabeth, congregating primarily in the Peterstown section of town, known to locals as "the Burg." Peterstown is located between First Avenue and the Arthur Kill. The Elizabeth River, a small tributary of the kill, runs along the southwest border of the neighborhood. The close-knit community continues to thrive to the present. And though many of the latter generations have moved to other areas, they still come back to the neighborhood for weddings, events, and church functions and to eat and shop in the cluster of Italian restaurants and markets.

It was from this close-knit community that the Elizabeth family emerged. One of the family's strengths was that so many of the members were from, or had ties to, Ribera, and this connection allowed the crime family to keep outsiders, and the prying eyes of law enforcement, away from its operations, at least in the early years. The Ribera core group that formed this early Mafia family was bound by a shared heritage, making the group somewhat insular for much of its existence. And Badami did not come from Ribera or live in the neighborhood.

The Elizabeth family is also considered among one of the oldest crime families in the United States, though that sentiment is believed more by their own members rather than researchers who point to crime families in New Orleans and New York as being around for as long, if not longer. Charles "Beeps" Stango, an Elizabeth mobster arrested in 2015, was caught on a wiretap talking about the crime family, specifically a member named "Milk,"[18] whose family "started the whole thing. See his uncle the underboss of consiglieres since the beginning of time. They come right from Sicily to here . . . This is *sii* . . . okay this proves he's the oldest crew in the country. They start, they originated the Five Families. Okay?"[19] Another crime family member, Anthony Rotondo, testifying in 2005 was asked if the Elizabeth family was a proud crime family:

(ROTONDO) ANSWER: Yes

Q: Well, they were the oldest Mafia family in the country, yes?

A: Yes.[20]

So, while the original boss is not definitively known, one of the earliest bosses in the Elizabeth area was definitely Phil Amari. He was born in Ribera and arrived in Elizabeth in the early 1920s via New York. When Amari made the move to Elizabeth, "other individuals who were originally from Ribera, Sicily, moved to Elizabeth from the New York area,"[21] joining the small existing Ribera community there. An informant later disclosed to the FBI that Amari, in his opinion, was "the one-time boss of the Mafia in the Elizabeth area."[22]

Amari's legitimate job was in the finance industry, as a loan officer, but his income stream diversified to include a variety of rackets including gambling, narcotics, and labor racketeering. Amari recruited from the neighborhood and stocked the crime family with members whose names carried the family's mantle, and leadership, through the ensuing decades. Soldiers and capos like Louis Larasso, Frank Majuri, and Emmanuel Riggi came up under Phil Amari. And under Amari's leadership, the Elizabeth crime family became a permanent part of the Jersey gangland scene.

This early mix of Mafia families, Jewish syndicates, and miscellaneous gangs spread across northern New Jersey was far from the only underworld activity going on in the Garden State. Starting on January 17, 1920, with the Eighteenth Amendment and the prohibition of the manufacture, transport, and sale of alcoholic beverages, the various bays, inlets, and waterfronts down the Jersey Shore and up into the Delaware River became hotbeds of bootlegging and the criminal empires moved out of the confines of the big cities and onto the beach.

Chapter Two

Dry Years in Jersey

The Jersey Shore is deceptive in size, seemingly insignificant, but measuring approximately 130 miles long. From Raritan Bay down to the tip of Cape May and around into the Delaware River, the shore is interspersed with inlets and coves, protected by long stretches of barrier islands and some of the most famous beaches in the United States both from an historical perspective (e.g., Atlantic City) and pop culture (e.g., Seaside Heights of *Jersey Shore* fame).

Today beach communities dot the shoreline up and down the coast. But in the 1920s, though some areas were tourist attractions, there were large stretches of open shoreline on the Atlantic, as well as areas in the back bays with little habitation. These areas became well-used drop-off points for boot-leggers running whiskey from offshore moored vessels transporting the liquid gold from Canada, Ireland, and the United Kingdom during Prohibition. Those intrepid seamen were collectively known as rumrunners, though rum was not the major liquor being smuggled into New Jersey (whiskey topping that list).

The rum-running system was simple in scope but relied on a series of well-timed maneuvers and machinations to make it all work. Smuggling ships laden with illicit alcohol from Europe, Canada, and even the Caribbean, would drop anchor twelve miles offshore in international waters. From there speedboats would be dispatched to meet up with the ships, which in turn offloaded their shipments to the smaller, swifter boats. The boats, able to outrun the US Coast Guard's fleet, would speed to shore where they would be met by trucks that would take the crates of booze to warehouses dotted across New Jersey, especially in Newark. The men recruited to unload the boats and drive the trucks to the warehouse were paid up to twenty dollars a night, which was a big paycheck for that time.

The speedboats that the rumrunners used were a uniquely New Jersey creation. Dubbed "Jersey speed skiffs," the boats, still raced and operated up and down the Jersey Shore today, were created in the early 1920s by Harold "Pappy" Seaman for racing out of his Long Branch base. The sleek wooden boats quickly gained favor among the bootlegging syndicates. The earliest boats were around fifteen feet long and powered by a twenty-two-horsepower engine, reaching speeds over twenty miles per hour. Modifications to that design increased the size of the boats and enhanced the top speed to over forty miles per hour.

It was off the coast of New Jersey that one of the most celebrated rum-running captains would run into trouble, twice, that ultimately ended his legendary career. William McCoy, born in Jacksonville, Florida, was a boat-yard owner who was approached to run some booze onshore from past the three-mile limit. Soon Bill McCoy was off and running with a large smuggling operation, first with his schooner, the ninety-foot *Henry L. Marshall*. He found success with a simple business model: deliver high-quality booze at a good price. "From dealing with bootleggers I found that they were mostly thieves and thugs and I concluded that a man running whisky on an honest basis and within the law could make money. I sold Scotch for twenty-two dollars a case and made four dollar profit on the case. Buyers always knew Scotch I sold was good and they would get a full case of twelve bottles. No short-changing or short cases."[1]

He called himself the King of the Rumrunners, and the press ate it up. One newspaper lavishly fawned over his appearance, noting, "His bearing is regal and assured. He has the manner of a man born tall, strong body and a muscular, good-humored face. His skin has been tanned to the color of leather by tropical sun and wind. His eyes are keen and intelligent. White wrinkles at the corners indicate that they have looked for a long time across wide waters, and laughed."[2] Another called him a "Volsteadian hero" who was "handsome, glamorous, soft spoken, well educated," and, essential for any self-respecting rumrunner, "perfectly manicured."[3]

But the *Marshall* ran into trouble on August 3, 1921, when the *Seneca*, a 240-foot-long coast guard cutter, intercepted the ship four miles off the coast of Atlantic City. Sailing under a British flag, the *Marshall* was towed back to New York Harbor after the coast guard found over fifteen hundred cases of liquor onboard. The ship was actually seized four miles off the coast, outside the three-mile maritime limit, but the coast guard insisted they had the right to seize the vessel because they had evidence of a conspiracy, likely referring to the fact they had spotted the *Marshall* being visited by smaller motorboats that then ran back to shore.

After the *Marshall* incident, McCoy relocated to the island of Saint Pierre, near Newfoundland. He made good money on the island with his other ship, a 130-foot schooner, the *Arethusa*. But the allure and money to be made from smuggling to the Jersey Shore was a lot to pass up. McCoy rechristened the *Arethusa* the *Tomoka* and started smuggling back in US waters.

In the early morning of November 25, 1923, the *Tomoka* was off the coast of Sea Bright, New Jersey, when, once again, McCoy came to square off against the US Coast Guard boat *Seneca*. After a chase of a few miles, the *Seneca* lobbed four shells into the water in front of the *Tomoka*. The smuggling vessel stopped, and the coast guard overtook it. When the Coasties went aboard and searched the ship, they found McCoy down below, surrounded by four hundred cases of whisky. According to the coast guard, it was all that was left of a massive 4,200 case shipment the *Tomoka* was bringing up from the Bahamas. McCoy had sixty thousand dollars on him when the coast guard searched him. The *Tomoka* seizure set off a diplomatic row when both Great Britain and Canada demanded the release of several British and Canadian sailors on the vessel. The men of the *Tomoka* were charged with smuggling. McCoy went through a couple years of legal back-and-forth and ended up serving a short stint in jail. When he got out, in part due to increased competition, he withdrew from the rum-running game. But there were always thirsty people at the Jersey Shore.

One of the first beach communities to benefit from the illicit liquor trade that developed in the wake of Prohibition was the resort town of Atlantic City. The city was run on tourist dollars. As far back as the late 1880s, over half a million people came to Atlantic City in the summer to walk up and down its famous boardwalk, at its height over four miles long. Luxury hotels were built to accommodate the swelling crowds, and tourist attractions of all kinds, from night clubs and family entertainment to the iconic Lucy the Elephant, still standing today as a symbol of Atlantic City's past. The boom continued into the early part of the 1900s as Atlantic City became the go-to vacation spot for residents from across the southern tier of New Jersey, especially Philadelphia.

Then there was the Steel Pier. Still a focal point of the boardwalk, back in the early 1900s the pier was home to an amusement park, movie theaters, shows, and the famous diving horse. Dubbed the "Showplace of the Nation," the pier jutted over fifteen hundred feet into the ocean and featured hundreds of soon-to-be famous actors and musicians over the years. The pier was part of the Atlantic City appeal, the engine that drove the economy of the town—and one that was, at least on paper, billed as family fun. But there was a different attraction to Atlantic City for a certain segment of the tourist population. This attraction was based on vice, and Atlantic City offered it up in spades. From gambling to prostitution to drinking on Sunday (not allowed in other parts of the state), the city was a Vegas-style nonstop party for those seeking forbidden pleasures.

And when Prohibition became the law of the land, what better place than Atlantic City to flout the law, setting itself up as the illicit-liquor capital of New Jersey? Many of the restaurants openly served liquor in defiance of the new law, while others sought to maximize the city's geographic location to bring booze onshore and reap the rewards of smuggling. At the center of it all stood the undisputed boss of the city, who had one foot in the underworld and the other in the upperworld.

The book and HBO TV show *Boardwalk Empire* fleshed out the story of Prohibition-era Atlantic City through the story of Enoch "Nucky" Johnson, a political powerhouse and gangland figure who ran the seashore resort town for decades (on the show, his name was changed to Nucky Thompson). The Hollywood images of a corrupt, very wet Atlantic City during Prohibition is pretty close to the truth. From July 1, 1922, to June 30, 1923, 114 people were arrested by the Atlantic City Police for violating the Volstead Act, not counting the numbers arrested by federal agents. And during Prohibition, "some 40 percent of all alcohol smuggled into the country was estimated to come through Atlantic City's shoreline, coves, and beaches."[4] And Nucky Johnson tried as hard as he could to make sure he got a dip into every barrel that went through his kingdom.

Enoch "Nucky" Johnson was born in Smithville, New Jersey, just outside Atlantic City, in 1883. He had clear ambitions and goals since his youth to become something more than another face in the crowd. He was sworn in as sheriff on November 12, 1908, becoming the youngest sheriff in New Jersey, at age twenty-five. A lifelong career in law enforcement was not in the cards for young Enoch, though his father had served four terms as sheriff. Following his law-enforcement stint, Nucky became active in local and state politics. By 1924 he was a rising star in the Republican Party and was solidifying his hold on his political career as well as his foray into the new and lucrative world of rum-running.

Eventually becoming city treasurer, Johnson had his finger on the pulse of all areas of the town and all of its power players. Through his influence with the local Republican Party, he was able to deflect suspicion of his activities with outsized efforts to ensure Republican control of the city as well as the state, and even into the White House. And his power extended to the smaller independent criminal operatives. Rivalries and violent flare-ups were rare in Atlantic City at this time. Johnson knew that a smooth operation with minimal violence was the best way to avoid exposure. "Fighting only gets you fighting,"[5] he once told a newspaper reporter.

Johnson enjoyed the luxuries afforded by his new income stream. The tall, dapper-dressed power boss often walked up and down the boardwalk, always with a red carnation in the lapel of his bespoke suits, using a walking stick with a gold top. Nucky often rented the ninth floor of the newly constructed Ritz Carlton. He was also fond of women and remained a bachelor until later in life. Johnson's appeal also came from his power over the hiring of city staff. He controlled everything such that if someone was looking to get a job with the city, they would have to see Nucky. He had control of the local government that in many ways was far greater than that of any other organized crime boss before or since.

The underground liquor scene in Atlantic City was actually a boon to the city's tourism, attracting revelers and vacationers all year round and helping jump-start the convention industry there. However, just a few years into Prohibition, Atlantic City's reputation was already taking a hit from local activists who saw the growing influence of purveyors of vice in gaming the political system to their advantage. A 1924 newspaper article bemoaned, "We have open gambling in our city, rum-running flourishes and I have good reason to believe that there are men walking the streets with no visible means of support who are getting at on the proceeds from the red light districts."[6] But to organized crime, the scene was paradise by the sea. "Atlantic City was always a good source of income, especially in the 1920s–1950s era."[7] And Nucky Johnson was bullish on the city, defending it to anyone within earshot. "We have whisky, wine, women and slot machines. I won't deny it and I won't apologize for it. If the majority of the people didn't want them they wouldn't be profitable and they wouldn't exist. The fact that they do exist proves to me that the people want them."[8]

Enoch Johnson's political opponents were not kind to the power broker. In 1929, Senator Alexander Simpson of Hudson County railed against Johnson and his ties to then-governor, Morgan Larson. "Affidavits I have establish the fact that the Sodom and Gomorrah conditions in Atlantic City . . . have existed so long and so openly that everybody in authority should have known them."[9] Atlantic City was viewed as such a friendly place for gangsters that a large meeting was called there in 1929, a meeting that has gained mythical status in Mafia lore.

The storied Mafia meet-up at Cleveland's Statler Hotel had taken place a year earlier, but the Atlantic City Conference—called a historic summit of organized-crime leaders—was attended by dozens of Italian and Jewish gangsters from across the country. From New York, Lucky Luciano, Frank Costello, Meyer Lansky, Dutch Schultz, and Owney Madden. Representing Newark were Waxey Gordon and Longy Zwillman. The meeting itself was covered by local papers, one of which, the *Atlantic City Daily Press*, ran stories of the gangsters in town, particularly Al Capone, who was at the apex of his notoriety and infamy. Johnny Torrio called the meeting, and the Chicago-centric focus, including the battles raging on the streets of the Windy City, was a main topic of conversation.

The story went that the attendees were originally going to stay at the Breakers Hotel, but the hotel would not let the Jewish gangsters stay there. The gangsters then reached out to Enoch Johnson to help them out. Johnson quickly got a number of rooms booked at the Ambassador and Ritz hotels. It's not clear if the implication in the story was that the men were not allowed to stay at the hotel because they were gangsters or because they were Jewish. The latter excuse would seem out of character for the Breakers, known colloquially as the "Aristocrat of Kosher Hotels."[10]

The Atlantic City Conference is often called one of the most important mob meetings in history, the one that cemented the "modern" structure of traditional organized crime, moving it away from the older bosses' old-school mentality into a new age where Jews, Italians, and Irish (though by this time Irish influence was waning) could work together as a syndicate to control the rackets. Other purported reasons for the meetings were the increased cooperation in the bootlegging rackets between Jewish mobsters and Italians, as well as discussion of combining forays into gambling. Or so the story has evolved over the years. The conference has taken on a mythological aspect that has overshadowed a lot of the contemporary accounts. "All the contemporaneous accounts of the Atlantic City Conference unanimously say that it involved Chicago gangsters only, with the limited goal of making peace between Capone and Moran. And then, at some point, the story transforms into one where dozens of rackets leaders from all over the country are summoned to a meeting that created the architecture for a national government of thugs."[11]

Damon Runyon was there when the conference was going on and wrote about the meeting in one of his short stories, "Dark Dolores." There is a belief that some of the reported events of the conference—the men being pushed in rolling chairs to the end of the boardwalk where they would get into the water and have their meeting—may have been, if not outright created, at least exacerbated by Runyon. And while the gathered gangsters ate, drank, and partied with hookers supposedly supplied by Johnson, there was no doubt they were also there to talk business. But the combination of press reports, Runyon's story, the passage of time, and the fact that none of the actual attendees ever talked about what was said at the meeting created a lot of speculation in the ensuing years. In fact, the exact list of attendees is up for question.

But there definitely was a meeting, and Al Capone was in Atlantic City at the time. The police first got a report of Capone in a nightclub, telling the newspapers that, if "Capone is found he will be given the choice of leaving the resort or going to jail."[12] Capone told the director of Public Safety in Chicago that "I met Bugs Moran and two other men in Atlantic City after we previously determined to declare a truce. We talked things over for a week and finally agreed to certain conditions."[13] Capone confirmed that the men had stayed at the President Hotel and that they had worked on a deal for six days, adding "The gang war, or at least the feud between Moran and myself, is ended for all time."[14]

With uncertainty regarding the exact attendees, it is likely that Nucky Johnson was there. One of the main pieces of evidence is the famous photo of a smiling Enoch Johnson walking arm-in-arm with Al Capone down the Atlantic City Boardwalk. The photo appeared in the *Atlantic City Daily Press*. Johnson assured everyone within earshot that the photo was a fake, that he had been superimposed on the scene. But the fact was that Capone had been in Atlantic City that week in May, and the newspapers were reporting it. And Nucky Johnson was a major power in town and would certainly have been the go-to resource for Capone and Torrio.

The Atlantic City Conference certainly put the city on the map for exactly the wrong reasons. The availability of liquor made the area infamous and its participants rich, but it also fell under closer scrutiny by the US Coast Guard. The old smuggling routes were now being shut down, and Atlantic City was not as easy to get into for the Jersey skiffs as it had been in the past. Rumrunners started creeping down the coast to the town of Wildwood, located just above Cape May at the southern tip of the Jersey Shore. This location, right near the entrance to Delaware Bay, provided ample back bays and coves, like Ottens Harbor, for smugglers to hide in while unloading from the supply ships off the coast. The back roads and rural towns just outside Wildwood were home to moonshining.

Since Wildwood, like Atlantic City, hosted visitors during the summer, speakeasies and drinking clubs sprouted up to quench the thirst of daring visitors who braved secret passages and scrutiny by local police. However, some of the businesses in Wildwood openly advertised beer for sale, while raids from police were not too common. One local legend concerns a nightclub proprietor, Louisa Booth, who owned the club Lou Booth's Chateau Monterey. The story goes that, during Prohibition, Louisa wanted to get in on the action and so set up business deals with smugglers. She feared, however, they wouldn't do business with a woman, so she shortened her name to Lou. There currently is a Lou Booth Amphitheater in Wildwood, memorializing her.

As the booze was flowing into South Jersey, the coast guard was looking to the sky—and Washington, DC—for help in thwarting the smuggling operations. In 1926, Congress approved funding for the US Coast Guard to purchase Loening OL-5 seaplanes. These two-seat seaplanes, first made in 1923, were some of the earliest amphibious planes and were made specifically for the US Navy and Air Corps. "The flying enforcers focused on stopping the liquor traffic at sea along the northeast and southeast coasts."[15] The flights originated out of the Cape May airbase. Also at the US Coast Guard base in Cape May were eight seventy-five-foot ships that patrolled up and down the coast.

But South Jersey did not boast the only drop-off point for liquor along the shoreline. The borough of Atlantic Highlands, located on the south shore of

Raritan Bay, became a hotbed of rum-running activity throughout Prohibition (mob boss Vito Genovese would later call the Highlands his home). Larger vessels would park offshore, and smaller boats, with shallower draft, would speed out to the ships, load up on cases of booze, and zip back to shore, all under the cover of darkness. Atlantic Highlands boasts the highest points on the eastern seaboard south of Maine, looking out far and wide over the bay, giving an advantage to rumrunners keeping an eye on ships coming in with cargo and any approaching law-enforcement vessels.

On the night of September 21, 1923, the relative calm of Atlantic Highlands was shattered as a gun battle erupted between a group of bootleggers and a gang of hijackers out of Newark who had been pilfering the locals' liquor shipments as they had come in to either the port area of town or nearby Wagner Creek, itself a busy route for small boats with smaller loads of illicit alcohol. The Newark hijackers were led by the LeConte brothers, Joe and Frank. They had been caught in a gun battle with a local bootlegging operation run by Walt Keener. The battle took residents by surprise. "Gangsters took cover behind cars, doors, trees and light poles, while residents hugged the ground behind cars, horse troughs, barrels, and buildings."[16] The Keener gang shot Frank LeConte in the stomach, the bullet lodging just under his back. Though LeConte was dropped off at a local hospital, he died the following Monday morning. Both sets of gangsters were arrested, but because none of them would talk and the shooting happened in the cover of darkness, murder charges were dropped against two of Keener's men, Ralph and Edward Bitters.

But that hardly stemmed the flow of liquor into the Highlands. Just a couple months later, after the shooting, the day after Christmas, the *Asbury Park Evening Press* reported that "twice as much liquor was landed for yesterday's Christmas celebrations than last year."[17] That was in part due to another extensive operation run by two local brothers.

Al and William Lillien controlled a bootlegging gang that extended from Montreal down to Virginia and was based out of Atlantic Highlands. The Lilliens' operation was raided in October of 1929. Federal agents estimated that his operation had taken in over two million dollars over the course of six months, based on figures they found in a notebook taken from the Lillien headquarters in the Highlands. Al Lillien was indicted with thirty-eight others in 1931 but was acquitted of smuggling. But the Lilliens' rum-running operation came to an end in March of 1933 when Al was found in his spacious mansion in Middletown Township, three bullet holes in the back of his head.

But there was more. There was the *Napeague*, a boat carrying fifteen hundred cases of whisky (thirteen hundred cases of Durand rye, two hundred of Canadian Club), which was raided by the US Coast Guard off the coast of Sandy Hook in 1923, the eleventh raid that year alone by the Sandy Hook station. On the western end of Raritan Bay, in Perth Amboy, the four Mikkelsen brothers (also relatives of the author) would gas up their boat on Saturday morning and head out into the bay to meet the supply ship offshore and bring the booze back into the city.

The complicity in bootlegging with politicians was not relegated to simple corruption. A lot of them simply turned their backs and looked away while the sand dunes were traversed by crews offloading cases of booze. In 1929 a grand jury went so far as to indict the mayor and twenty members of the police department in the resort town of Ocean City, which was hardly a unique incident in an era when the profit from a few cases of booze was more than many people's weekly, or even monthly, salary.

The Jersey Shore is littered with the stories, and ghosts, of the rum-running era. But for all the high-seas adventure and high-speed chases, the Shore was sometimes just one part of a bigger operation. In fact, one of the largest rum-running operations in Atlantic Highlands started around 1925 when Joseph and Saul Reinfeld began bringing liquor into port with the help of a partner from Newark—who also brought in Joe "Doc" Stacher into the partnership—who managed to bring his name and reputation to the forefront of Prohibition-era crime in New Jersey. In fact, this partner's name became so synonymous with the underworld at that time that he earned the moniker "the Al Capone of Newark." His name was Abner "Longy" Zwillman, and he became one of the most influential mobsters in the Garden State.

Chapter Three

Zwillman

In the lore of the New Jersey underworld, few figures loom as large as Abner Zwillman. Nicknamed Longy, due to his tall stature, Zwillman was one of the—if not the most—influential figures in organized crime in the first half of the twentieth century.[1] His presence both figuratively and literally set the course for the expansion of the mob in New Jersey and across the United States, touching into Florida, Las Vegas, and pre-Castro Cuba. In the historically Jewish section of Newark, the Third Ward, Zwillman was both feared and beloved, wielding enormous political and criminal influence over the neighborhood, while standing up for the neighborhood denizens, often against anti-Semitism, especially in the years leading up to World War II.

Zwillman moved effortlessly between the mob he controlled in Newark, the Mafia families of the New York/New Jersey metro area, politicians, and businessmen. He cultivated an image of success and, unlike many of his contemporaries, was able to leverage his activities during Prohibition into successful legitimate businesses throughout the Garden State.

Abraham "Abner" Zwillman was born on July 27, 1904, in Newark, the third child of seven. His parents were Russian immigrants who had settled in the heavily Jewish Third Ward. The neighborhood ran through a patchwork of streets bounded today by Avon Avenue and Springfield Avenue to the west and east and Irvine Turner Boulevard and Dr. Martin Luther King Jr. Boulevard to the north and south, respectively. Though few remnants of the area's Jewish influence remain today, at the time of Zwillman's birth the crowded neighborhood was teaming with Jewish merchants, poultry and produce dealers, kosher butchers, and all kinds of peddlers walking the streets selling all manner of goods. Prince Street was the main thoroughfare and is where Zwillman got his start.

When Abe was only fourteen, his father passed away, forcing the boy to leave school early to work and provide for his family. He became a produce peddler and realized quickly that his best customers weren't the poor immigrants in his neighborhood but wealthier clients in other parts of Newark. But his loyalty to his fellow neighbors was strong, and when elderly Jews and merchants of the Third Ward were harassed by roving outside gangs, they would seek out Abe's help. They would send out the call for the *Langer*, a Yiddish word for "the tall one." This morphed into the nickname Longy.

Though he hadn't graduated from school, Longy's considerable street smarts were matched by his overall intelligence. He quickly saw that the path to fortune was not in selling produce alone. "The men in the Third Ward who made real money, the kind of money Longy was after, were either in politics or gambling."[2] And it was gambling, specifically the numbers game, that Longy took on as his first organized racket.

The numbers racket, known by a variety of names from *policy* to *bolita*, is essentially the same as a pick-three lottery. A bettor would pick a three-digit number and bet a penny, nickel, or dime. The bet would be made with a collector, who would give the betting slips to a runner, who, in turn, worked for a seller or bank where the money was collected, the betting slips indexed, and the winning number drawn. Depending on who ran the bank determined where the winning number was drawn. Some policy games took their winning number from the last three digits of the stock market, others from horses at the racetrack, while some simply made the number up, though that last group was rare. In order for the game to work well, and for the bettors to keep coming back, the game needed to be straight and run well, which many were not. Another essential part of keeping the numbers game running smoothly was cooperation from local police. In some cities, police even worked hand-in-hand with policy banks selling numbers as well as protecting the operations.

To the enterprising young produce dealer and numbers racketeer, the same customers, mainly housewives, to whom he sold vegetables door-to-door were also his best customers. And Zwillman's door-to-door service meant that some of his more discreet customers did not need to venture out to a centralized betting location to make their policy pick. This type of customer service helped the operation flourish, and before long Zwillman had a small crew that worked with him, expanding his numbers game across Newark—though at that time the terminus of his territory was the nearby First Ward, under the control of the Italians.

Among the early recruits to Zwillman's gang was Joseph "Doc" Stacher, a Ukrainian-born Jew whose family had immigrated to Newark in 1912. Over the next few years after joining Zwillman's group, Stacher became an essential element to the gambling enterprise's success. "Doc was not a refined gentleman. He would wipe his mouth on the tablecloth after he ate. He didn't care. He also scared the shit out of a lot of guys. However, at the same time he could be extremely charming. He was highly intelligent and was close to Longy Zwillman and to Meyer Lansky."[3] Another member of Longy's gang was Abe Green, described as "very powerful. He was originally with Longy and sold alcohol with him. Abe dressed like he belonged in *Esquire* magazine. He didn't talk much. He was very quiet."[4]

But, while gambling was bringing in a good payday for the gang, the advent of Prohibition brought about an outstanding opportunity to make more money than either Longy or Doc could have ever dreamed of. And Longy was in the right place at the right time. Newark was well situated as a waypoint between New York and Philadelphia, with access to major roads, trains, and the port. "By 1922, Newark, New Jersey, was the bootleg capital of the country. Newark was chosen over other cities for good reason. It had the most corrupt police, prosecutors, and courts in the country."[5]

Zwillman started off by providing transportation and protection to other bootleggers in town. "Zwillman's men proved to be the best protection available; the only attempt to hijack a shipment they were transporting was met with a fusillade of bullets."[6]

One of the early bootleggers that Longy's gang worked for was Joseph Reinfeld, who owned a tavern in Newark. Reinfeld's operation involved smuggled whiskey coming across the Great Lakes from Canada. Longy became one of his most trusted workers, helping the Reinfeld operation make significant inroads into the bootlegging business and solidify ties between Reinfeld at the Bronfman family in Montreal, who owned Seagrams.

The young Zwillman showed his fortitude around this time by shooting Leo Kaplus, a well-known local bootlegger who had been harassing Zwillman and his operation. He shot Kaplus in the leg in 1923 and thereafter "gained some prominence among racket people in North New Jersey . . . and was associating with well-known gangsters in the area."[7] Kaplus disappeared from the scene, surfacing only briefly in 1937 when he was indicted for, and ultimately acquitted of, a land-deal conspiracy that included then–Newark mayor Meyer C. Ellenstein (also acquitted), one of Zwillman's political allies, who Longy helped get elected according to some sources.

But Longy was too ambitious to stay working for someone else. He wanted his own business. So he approached Reinfeld with an offer that either Reinfeld take Longy on as a fifty-fifty partner or Longy would walk and take all of his men, and their protection, with him. Reinfeld, not wanting to start any violent altercation, and sensing Zwillman's potential, reluctantly agreed. Zwillman now had a part in a liquor-smuggling operation, his own gang, and growing respect among the local gangsters.

Zwillman and Reinfeld's operation was a huge success. Between the two men and their respective gangs, they dominated the illegal liquor scene in Newark and branched out to nearby communities. "The Internal Revenue

Service estimated that the Reinfeld-Zwillman combine earned forty million dollars from rum-running during the five-year period between 1928 and 1933."[8]

As expected, Longy was increasingly the target of law enforcement as his star rose. From 1925 through 1928 he was picked up four times on minor charges, though none of the charges stuck. Within a day of his arrests, Longy was back out on the streets of the Third Ward. But in June of 1928, he was accused of assault by local crime figure and runner for his numbers racket, Preston Buzzard. Longy was accused of hitting Buzzard with a blackjack. Supposedly Buzzard himself went into the police department and demanded they arrest Zwillman for the attack.

The police knew who Buzzard was and were not overly enthused about having to go round up Zwillman just to appease another criminal, but when Buzzard came into the police department demanding action, there happened to be a couple local reporters there. The police knew that they were going to have to take Buzzard's complaint seriously, so they sent out two detectives to find and arrest Longy. The detectives took their time; it was a week later that Longy was finally brought to the police station, where he promptly paid a thousand dollars for the bail and walked back out on the street, though this time with an assault charge hanging over him. Years later Zwillman looked back at the incident. "Well it's a long story. It goes back I think to about 1925 or 1926. And some man up in the old ward that time got hit with a blackjack, and they said I did it. A lot of circumstance surrounded that."[9]

A curious spectacle occurred in the ensuing months between the time Zwillman walked out of the police station and the beginning of his trial. Three different men all came in and confessed to being the one who had beaten Buzzard. It wasn't clear from the police whether any of the men was telling the truth or simply covering for Zwillman. But the additional confessions were not enough to sway the judge overseeing the case. He pushed for it to move ahead, while Longy declined a trial by jury, probably assuming that he would get off right there on the spot.

The indictment he faced was atrocious assault, battery, and assault with intent to kill. These charges were serious, and Zwillman faced the prospect of real jail time. On February 11, 1929, he was convicted of the charges, though the sentencing phase was suspended. Zwillman's lawyers quickly went about working to apply for a new trial. They appeared before the court on March 12, but the court took it under advisement for another year and a half. By the time they reached a decision, on December 12, 1930, the motion for a new trial was denied, and a judge sentenced Zwillman to six months in jail and a fine of one thousand dollars for the beating of Buzzard.

Zwillman was sent to serve his time at the Essex County Penitentiary. Though the sentence called for hard labor, Longy managed to avoid that by working as an orderly in the prison hospital. He was able to leave on weekends through an arrangement that he made with the warden, staying at the home of his bodyguard, Sam "Big Sue" Katz. Zwillman also "had a telephone in his cell, had outside meals brought in, and enjoyed unlimited visiting privileges."[10] He was released from the penitentiary at 8 a.m. on March 31, 1930, having had some time shaved off for good behavior. Though his time in prison was not what anyone would consider "hard time," Zwillman was determined to avoid going back. The word on the street was that he was done getting his hands dirty and would rely on his crew to take care of things, remaining above the fray and with a degree of separation from the law.

Zwillman's base of operations was the Riviera Hotel on Clinton Avenue in Newark. The hotel, built in 1922, was one of the largest in the area at the time and a prominent gathering place for local politicians, the exact type of people that Zwillman wanted to hobnob with. Though now past its prime, during its heyday the hotel was an architectural landmark for the area and walking distance from the retail strip of the Third Ward. It was here that Zwillman would host fellow mobsters from New York City as well. "Meyer Lansky would come into Newark and stay at the Riviera with his brother Jake. Bugsy [Benjamin Siegel] used to come as well."[11]

Just up the street from the Riviera was the Blue Mirror Lounge, a nightclub that was a "well known meeting place of Newark and New York City mobsters as well as a payoff spot for graft."[12] Zwillman and his crew hung out here often as well. It was here, according to underworld lore, that Dutch Schultz was drinking the night before his murder in 1935 at the Palace Chop House in Newark.

One of the reasons that Longy was able to gain such power in New Jersey was related to his prowess at working with politicians and the judiciary to his benefit. His alleged involvement in political corruption was reported on religiously by local papers at the time. Longy was questioned in a 1932 voting scandal in Newark. Ballots had been stolen from boxes that had supposedly been safeguarded in the basement of Newark City Hall. The thefts had been "to cover up alleged voting frauds in the Third Ward."[13] By controlling the voting and the political appointments, the lanky kid from the Third Ward was becoming a force unto himself.

One of the political establishments with which Zwillman aligned himself was the Third Ward Political Club. Opened in 1927, and located at 88 Waverly Place,[14] the club was an important hangout for politicians from both ends of the political spectrum. But "party affiliations didn't matter to Longy. If you needed a favor, you got it, regardless of political affiliation."[15] The club had several hundred members and was an active part of the social scene in the Third Ward; Zwillman was the man in charge. "Well, I had a club, and I was living out in my old neighborhood, which is the ghetto, a very poor neighborhood, and everybody needed help, everybody needed jobs, and we were making a little money, so we started a club and got everybody into it . . .

it more or less started off as a charitable thing and then wound up in a political club . . . nonpartisan."[16]

Another side of Zwillman often lost to news reports of the day was his charity and hospitality in the neighborhood. The Robin Hood image of the old-school gangster may have been best exemplified by Capone and his soup kitchens for the less fortunate of Chicago during the Depression, but other underworld figures would, sometimes quietly, give back to their communities—the same community that gave them their best customers when it came to gambling or loan-sharking. It seemed kind of a penance for the Irish and Italians, a mitzvah for the Jews, and a general way of currying favor with the neighbors in general that a local gangster might expect to look out for the neighborhood, keep an eye on police, and offer an additional layer of protection from rivals.

Zwillman was no stranger to such outreach. From his earliest days defending the Jewish merchants from roving gangs of thugs Zwillman sought to better those around him, as well as himself. Known as an avid reader who, before he left school to start supporting his family, had excelled in his classes, Longy was very different form the archetypical street urchin. His charity, while unable to be confirmed to the dollar, was expansive, giving "millions to charity over the course of his life, sponsoring scholarships and orphanages and soup kitchens in Newark, buying matzo for indigent Jews at Passover."[17] Jewish charities were not the only beneficiaries of Longy's largess. He reportedly donated a thousand dollars a week for years to the Mount Carmel Guild of the Catholic Charities and "provided a yearly Christmas carnival at Laurel Gardens for orphans of all colors and creeds through the Third Ward Political Club."[18]

This civic-minded attitude, especially toward members of the Jewish community he grew up in, was on full display in the years leading up to World War II. Newark at the time had one of the largest Jewish populations in the United States, and it became the target of marches by the German-American Bund, an offshoot political party that emerged in the 1930s and was "for all intents and practical purposes the American Section of the Nazi Party."[19] Jewish merchants and citizens banded together, with assistance from underworld figures. Meyer Lansky and his crew disrupted Bund meetings in the Yorkville section of Manhattan. Zwillman did the same in Newark and nearby towns like Irvington. The goal was to drive out the Bund from the community and show Longy's allegiance to the citizens.

But even with the clout he wielded, he was still playing in the shadow of New York City. Newark's proximity to New York, and the easy travel between the two cities, even at that time, brought about collaborations and partnerships between sometimes-rival factions and bosses. Zwillman was no exception, allying himself with other smuggling kingpins like Irving Wexler—aka Waxey Gordon—and future Mafia boss Nick Delmore. Zwillman's partnership with Gordon extended not only to the vast smuggling and transport operations throughout the New York metro area but also to control of "closed" breweries.

The New Jersey breweries controlled by the Zwillman/Gordon combine included Hensler Brewery (Newark), Orange Brewery (Newark), Union City Brewery (Union City), Peter Hauck Brewery (Harrison), Eureka Brewery (Paterson), Hygeia Brewery (Passaic), Peter Heidt Brewery (Elizabeth), and the Rising Sun Brewery (Elizabeth). Though they had all been closed at the start of Prohibition, the buildings were used by the combine to store and, in some cases, manufacture illegal liquor and beer.

One of the breweries, the Rising Sun, located on Marshall Street in Elizabeth, was raided in 1930 by Prohibition agents. The agents came up from the Philadelphia office of the federal Prohibition administrator. On the way up to the raid, agents were involved in a car crash. An unknown vehicle sideswiped them and drove off. Suspecting their raid had been leaked to the brewery operators, they continued on anyway, arriving in Elizabeth. The agents drove around the large brick building where they "detected a strong odor of beer brewing emanating from the premises" and "saw smoke rising from the smokestacks . . . steam coming out of said premises at the top of the building from two different pipes."[20]

When agents stormed the brewery, they rounded up eleven employees. But they did not realize that a number of other men were camped out across the street in another building. The other men came in to the brewery, surprising the agents, which included John G. Finiello, a noted agent who had been on a number of raids of illegal liquor establishments in both New Jersey and eastern Pennsylvania. One of the gangsters took an agent's gun and turned him around as a human shield, making the other four agents line up against the wall to be disarmed and searched. Just then, one of the unknown gangsters saw Finiello standing just apart from the other agents. Recognizing the enterprising dry agent, who had made his career as the continual thorn in the side of brewery operations in New Jersey and Pennsylvania, the man shouted "There's Finiello—give it to him!"[21]

Gunshots erupted. Three shots hit Finiello, a fourth killing him as he fell forward. Then the place "became a turmoil with shots being fired right and left."[22] In the ensuing pandemonium, the gangsters fled the scene, though they ran into a sixth agent entering the brewery and disarmed him, leaving the agents to care for their fallen compatriot. The gunmen were believed to have escaped with waiting cars, just as over a hundred police officers with guns and teargas descended on the brewery. The spectacle drew the attention of the neighbors as well as the local press. The headlines for the next several days in newspapers across New Jersey and Pennsylvania were focused on the Finiello murder.

Suspicion was directed toward members of Zwillman's crew and an upstart Italian gangster who was working with Zwillman and had ties to the Elizabeth crime family, Nick Delmore. At the time. Delmore was the owner of the Maple Shade Inn in Berkeley Heights, New Jersey, but he was also widely regarded as a major beer baron in the state and operator of the Rising Sun. Within a day of the shooting, police believed that he was not only involved in the incident but also may have been the one who fired the fatal shot that took Finiello down. Delmore, "said to have intensive political and social connections," allegedly "fled in one of his three expensive limousines shortly after the killing of the agent."[23]

Police went both to his house and an apartment above the brewery in search of Delmore, but he was not around. What they did find in the apartment was a complex set of buzzers and wires that connected his apartment to the rest of the brewery, as well as a signal tower from which all areas of the brewery and surrounding grounds could be surveilled. The police were also searching for Philadelphia-based gangster Mickey Duffy and some of his associates, and brought in the brewmaster John Liebert for questioning.

Years after an informant told the FBI that he had overheard Herman "Red" Cohen reminiscing about the old days in Newark. Cohen said that the night of the shooting Delmore "came into the Riviera Hotel in old clothes one night many years ago and told the late Longy Zwillman that they had just shot a Prohibition agent."[24]

By September 23, 1930, the FBI was in on the hunt for Delmore. As evidence and tips poured in, law enforcement did what it could to not only stay on the trail of Delmore but also crack who the other gunmen were. In addition, the fallout from the Rising Sun shooting was causing serious disruptions in rum-running activities across New Jersey and Pennsylvania. The other Treasury agents were taking their frustrations out on the gangland operations. Some of Delmore's breweries, like the Harrison brewery near Newark, were shut down, and raids intensified against still operations.

As 1931 yielded to 1932, indictments started coming down on Delmore's accomplices. One of the first to be indicted was Martin "Red" Podolsky, who had allegedly been the lookout man outside the brewery when the shooting had occurred. But Podolsky was released on bail when the prosecutor declined to proceed with his case until he had more of the gang in custody, including Delmore, who was still a fugitive. But the winds of fortune were turning in Delmore's favor in the fall of 1932. August Gobel was one of the men arrested back when the raid had occurred. He was a fireman in the brewery. Police then brought him in as a witness and in anticipation of Delmore's trial, though Delmore was still a fugitive.

By November of 1932, Gobel was working in a factory in Newark. Police had been tipped off that there might be an attempt on Gobel's life, so a patrolman was sent to guard the witness. The patrolman was talking with

Gobel by a boiler in the plant when Gobel walked outside, out of the sight of the patrolman, for a moment. Then he screamed out, "They got me." When the police officer ran outside, he was met with a barrage of bullets that took him down, wounding him. Gobel was not so lucky. The star witness to the murder of John Finiello was dead.

With his resources, it would have been simple for Delmore to disappear to another part of the country, but when police finally arrested him on October 19, 1933, they found him asleep in his own bed at his house in Berkeley Heights. When police woke him up, he asked them, "What rat turned me up?"[25] He told the police that he would be happy to accompany them to the station. He was put in a lineup and identified by a dry agent as one of the gunmen at the Rising Sun. At his arraignment Delmore discovered that he was charged with first-degree murder and that the prosecutor was going to pursue the death penalty.

The turnaround time was quick. A month later, on November 20, the trial was underway. Some of the agents who had participated in the raid were called as witnesses. Delmore himself was called to the stand. He told the courtroom that he had an airtight alibi for the day of the Rising Sun shooting. He said he had been nowhere near the brewery when the shooting had occurred. Upon hearing of Finiello's death, he had visited another beer baron, Max Hassel, in a hotel in Elizabeth and then gone to New York City, where he lived in a private home for three years. He didn't offer any explanation as to why he had decided to come back to New Jersey when he did.

Overall the trial lasted eight days. Jurors went into deliberation on November 28 and came back to the courtroom after only two and a half hours. Delmore and Podolsky were acquitted of murder. Applause erupted in the courtroom as the verdict was announced. Though Podolsky was immediately released, agents rearrested Delmore and charged him with conspiracy in the operation of the Rising Sun Brewery, resisting a federal officer, and use of a deadly weapon.

Before Delmore's trial even opened in January of 1934, four men—including one of Longy Zwillman's right-hand men, Jerry Catena—were arrested for attempting to bribe a juror. The men had gone to the home of one of the jurors and given him a hundred dollars, with the promise of another four hundred if Delmore was acquitted. Catena received three months in jail for the bribery attempt. However, he was lucky once again, as jurors acquitted him for the second time in less than six months.

Delmore's alibi in the Finiello murder case brought a new name to the New Jersey bootlegging scene. The beer situation in central Jersey was firmly under the control of Zwillman, Waxey Gordon, and Ritchie Boiardo, as well as New York mobster Vito Genovese. Another brewery owner making headway in New Jersey was Max Hassel, based in Reading, Pennsylvania, and the man Delmore said he had visited the night of the Rising Sun raid.

According to sources, Hassel had been pushed out of Reading, forced to give up his operations there, because of the intense pressure agent Finiello was exerting. Hassel had relocated to Elizabeth, New Jersey, in 1929 to start anew. He set himself up in the Elizabeth Carteret Hotel and teamed with Max Greenberg and Waxey Gordon to operate over a dozen breweries. But success can breed envy, especially in the rapidly shifting world of Prohibition-era gangland.

The Elizabeth Carteret Hotel was one of the largest hotels in the city of Elizabeth. Located at 1156 East Jersey Street, it had over two hundred rooms with baths and advertised its air-conditioned coffee shop. On the ground floor was a luxurious ballroom where dances and social events were held. Today a senior citizen center, at the time the Elizabeth Carteret building was at the forefront of luxury and an attractive place for underworld figures to stay, what with its proximity to Newark and New York City.

Late afternoon in April of 1933 Hassel and Greenberg were relaxing in their suite on the eighth floor of the hotel. Across the hall was Waxey Gordon. Hassel and Greenberg were surrounded by highball glasses and bottles of liquor. Sometime just after 4 p.m., shooting started. Gordon later recounted, "I heard a noise around 4:15 in the afternoon that sounded like breaking glass or someone dropping dishes. I then beat it as quick as I could, for I know that if I had been in that room I would have got the works too."[26] Another hotel guest ran downstairs to the front desk and told them to call the police. Within minutes detectives swarmed the building.

The suite where Hassel and Greenberg were staying had a code and an electronic lock that could only be opened by the front desk. Detectives believed the shooter was either someone already in the room or someone known to the two men. Theories abounded. One investigation "disclosed that the killings were perpetrated by persons who either were seeking to murder one Irving Wexler, also known as Waxey Gordon, or killed Hassel and Greenberg, who were known to be henchmen of Gordon's, in a gang war waged between Gordon and his followers and rival factions in the so-called 'beer racket.'"[27]

Police had another theory and in 1935 arrested a young mobster by the name of Frankie Carbo. Frankie had previously been arrested for the murder of Mickey Duffy, who had previously been implicated in the Rising Sun brewery shooting. Carbo was arrested and charged with Hassel's and Greenberg's murders, but the charges were eventually dropped for lack of evidence.

Another possible suspect, named fairly recently by two authors in Pennsylvania, was Joe Stassi, a Newark gangster who would go on to work at hotels for the mob in pre-Castro Cuba. Before he died, Stassi told one of the authors that he knew Hassel and that Meyer Lansky was behind the shooting.

But Stassi had a closer connection: he was living in a room just below Hassel and Greenberg at the hotel. He also had the means and motive, if ordered by Lansky, to murder the two men. Stassi confessed that he was there when the murder was ordered and intimated that he may have carried it out, though he never came right out and implicated himself.

Hassel and Greenberg may have been merely the latest in a string of gangland hits that seemed to be occurring as Prohibition was in the process of winding down. Just a month before Hassel was killed, one of his close associates and former Jersey Shore beer baron, Al Lillien, was shot and killed on a flight of steps leading up to the old Hammerstein mansion in Atlantic Highlands. And after the Hassel and Greenberg killings another murder rocked Newark, the victim a notorious mobster also alleged to have threatened Hassel, Greenberg, and Gordon over their operations.

Chapter Four

Dutch, Longy, Jerry, and the Boot

Arthur Flegenheimer was a gangster's gangster. The brash policy kingpin and beer baron, who went by the moniker Dutch Schultz, was a New York crime figure who managed to bump up against most of the major underworld figures of the day, as well as law enforcement. One of his most heated rivalries was with Thomas Dewey. As special prosecutor in New York City, Dewey made it his mission to root out organized-crime elements in town. Among his top targets was Schultz. Dewey had previously successfully prosecuted Zwillman associate Waxey Gordon, and now his sites were set on the empire of Schultz, who had managed to escape conviction on two previous trials.

Dewey sent out word that he wanted Schultz arrested on sight. In August of 1935 Dewey officially started the investigation into Schultz's doings. The investigation promised to build a "million dollar microscope to trace an estimated $1,000,000,000 exacted yearly in the metropolis through vice and racketeering."[1] Schultz—who at the time was celebrating the birth of his son in upstate New York, near the scene of his tax trial, where he was acquitted, much to the chagrin of authorities—decided to relocate to Newark in the late summer of 1935 and started taking potshots against the prosecutor. In a breach of mob protocol, Schultz sent out word that he wanted Dewey killed. This did not sit well at all with the syndicate. Luciano, Lansky, Lepke Buchalter, and others feared that any attempt, successful or not, on Dewey would have significant repercussions for all of their operations. Schultz needed to either back down or be removed from the situation, permanently.

While in Newark, Dutch Schultz was a regular at the Palace Chop House, located at 12 East Park Street, in downtown. His regular meal was steak and fries. In the early evening of October 23, 1935, Schultz walked into the Palace, flanked by his two bodyguards, Bernard "Lulu" Rosenkrantz and Abe

Landau. They walked past the long bar and sat down in the back of the restaurant. A bail bondsman, Max Silverman, came in to collect some money from Schultz and walked out just before 8 p.m. Schultz was then joined at his table by the affable Otto "Abbadabba" Berman.

After 10 p.m., a bartender at the front of the house was stirring some coffee when the front door opened. "A heavy set man walked into the barroom and I heard a voice order, 'Don't move, lay down.' I could hardly discern his face as he pulled his topcoat up to hide it. I saw him place his hand on his left shoulder and whip out a gun from a holster. I didn't wait any longer. I dropped to the floor and lay behind the bar."[2] The man he couldn't identify was Emanuel "Mendy" Weiss, who had arrived with fellow gangster Charles "the Bug" Workman.

The two gunmen had been expecting to find Schultz sitting with three other men at the table. But when they entered, they were only able to make out three of the four men in the back room. And so Workman had Weiss stay in the front as he walked into the washroom. He didn't even look at who was in there, figuring it had to be one of Schultz's men, and shot the man with a .45. The other three men at Schultz's table—Berman and his bodyguards Rosenkrantz and Landau—didn't even know Weiss was there until they heard the shots from the washroom. Lulu Rosenkrantz went for his gun but was stopped before he could return fire. Weiss blasted the three men with his shotgun as Workman came out of the washroom with his .38 and .45, firing across the table as well, knocking each of the three men to the ground. When Weiss and Workman went over to look at their victims, they realized that Schultz was not among them. Workman went back into the washroom to find Dutch Schultz bleeding on the floor. "Schultz was hit with a rusty steel-jacketed .45 slug that crashed into his husky body just below the chest, on the left, and tore through the abdominal wall into the large intestine, gall bladder, and liver before lodging on the floor near the urinal he had been using when the door opened."[3]

Weiss ran outside the bar, but Workman was still looking over Schultz, who miraculously was still alive. But so were his bodyguards. Rosenkrantz started shooting at Workman, and then Landau followed suit; though both were seriously wounded, they managed to stagger up and toward Workman, who ran outside to find the getaway car had left without him. He took off on foot into the balmy October night.

Schultz managed to claw his way out of the washroom and over to a table. "He didn't say a cockeyed thing. He just went over to a table and put his left hand on it kind of to steady him and then he plopped into a chair, just like a souse would."[4] When the police arrived, they found Schultz still slumped in the chair, head hanging over the table. But he was conscious enough to tell them his name and that he didn't know who had shot him. Three ambulances arrived and carted the men to Newark City Hospital, which by then had filled with police, certain the men who had attempted to assassinate Schultz would likely try again.

Police officers and detectives took turns questioning Schultz and his men, but information was piecemeal at best. Schultz, growing annoyed, told the police to get out of his room and bring him an ice-cream soda. Though seriously wounded and in pain, Schultz managed to keep his defiant attitude against authority. But his fever was climbing, and he started to speak, irrational outburst punctuated with rare moments of clarity. The police sent for a court stenographer to record the Dutchman's last words. The full account is long, but a small sampling of his musings gives a feel for what the police, stenographer, and family members heard in the last conscious minutes of the underworld kingpin.

> I know what I am doing here with my collection of papers, for crying out loud. It isn't worth a nickel to two guys like you or me, but to a collector it's worth a fortune; it is priceless. I am going to turn it over to . . . Turn your back to me please, Henry. I am sick now. The police are getting many complaints. Look out. Hey, Jack; hello, Jack. Jack, Mamma. I want that G-note. Look out for Jimmy Valentine, for he is an old pal of mine . . . Look out! Mamma, Mamma. Look out for her. You can't beat him. Police, Mamma! Helen, Mother, please take me out . . . The Chimney Sweeps. Talk to the Sword. Shut up, you got a big mouth! Please help me up, Henry. Max, come over here . . . French Canadian bean soup . . . I want to pay, let them leave me alone. [5]

Before long, Schultz fell into a coma and was pronounced dead at 8:35 p.m. on October 24, 1935. He had been preceded in death by Otto Berman and Landau, who had succumbed to their injuries earlier that same day. Schultz's last words became subject for a number of novelizations and works of prose over the years. Most notably William S. Burroughs used Schultz's ramblings as the jumping-off point for his screenplay *The Last Words of Dutch Schultz*, which was to use Schultz's ramblings as a constant soundtrack to the film. In 1993 hip-hop group The Disposable Heroes of Hiphopricy released a spoken-word album featuring Burroughs speaking Schultz's last words, laid over a hip-hop beat. [6]

At the time police had a list of suspects and eventually caught up to Weiss and Workman, the two gunmen. But Longy Zwillman was also brought in for questioning by Newark police, as well as by the FBI. Each agency took a turn questioning Zwillman, but he insisted he had no knowledge of Schultz's murder. The authorities felt that the kingpin of the Newark rackets should have some inkling as to who had been planning such a brazen gangland hit on such a high-profile target, right in Longy's backyard, no less. Two nights before the shooting, Dutch Schultz had been seen in the Blue Mirror nightclub, a known Zwillman hangout. And according to a source that night, Doc Stacher had had one of his associates go out and make sure his gun was ready in case there was any trouble. There had definitely been tension in the air in Newark with Schultz escalating his war of words on the authorities. And if a plan had been in motion with Zwillman's knowledge, Stacher would almost certainly have been privy to it.

In the early 2000s, before his death, Newark mobster Joe Stassi gave an interview to a reporter for *GQ* in which he claimed to have inside knowledge of the Schultz killing. Stassi said that the mob called for Schultz's death in part because of his vow to retaliate against Thomas Dewey but also because of his temper and out-of-control ways, which many in the "new mob" saw as an out-of-date way of doing business. The cowboy days of Prohibition were over, and the new era of the businessman gangster was beginning. Stassi maintained that he was the one who set the deal in motion, recruiting Workman and Weiss for the killing. But he claimed that he personally received the order from Meyer Lansky, Lucky Luciano, and Longy Zwillman.[7]

In the aftermath of the Schultz killing, and with the swift move away from the era of Prohibition, Zwillman was juggling a lot of balls in the air. His move into legitimate businesses were still weighted by a lot of baggage from the Prohibition years. In the interim he had managed to improve his personal life, marrying Mary Mendels Steinbach on July 7, 1939. But the ghosts of the Prohibition-era gangsters still hung on, despite his efforts to distance himself.

Just a month after his marriage, Zwillman was called before a federal grand jury investigating the activities of Louis "Lepke" Buchalter, notorious New York mobster and head of the hit squad Murder, Inc. Buchalter had been indicted in 1937 and so fled. Authorities had looked for him for two years, finally discovering that he had never left New York; he was apprehended in August of 1939. The federal grand jury believed fellow gangsters had been aiding and abetting Buchalter's flight from justice, Zwillman among them. Before the judge Zwillman was "particularly adamant in his refusal to testify when asked about the nature of his work and for whom he worked in 1933,"[8] garnering a citation for contempt.

The judge overseeing the grand jury sentenced Zwillman to six months in prison for refusing to testify but allowed Longy out on a ten thousand dollar bail. Longy's lawyers appealed the sentence, and within a month it was ruled that he was within his right to refuse to testify to the grand jury. Zwillman was a free man, and the victory over the government enhanced his already-growing reputation among the underworld. It also made Zwillman the focus of even more law-enforcement scrutiny.

In an FBI memo to Director J. Edgar Hoover, a local agent at the time relayed a conversation he'd had with a US district judge who'd asserted that "Newark has been a little bit neglected by the [Justice] Department, and the result of that is that all these gangsters have now all come over here."[9] As a result, the FBI, in conjunction with local law enforcement, started paying closer attention to the Newark racketeers, though, unbeknownst to the feds, some in the Newark police department were on Zwillman's payroll.

According to FBI files, Zwillman "branched out in control of slot machines, cigarette vending machines, gambling, numbers rackets, and several restaurants and cafes."[10] This diversification only increased after the repeal of Prohibition in 1933. By 1938 his portfolio of legitimate business included the Star Bowling and Billiard Academy, Borok's Furniture Company, the United Brewing Company, and a 40 percent stock holding in the USA Yeast Company. He moved into other areas of the liquor industry as well, investing in liquor distributorships and wholesalers like J&J Distributing and Browne Vintners, the latter a firm run by Longy's old partner Joseph Reinfeld, who had parlayed his ties with Canadian liquor merchants during Prohibition into a prosperous legitimate business.

Real estate and development was another sector Longy viewed as a wise business investment. He had the nightclubs, the Blue Mirror and the Casablanca, as well as the Tavern Restaurant in Newark. Zwillman added Club Greenacres in Miami Beach to his portfolio, as well as Hotel Versailles in Long Branch and Colony Surf Club, both on the Jersey Shore. His operations also extended out west to Las Vegas, where less-legit operations included skimming casino profits from the Fremont Hotel on Fremont Street in downtown Vegas. His bagman was a New York City theatrical producer who arranged entertainment for many of the casinos and hotels in Vegas. On his return to New York he would bring cash back for Longy. Longy's longtime friend Doc Stacher was also involved with the Fremont. In fact, an informant told the FBI that "almost all of the gambling casinos take their orders from Meyer Lansky and Joseph 'Doc' Stacher."[11]

Longy also was involved in an unusual subgenre of the music industry: He controlled a company called Music by Muzak. The Al Capone of Newark was in charge of a Muzak company that supplied soothing vocal-free music to office, restaurants, and elevators throughout central New Jersey. The burgeoning gaming and music-machine business was emerging as a major business line, and racketeers were quick to size on the potential. One such company was the Runyon Sales Company.

The company was started by Barney Sugerman and Abe Green. According to Barney's son, Myron, "My dad and Abe Green (Longy's guy) were the original partners. Doc Stacher got involved because they needed finance and connections. They eventually had a major jukebox, pinball, arcade games, vending machine operation. Everybody knew their name around the country. But my father was a better visionary and salesman than a businessman. In 1946 Doc Stacher sold his shares to Jerry Catena when Doc moved west to Los Angeles. And when my dad died in 1964 my mother was bought out by Abe and Jerry in 1966."[12] As for Zwillman's alleged involvement in the company, "The FBI thought that Zwillman had part of Runyon and that my dad was holding shares for him. I'm not sure if that's the case."

Longy also owned half of a tobacco operation, Public Service Tobacco Company, in an industrial section of nearby Hillside, New Jersey. Zwillman had bought into the company in 1937. It was previously owned by Doc Stacher and Jerry Catena. Another owner of the company was Mike Lascari, longtime associate of Lucky Luciano. Zwillman defended his partner in testimony before Congress against accusations that Lascari was involved in the rackets. "He came to Jersey and worked all day and night on the Public Service thing," insisted Zwillman. "Now certainly that does not spell out an underworld man who works 20 hours a day."[13]

The automobile industry was another business line that interested the enterprising gangster. He owned a number of General Motors dealerships, one of which sold over $375,000-worth of cars to the city of Newark in 1948 alone. Zwillman had a 97 percent stock holding in E&S Trading Company, a steel- and scrap-metal dealer, and in A&S Trading, which bought and sold automobile part and accessories, and even had a company that rented out washing machines for use in apartments and housing complexes. In addition to the companies held in his name, there were others he helped run from behind the scenes, including a movie-production company, a post office, and a railroad.

It's easy to apply the label *gangster* to Longy Zwillman if one looked strictly at the way he made his money before and during Prohibition. But his activities in legitimate business industries show a man who, if he decided to solely concentrate on business matters, may have been a successful entrepreneur or even CEO. There is a definitive dividing line when discussing and analyzing the activities of organized crime, especially older mob figures. There are those who started out as street gangsters and never really rose to anything greater than that. They were the low-level hit men, the workaday gangsters who would steal a couple thousand dollars, spend it, and then go steal more. Bookies, loan sharks, and fences were probably the next rung up on the ladder, but for the most part there was, and still is, a large portion of mobsters who did it because they like to thumb their nose at the law and had little to no aspiration to change. But Zwillman had a broader knowledge of things and was certainly more intelligent than most mobsters of his generation. Even the men he surrounded himself with (Catena) and associated with (Lansky) shared those traits. Zwillman had all the makings of a captain of industry.

In addition to his forays into the business world, Zwillman's work in the political realm continued as well. This was an area where he started back with the Third Ward Political Club, bringing politicians and elected officials under his wing and influence. In the run up to the 1949 New Jersey gubernatorial elections, Zwillman reportedly offered Democratic candidate Elmer

Wene a campaign contribution of three hundred thousand dollars. In return Zwillman wanted say over who would be picked as state attorney, "because Zwillman does not want the Wene administration to hurt him."[14] Wene declined the offer and did not end up winning the election, so Zwillman ended up saving his three hundred thousand. It wasn't Zwillman's first activity in the races for governor. In 1946 he was approached by Governor Hoffman's office for help in securing the vote in Essex County.

In 1950 the congressional Kefauver Committee, established to investigate organized crime, turned its attention to Longy and subpoenaed him to testify before the Senate. He did, though he did his best to give as little information as possible, pleading the Fifth numerous times. When pressed about his moniker as the "Al Capone of New Jersey," Zwillman replied, "That, Mr. Senator, is a myth that has been developing for a good many years, and during the time when I should have had sense enough to stop it, or to get up and get out of the state, I did not have sense enough."[15]

He also delivered a prepared statement to the senators quizzing him.

> It is, and has been, my intention in coming here as a witness to answer every proper question to the best of my ability but without waiving any rights which I may have under the Constitution and under the law.
>
> If I understand the scope of this committee's function correctly, it is to investigate organized interstate crime. Therefore, one might conclude that I was called here either on the assumption that I have some facts concerning such crime or that I myself are [sic] engaged in interstate crime. However, when one considers the nature of the questions asked of the witnesses who preceded me, and one has followed their appearances here, one wonders whether he is only a witness when he appears here. I have a feeling that this committee, or in any event one of more law-enforcement agencies of the government, are seeking to implicate me in federal offences. I know that many enforcement agencies of the government have for a long time been engaged in an extensive investigation of my affairs and those of my business associates and even my friends and relatives for many years.
>
> My attorneys have been told, directly by responsible officers of the government, that they have a suspicion and feeling that I have committed federal crimes and that they seek to prosecute me . . .
>
> . . . I have come to the conclusion that it would be impossible for an average person, not trained in the law, and who has been actively engaged in many businesses and endeavors over a period of years, particularly in association with other people, to be fully aware of all the federal laws which might govern or control these matters . . . These and other factors contribute to my fear that the answers to some of the questions which may be put to me may tend to incriminate me.[16]

The Kefauver Committee, in turn, had this to say about Zwillman: "Like Frank Costello in New York, Zwillman exercises his influence in New Jersey in a manner that makes detection almost impossible. He makes it a practice never to attend any public function, and he avoids wherever possible having his name appear openly in any financial transaction."[17] Zwillman told the committee when asked if he was going legitimate that "From that period of 1935 or 1936 up, I have been trying, Mr. Senator. I am trying . . . trying hard."[18]

The Kefauver Committee did not put Zwillman alone on the spot. It pulled open the curtain on the existence and depth of organized crime in America. Zwillman just happened to be one of the more notable people who testified. The experience rattled him and would continue to plague him through the 1950s. Just as Longy thought he had put his gangster image behind him, it was right back in the headlines—and now on television—something he hadn't had to contend with back in during Prohibition days.

While Longy was trying to erase the stain of Kefauver, two of his associates were busy building their own empires. The first, Ruggerio Boiardo—aka Richie "the Boot"—had risen out of the same Newark streets that had produced Zwillman, though Boiardo had grown up in the First Ward, the heavily Italian neighborhood that hugged to bend of the Passaic River where it turns north. The close-knit neighborhood was the epicenter of the Italian community in Newark, though few vestiges remain today. Like Zwillman, Boiardo had cut a Robin Hood–type persona in the neighborhood. Seeing himself as merely a backer of gambling and bootlegging, and eschewing violence and prostitution—not to mention drug dealing, which was starting to become an issue in the United States at the time—Boiardo entrenched himself in the neighborhood.

Boiardo started his criminal career as a member of a gang led by the Mazzocchi brothers—Dominic, John, and Frank. When Boiardo moved to align himself with the Mazzocchi brothers in 1925, they were big players in the bootleg liquor scene of the First Ward. They operated the Victory Café and a billiards parlor. The brothers and the Boot also "ran alky cookers in the city. One of the most profitable, said to be owned by the Boot, was located in the back of a tenement house on Wood Street in the First Ward."[19] These still operations were common in many parts of the country though they could be dangerously combustible, not unlike the meth labs of today. In October of 1927 the still exploded with two men inside, Sam Angelo and Carmine DePalma. The blast shook buildings for blocks around, with reports that "The walls, doors, windows, and ceilings of the garage were shaken and almost shattered."[20]

By 1928, the Boot was looking to form his own gang and opened up his own speakeasies. His move toward independence from the Mazzocchi gang did not go over well with the brothers, especially since he took some of their own men with him. The Boot was expanding while the Mazzocchis were suffering. This type of disparity in the racket inevitably led to conflict. The

Boot furthered angered the brothers by setting up his own headquarters, the Richie Association, just up the street from the Victory Café.

Skirmishes started with incursions on one another's turf, followed by the hijacking of liquor shipments. Things took a turn on the night of August 19, 1929, when two Mazzocchi men, Agostino Dellapia and Vincenzo Follo, were chased by Boot gunmen right past a police station, where they were shot. Dellapia was shot twice in the chest, twice in the stomach, and once in the back and died soon after arriving at City Hospital. Follo never made it; he'd been shot three times in the chest. The following year, Frank Mazzocchi was shot in front of the Victory Café. He'd been talking with friends in a car when "another machine drew abreast of the party and Mazzocchi dropped under the [hail] of bullets."[21] He was rushed to the hospital with four bullet wounds but died, after refusing to talk to police. John Mazzocchi was killed in March of 1932 with a gunshot to the back of the head. Thereafter the remnants of the gang were no longer a threat to Boiardo.

But Boiardo identified a potential rival across town: Longy Zwillman. Boiardo suspected Longy might have aligned himself with the Mazzocchis. Boiardo's reasoning was that Longy was smart enough to see how quickly the Boot had been engulfing existing liquor and gambling operations and so it was only a matter of time before he came knocking at the Third Ward's door. According to sources, Zwillman started the salvo when he sent his men to capture three Boot soldiers and literally kneecap them, hitting them so hard in the legs that they were crippled for life. There was another story of two Boot hitmen who had decided to visit Zwillman at the Riviera Hotel, dressed as women. The young men were taken upstairs to Zwillman's room, where they were "unmasked" and threatened. Longy reportedly told them, "I'll give you a number. You tell Boiardo if he doesn't call it in twenty-four hours, you're all dead. My people will clean every one of you rats of the streets of Newark. Now, get out of here."[22] It's unknown whether those were Longy's exact words or if the story is even totally true, but it's become part of the lore of the Boiardo-Zwillman war. What is known is that the two men decided to make peace.

The meeting took place at the Nuova Napoli restaurant in October of 1930. The "peace banquet," as the newspapers called it, lasted for three days and was a feast of food, wine, women, and discussion over sharing the Newark rackets and working together rather than apart. Zwillman had the backing of Lucky Luciano and many of the major New York bosses. Zwillman showed up the second day of the event and was accosted by reporters who wanted to take a photo of Longy shaking hands with the Boot. Such was the prestige of the bootlegger in Newark in those days. Whereas paparazzi in Hollywood were fawning over movie stars like Jean Harlow (who would later date Zwillman), the Newark press corps hung on every word, every sighting, every event in the never-ending saga of the rumrunners, bootleggers, and racketeers that populated the city. Strengthened by the popularity of gangster movies, the pop-culture connection between wiseguys and the public was apparent even in these early years. While many would look at it as glorification of criminality, the fact is that if nobody had bought the newspapers the press wouldn't have covered the event. Same went for the movies of the day: Gangster films brought in the crowds at the box office. And so reporting about a peace meeting between two of the city's biggest crime lords was just another scoop.

Zwillman left the meeting certain that peace had been achieved. But events unfolded that challenged the success of the meeting. Boiardo was stepping out of his bulletproof limousine in front of his apartment at 242 Broad Street in Newark on November 26, 1930, when machine-gun fire tore through him, eleven bullets ripping through his head and body. The Boot was rushed to City Hospital where he miraculously survived, though he was in dire shape. Papers of the day dramatically reported that the "overlord of First Ward gangdom, whose dominions he sought to widen, lay near death today, victim of foes who raked him with shotgun fire as he stepped from his bulletproof automobile."[23]

Suspicion fell almost immediately on Zwillman, but in reality Longy would have had little to gain in hitting the Boot at that time, when the press had just fawned over the two men joining hands. It would have been a smarter move, had he indeed been looking to move in on the Boot's rackets, to wait until the press coverage, and attention from the police, had died down. There were also many who thought the attempted hit on Boiardo was the responsibility of an associate of Dominic "the Ape" Passelli, another local crime lord who had been killed a few weeks earlier. Shot and injured on November 2, Passelli had gone to the hospital, where he asked for a private room for the night. Two gunmen strolled past the hospital's information desk and found Passelli in his private room. They shot the Ape three times, killing him. And this is how gangsters Sam Monaco and Louis Russo came to be suspected of involvement in the Passelli murder. However, a nurse at the hospital later identified Jerry Catena as one of the men who had visited the Ape between the time he had been admitted and when the second wave of gunmen had killed him in his hospital bed. That Catena may have been involved in the Ape's death places some suspicion in the Zwillman/Boiardo camp.

With each passing day, and ultimately year, the ties between the Boot and Longy grew. Catena became close to the Boot as well, even serving as best man to Boiardo's son, Anthony, at his wedding. Boiardo's empire grew after he recovered from the shooting. One of his earliest headquarters was the Vittorio Castle, a spectacular Italian restaurant on the corner of Summer Avenue and Eighth Avenue, in the heart of the First Ward.[24] Opened in 1937, the restaurant was far grander than anything in the area. Billed on its menu as

"The Home of Fine Italian Food and Wines," the Vittorio Castle's exterior was "an undulating flow of towers and sturdy Flemish bond brickwork, tall arch windows, and a canopied turret entrance, like a medieval citadel."[25] The Boot's business partner was Henry Abrams, a former boxer with a criminal record, like Boiardo's, which prevented their applying for a liquor license. The solution was to transfer ownership of the restaurant to Boiardo's son, Anthony "Tony Boy." In time, the Vittorio became a popular eating establishment for local officials and politicians, celebrities and sports stars (like Joe DiMaggio), and many of Boiardo's fellow Jersey criminals.

As Boiardo's stock rose, so did Jerry Catena's. Zwillman's right-hand man had been plucked out of the Ironbound section of Newark, along with his brother Eugene. Like Zwillman, Catena played the part of gentleman gangster. He was courteous, rarely used profanity, and dressed impeccably. He also shared Zwillman's business acumen and became heavily involved in legitimate businesses throughout New Jersey. Catena amassed an extensive rap sheet through the 1920s and '30s, with ten arrests ranging from gambling to bribery to grand larceny. He served time in Ann Reformatory, Essex County Penitentiary, and Rahway State Prison. To law enforcement, Catena's profile rose right alongside Zwillman's. The FBI considered Jerry Catena "a top hoodlum of the Newark office."[26] As the 1940s and '50s rolled on, Catena became business partners in some of Zwillman's legitimate ventures and branched out on his own, primarily into the world of gambling machines and jukeboxes. Later Myron Sugerman, son of Zwillman and Catena's contemporary Barney Sugerman, had this to say:

> Jerry Catena was the one who put the Bally gaming deal together. My father was the key player. He was the Bally distributor for New Jersey, New York, Connecticut. Bill O'Donnell, the general manager of Bally at the time, came and asked my father to introduce him to Catena. They had now the hopper that they were able to put into slots, and this would revolutionize the slot-machine business. Catena picked up the phone and contacted Sam Klein, owner of Stern Vending in Cleveland, Ohio, who in turn contacted the Jacobs family, owners of Emprise from Buffalo, New York. Together with Jerry Catena, Barney Sugerman, Abe Green, Irving Kaye, and Bill O'Donnell they bought the Bally factory out of foreclosure from the bank. That's how they put the Bally deal together. They revolutionized the slot-machine industry and had complete control over it. But they were all forced out of the company when they went public because they all had criminal records.[27]

In the post-Kefauver days, Zwillman's crew did not have as deep a bench as it once had, but Zwillman still had some heavy hitters on the payroll. Mob hitmen and tough guys are the stuff of gangster-movie legend and lore. But in the annals of New Jersey mob history, Harold "Kayo" Konigsberg was a true tough guy and hitman who was originally under the wing of Zwillman.

Whereas the dapper Zwillman cultivated an image of the businessman, Kayo was the opposite. Ruthless and effective, he is alleged to have racked up over twenty gangland killings. And he had a vicious temper. People that were around him kept their distance, afraid of saying anything to set off the bruiser.

> Max "Puddy" Hinkes was a well-known Newark, New Jersey, Jewish gangster who was part of the Zwillman-Stacher mob from early youth. Puddy operated a card room and sports-betting operation on Chancellor Avenue in Newark. One day out of a clear blue sky appeared Kayo Konigsberg and beat up a guy in the place who owed Kayo money and had been ducking him. Besides working this guy over, Kayo trashed the place. Longy was no longer on this earth, so Puddy ran to Tony Bananas Caponigro, who in turn contacted Bayonne Joe Zicarelli to put a leash on Kayo so that Mr. Konigsberg wouldn't be making himself troublesome in the future. [28]

Since Zwillman had appeared before the Kefauver Committee, he was continually dogged by the IRS. They tore through his business returns and kept a close eye on new investments. Longy was getting squeezed constantly, and it was starting to affect the way he managed his affairs. Longy was indicted on two counts of tax evasion in May of 1954, based on his and his wife's tax records from the late 1940s. The trial was postponed until January of 1956. The IRS had been after Zwillman for close to a decade, scrutinizing his various business interests and tax returns going back to the days of Prohibition. The government thought they had an airtight case and so were taken aback when, on March 1, 1956, the jury came back and said it couldn't reach a verdict. It wasn't until two years later, in 1958, that a wiretap placed in the Supreme Beverage Company at 631 Bergen Street in Newark, a known hangout of Zwillman, revealed that two jurors in the trial had been bribed. A third potential juror had been paid off by Sam "Big Sue" Katz, [29] but that person was not empaneled.

Longy still held sway over criminal activities in Newark, "still an imposing figure, brainier than most of his contemporaries, wiser, more experienced in handling the daily problems that cropped up in any illicit undertaking— and few in the rackets wanted to try and toss him aside." [30] In 1957 an internal FBI report indicated than an informant told the feds that Zwillman was still one of the big kingpins of New Jersey organized crime, along with mafioso Ritchie the Boot, John "Big Pussy" Russo, Angelo "Gyp" DeCarlo, and Tony Caponigro. Zwillman was still sought after by Catena for advice long after the rising Genovese mobster would have needed to defer to him. Meyer Lansky still considered Longy a good friend, and the two often socialized in Florida or when Meyer was back in New York. Zwillman knew his days as the top racketeer were behind him, and he knew that the continued pressure of IRS investigations, press fixation on his every move, and the changing nature of the underworld scene were taking their toll on him both physically and mentally. But his fellow racketeers were not privy to his feelings. Longy kept them at arm's length, though he did occasionally let it slip how the court cases were draining him. His doctor later told police that Zwillman was suffering from high blood pressure, heart issues, and depression. And maybe in the back of Zwillman's mind was the concern that, what with all the pressure building, things would crack and he might fall out of favor with the very friends and business associates he had helped get their start.

On the night of February 25, 1959, Longy went to dinner with his wife. He left the restaurant early, telling her he had somewhere to go. He was driven to the home of his friend Jerry Catena, where he stayed for a few hours, talking. He got home and went to bed. His wife told investigators that she awoke around 2 a.m. and that Zwillman was pacing, saying he was having trouble sleeping. At 8 a.m. the next day, his wife awoke, assuming Longy had gone to work at the Public Service Tobacco Company. At 10 a.m. she went to the basement storeroom. There she found Longy, dressed in bathrobe and slippers, hanging from a cord looped around supports in the ceiling. He was dropped down to his knees. She immediately called the family physician, who arrived at the home just after 10 a.m. He pronounced Longy dead and called the police.

The prosecutor at the time was future governor Brendan Byrne. "The first thing I knew about Longy's death was when Dr. Edwin Albano, the medical examiner, called me. He and his assistant, a man named Kaehler, were at Zwillman's house with the West Orange police. He said Zwillman was hanging in the basement and that it looked like suicide."[31] Later that day, Dr. Albano officially declared Zwillman's death a suicide.

In keeping with Jewish tradition, Zwillman's body was prepared for a burial within twenty-four hours of his death. The funeral took place at the Philip Apter Funeral Home in Newark. The funeral drew a modest crowd of family, friends, curiosity seekers, and FBI agents looking for names and faces. It was a far cry from the lavish gangland funerals of other well-known racketeers, but enough of Zwillman's contemporaries showed up to make it known how well-liked he was in the neighborhood and the business worlds, legit and not. Some of his closest friends couldn't attend. Jerry Catena was in Florida, unable to make it back up in time; friends reported him despondent for days after Zwillman's death. Meyer Lansky and others were out of town but sent regards. A funeral procession of twenty-seven cars took his body to the B'nai Abraham Memorial Park off Route 22 in Union, just next to the Rahway River.

When Longy died, there were lots of questions: Did he really commit suicide, or was he murdered? One source said he had heard that a couple days before his death Longy had gone to see Eugene Catena, Jerry's brother and head of his own crew. Longy told Gene that he was really feeling the pressure from the IRS investigation and that they were squeezing him hard. There were other people who told of Zwillman's declining state. His stepson told reporters that he had been depressed and that Saul Kantz's indictment for bribery in his tax case had been the final straw.

Even entertaining the possibility that Zwillman was murdered, it's highly unlikely that a mob hitman or team would enter a house when a man's family was sleeping and kill him by making it look like a suicide. That is an idea wrapped in issues both moral and logistical—even for organized crime. Syndicated columnist Dorothy Kilgallen opined that "it's no secret in the underworld that when the mob boys want one of their tribesman erased, they know just how to do the job so it looks like a perfect suicide."[32] Brendan Byrne dismissed the idea that Zwillman was murdered. "From all our findings, that was nonsense. The autopsy, the man's actions on the night before his death, the fact that at fifty-five he was still strong enough to raise quite a racket if someone tried anything funny, everything pointed to suicide due to temporary insanity."[33]

But even though Longy was gone, business had to continue. And that meant a sea change in the way Longy's old rackets were divvied up.

> After Longy died, the Jews no longer had a roof over their head. Shortly after his passing, Messrs. Irving Berlin and Max Puddy Hinkes, who had a share of the Newark, New Jersey, numbers business, were being sought after by the authorities. They took off for the night and stayed at the Luxor Baths on Forty-Sixth Street in Manhattan. When they came back to Jersey shortly thereafter they were told that their numbers business was now in the hands of Jerry Catena, Tony Boy Boiardo, Gyp de Carlo, and Tony Bananas Caponigro. As long as Longy was alive, the Jews who were operating businesses outside the law were under his protection. Once he was gone, the Italians took over.[34]

But beyond the implications for Jewish members of the Newark crime scene, the death of Longy Zwillman was the final nail in the coffin of the old Newark gambling syndicate. Jerry Catena was now affiliated with a Mafia family, Longy's other associates partnered up with Mafia crews for protection and business ventures, and the Mafia's control over the other rackets expanded. Much like the Irish were pushed aside in many areas to make room for the Jews and the Italians, now it was the Jewish gangster of the Prohibition era leaving the scene. Most left the scene voluntarily or by natural causes. But within the world of organized crime, murder was still the ultimate way to take care of a problem.

Chapter Five

The Moretti Hit

The World War II–era Jersey underworld was a pastiche of existing Jersey-based mafiosi coupled with the presence of New York crime figures who had fled Manhattan in the face of increasing law-enforcement attention. These New York wiseguys set up operations across the Hudson River. The inter-Mafia ties established during the Prohibition years reached fruition as the underworld's focus turned toward the docks, drugs, labor unions, and the New Jersey Mafia's bread and butter of the time, illegal gambling. And with the expansion of gambling operations came loansharking, extortion, political corruption, and, when competition grew fierce, murder.

Essex County may have housed the largest number of crime figures, but it was in Bergen County that residents felt the New York syndicates' reach most directly. Bergen, New Jersey's northeasternmost county, is located across the George Washington Bridge from New York City. In the postwar years, the county had experienced a significant population boom, growing more than 30 percent between 1940 and 1950. The smaller towns tried to keep up with the rapid pace of suburbanization fueled by the influx of new residents, including the wiseguys.

Palisade Avenue in Cliffside Park, New Jersey, is one of Bergen County's major thoroughfares. The street runs parallel to the Hudson River and offers a scenic view of Manhattan. On this street sat the unofficial headquarters of Bergen County's major Mafia figures. The establishment was Duke's Restaurant,[1] on the corner of Palisade Avenue and Hudson Place. Duke's first became a popular hangout in the late 1930s, and by 1941 it was not only a regular hangout for wiseguys and politicians, it also served as the New York wiseguy diaspora's nerve center. From May 1948 to February 1949, 6,191 phone calls were made from Duke's to 509 different mob-connected numbers in New York City.

Duke's was owned by John "Duke" DeNoia, a mob associate who had as many friends in the underworld as he did in law enforcement and politics. DeNoia gained notoriety during exposés of organized crime's penetration of the New Jersey and New York docks, as well as the longshoremen's union. DeNoia had been hired by Dade Brothers, Inc., to oversee the nighttime unloading of ships at Jersey City's Claremont Terminal Channel. Investigators found that, under DeNoia's oversight, workers "shot dice, bribed, pilfered, peddled dope, and amused themselves by crashing Army forklifts into each other."[2]

Quite a few major Mafia powerhouses were based in Bergen by the early 1940s. Some arrived from New York City, having been edged out by a crusading mayor. When New York City mayor Fiorello La Guardia commenced his mob crackdown, he boasted that he would "dive the bums out of town." Later he warned, "Let the gamblers, tinhorns, racketeers, and gangsters take notice that they have to keep away from New York from now on."[3] To some extent, La Guardia succeeded. Still, the mobsters who had relocated to New Jersey were not about to let go of their lucrative customers. Combining the latest in telephone technology with bribes, the Bergen County mob crews set up a sophisticated network of phone lines throughout the county, paying some residents fifty dollars a week to access their phone lines for a few hours a day. The phone system was used to tap into the betting action in New York, as well as to take in calls from payoff bets around the country. It was reminiscent of the old nationwide wire services, but with a decidedly high-tech flair for the time. Authorities estimated that more than 2,600 Bergen County residents rented their phone lines out for the weekly payout.

The operations were orchestrated to perfection. Bellhops, bartenders, and concierges in hotels across Manhattan coordinated cab and limousine pickups for rich potential customers to be driven across the George Washington Bridge, where they were then ferried to clubs across Bergen County. These clubs ranged from low-class establishments known as sawdust joints to elegant, higher-end gambling palaces, called carpet joints. Particularly well-off gamblers were plied with free food and wine.

One of the more renowned higher-end establishments was the Riviera, owned by Ben Marden, a Longy Zwillman associate, as well as New York mob boss Frank Costello and Owney Madden, who owned the Cotton Club in Harlem. Marden's Riviera opened in 1931, but a fire destroyed the original building in 1936. Marden built a second, just to the south of the original, and it became a hub for top entertainers of the day, from Frank Sinatra to Lena Horne to the Andrews Sisters. Perched high above the Palisades, its large sign tilted toward the George Washington Bridge; the club became a mecca for New York City's well-to-do. It also became an underworld hangout. Marden himself was fined for contempt for his refusal to answer questions about mob involvement in the Riviera.

The nightly trips across the GW Bridge to places like the Riviera were inevitably noticed by elements of law enforcement on both sides of the state line. But while New York City District Attorney Frank S. Hogan sent his detectives to investigate the activities of the New York mafiosi in New Jersey, various local police departments in Bergen County also kept tabs on Hogan's men, and US Treasury agents looked into the vast gambling empire. The corruption of local police didn't extend to the New Jersey State Police as much, so mobsters in areas where the State Police held jurisdiction moved the games around frequently, trying to stay one step ahead of the law.

Several Bergen gambling halls were under Joe Adonis's thumb.[4] Already well known in Manhattan, Adonis was one of the top targets of local law enforcement, as well as of federal agents from the Bureau of Narcotics. Adonis's New Jersey empire was based in Fort Lee, West Paterson, and especially Lodi. The Lodi operation was centered on a palatial gambling hall called Costa's Barn. According to lore, Adonis spent lavishly to redecorate the interior.

While Adonis garnered a lot of the police and media attention, one of his partners was Guarino "Willie" Moretti, one of Bergen's most powerful crime figures. He seemed to have his hand not only in the gambling palaces but also in the pervasive payoffs to police, judges, and lawmakers.

Willie married and settled in New Jersey in 1928.[5] His early criminal career included a five-year sentence in Elmira Prison in New York for gun charges. Moretti only served part of the time. Of the circumstances, Willie told the Senate,

> In 1913 some barber said I tried to hit him and take money off him, so they charged me with robbery. It was no more robbery than sitting here . . . In 1915 I was convicted for— there was a gun charge of a misdemeanor. I got a two-year suspended sentence from Judge Rolasky again. And he made a speech there, and he said, "Being I sentenced you to Elmira Reformatory in 1913 and you obeyed my orders, I am going to give you a suspended sentence. Next time you hear shooting, turn and run the other way, and don't take any guns out of people's pockets."[6]

After he was released from Elmira, the teenage Moretti made most of his money on gambling, "just shoot craps, that's all . . . All kids gambled to make a living."[7] Moretti moved around the area, never staying in one place too long, "between New York and Buffalo—and I went all over, Newburgh, traveled around, wherever there was a crap game, I was there."[8]

Later on, Moretti became a legitimate businessman as well, owning a share of the United State Linen Supply Company of Paterson, New Jersey. Moretti dressed sharply and carried himself like a man of great importance. He was comfortable meeting with various Mafia chieftains and was also a regular fixture at the horse track, where he later told a Senate committee he pocketed up to fifty thousand dollars a year in winnings from the horses alone.

Willie had a close professional relationship with Essex County boss Longy Zwillman and with Jerry Catena and operated for a time out of Newark's First Ward, along with Richie "the Boot" Boiardo. Zwillman said of Moretti, "I have known the fellow a long time. He is a nice fellow."[9] Moretti was close with Vito Genovese, whose name eventually became the old Mangano crime family's "official name." Genovese had an interest in slot machines set up in bars throughout New Jersey. His point man for the slots was Moretti.

Moretti's connections also extended to Charlie "Lucky" Luciano, with whom Moretti met in Havana, along with Jerry Catena. Moretti said of Catena, "He knows Lucky well, too. We happened to be in Florida, and I took him along with me. I wanted to see Charlie Lucky, so they volunteered, just on a friendly basis."[10]

Willie's pop culture claim to fame was his friendship with Frank Sinatra. Unlike many of the singer's alleged gangland connections, the Moretti relationship was real. The story, fictionalized in *The Godfather*, was that Moretti put a gun up to Tommy Dorsey's head to force the bandleader to release Sinatra from a restrictive contract. Sinatra was eternally grateful, and Moretti gained a nice footnote in cinematic lore.

Moretti, his brother Solly, Adonis, Max Shargel, Frank Ericson—these were some of Bergen's bigwigs. But while the occasional local newspaper published a story detailing the Mafia's hold on the county, enough of a cloud of secrecy hovered over the Bergen Big Five, as they were called, to keep at bay any serious investigations. The hold over Bergen extended to the political establishment. Moretti knew a lot of powerful political figures not just at a local level, but the state level as well. This type of influence with political figures was essential for the mob in Bergen, and elsewhere, to maintain their business operations with minimal disruption by law enforcement. As long as things stayed quiet and no one uncovered too much, there was an air of plausible deniability.

But that lasted only so long before citizens across the country got a front-row seat to the story of how the Mafia was able to deeply infiltrate many of America's largest cities, courtesy of both the emerging technological marvel of television and the efforts of a senator from Tennessee, the coonskin-cap-wearing Estes Kefauver. The committee that informally took his name, officially titled the United States Senate Special Committee to Investigate Crime in Interstate Commerce, was established on May 3, 1950. Its stated mission was to investigate "whether organized crime utilizes the facilities of interstate commerce or otherwise operates in interstate commerce in furtherance of any transactions which are in violation of the law."[11] Many hearings were filmed for a television audience, and they aired more than those sessions attended by journalists from all the major newspapers and magazines. Up until the Kefauver hearings, the idea of a national crime syndicate had been a foreign concept to many Americans. But that was about to change.

The Kefauver Committee shed some light on the Mafia's activities in New Jersey (as well as in other cities, from Tampa to Kansas City) and, as previously noted, brought Longy Zwillman in for an appearance. The committee also paid particular attention to Duke's Restaurant and attempted to get some of its more infamous customers to share secrets about the establishment's allure. They called Solly Moretti (Willie's brother) and Joe Adonis, among others. They also called Willie, who turned out to be surprisingly candid about some details, including offering a who's who of his appointments at Duke's—from Jerry Catena to Longy Zwillman. At the time of the hearings, his brother Solly was in prison for gambling charges, and the rumor was that Willie was so incensed that his political connections were not able to get the charges dropped that he was prepared to bare all about the nexus between the Mafia and the law before the committee.

Moretti's questioning before the committee fell on Wednesday, December 13, 1950. His brother, as well as Joe Adonis, had been previously questioned but had offered little in terms of substance. Moretti, on the other hand, answered most of the committee's questions, admitting that he knew a cadre of underworld figures from Longy Zwillman to Los Angeles Mafia boss Jack Dragna. Moretti even had his own concept of the mob. "Well," he told the assembled senators, "the newspapers calls them the mob. I don't know whether they are right or wrong. If they would be right, everybody would be in jail; is that right?"[12]

While Willie kept many secrets—for example, when asked about the politicians he knew, he replied, "I know a lot of people . . . I don't care to mention any names"[13]—he was open about a wide range of intimate topics, such as his income, his business dealings, and his frequent visits to the horse tracks, from Jersey down to Florida. Later that day, newspapers described Moretti as "one of the most remarkable citizens to appear before the Committee."[14] Many in the Mafia weren't as taken with Moretti's appearance.

By 1951, Moretti was living in Hasbrouck Heights, a small Bergen County borough, adjacent to Lodi. He had a six-acre estate in Deal, on the Jersey Shore, where he raised ducks. As the immediate fallout from his Kefauver appearance seemed to wane, Moretti was back looking after his business arrangements. But he was also battling an enemy within. A case of syphilis he acquired when he was younger was starting to eat away at his brain. This caused bouts of dementia (some mobsters believed the illness explained his otherwise-inexplicable appearance before the Kefauver Commission). Rumors started flying that Moretti's behavior was growing increasingly unpredictable.

On October 4, 1951, Willie was set to meet some fellow mobsters at Joe's Elbow Room for lunch and business discussions.[15] Joe's was located down the block from Duke's—which had closed a year prior—and was basically a nondescript one-story building with a flat roof. As a waitress later recounted, two men entered the restaurant around 11 a.m. and sat down at the counter. They were joined by two more, and all four then took a table near the front window. Willie Moretti drove up in his Corona Cream–colored Packard.[16] One of the men went out, greeting Moretti, who wore a brown suit and maroon tie, ushering him inside. The men sat and spoke Italian while the waitress went to the kitchen to retrieve menus. The shots rang out seconds later in quick succession, filling the empty restaurant.

What exactly happened during the shooting is speculation. It is believed that at least two men stood and commenced firing on Moretti, hitting him in the chest and head as he fell from his chair onto the black-and-white-tiled floor. After cutting Moretti down, the men bolted from the restaurant. The waitress told police that by the time she gazed back into the main restaurant, the men were already gone, and Moretti was lying on the ground, dead.

"His left arm was crooked, thick, ham fist holding onto his heart long stilled; his ankles neatly crossed, a hint of sock showing, his eyes closed to the violence of that final moment, as his killers shot him, face on, a mark of respect—he had the right to see what was happening—the blood pooling out from under his shattered head, one of those awful ties, soaked in red, crumpled over the shoulder of his open jacket."[17]

Reporters flocked to the restaurant immediately. With the crime scene located only feet away from the Palisades Amusement Park's entrance, there was a somewhat comical juxtaposition: While Moretti was being killed, the deadly gunshots rang out across an amusement park brimming with families, many of which would have easily heard the shots, though they probably had no clue as to what was actually happening.

Willie's funeral was lavish, even by mob standards. The procession was comprised of eleven limousines and seventy-five cars. Flowers arrived courtesy of all the major Mafia figures. After the mass at Corpus Christi Church, over five thousand mourners descended on the burial site. One reporter observed that actual mourners seemed to be in the minority and that the rest came "to gape, trample the cemetery, and steal flowers off his grave."[18] Moretti was buried in an ornate tomb at St. Michael's Cemetery in South Hackensack. His tomb towers over nearby headstones, casting an ominous shadow.

The Moretti killing rippled through both the New Jersey and New York underworlds and made news around the country. Many mobsters felt that Moretti's worsening dementia and ever-opening mouth had definitely been unwelcome, especially with both law enforcement and the media beginning to exhibit renewed interest in their activities.

Some suggested alternative means would have been more appropriate to Moretti's stature. Angelo "Gyp" DeCarlo respected Moretti and "deplored the manner in which [he] was killed."[19] Even so, DeCarlo had understood that Moretti had to go, due to the advancing syphilis, but he offered that they should have simply injected certain substances into Moretti's arm and placed him in a car, creating the facade of a natural death by heart attack. Talking to another New Jersey mafioso, "Tony Boy" Boiardo, DeCarlo pontificated further: "They say, 'Tony Boy wants to shoot you in the head and leave you in the street, or would you rather like this, we put you behind your wheel, we don't have to embarrass your family or nothing.' That's what they should have done to Willie." To which Tony replied, "I don't think Willie would have went for that." And Ray responded, "I think he would. He would have tried to talk his way out of it, but he would have went for it."[20]

The leading motive for the Moretti killing of is generally thought to be related to his 1950 appearance before the Kefauver Committee and the view that his declining mental state had rendered him too unstable. Joe Valachi testified to Congress that "they expressed it that he was a sick man, and once Vito [Genovese] even told us, and he said, 'Lord have mercy on his soul' and that he said he lost his mind and that is the way life is." Valachi went on to describe how Moretti hadn't been killed out of anger but respect, citing the funeral as evidence. "He had lots and lots of automobiles, with flowers, and usually when a boss like Anastasia or even Maranzano, they were deserted, but Willie was not deserted, because it was sort of, as we put it, he was supposed to be a mercy killing because he was sick."[21]

But a highly interesting competing theory was posed by one informant.[22] Based out of the FBI's San Diego office, this informant told the FBI about the belief that Moretti had been an informant for the Federal Bureau of Narcotics, under George White. During Moretti's appearance at the Kefauver hearing, White had even sat behind Moretti in the audience.

The informant was suspicious. White had known about some of the informant's operations, and the only other person "in the know" was Moretti. And so, before a meeting of top Cosa Nostra figures in Los Angeles in 1951, the informant laid out his theory. Word was then passed back to New York to investigate the charge, and, according to the informant, it was found to be true.

White had regularly met with high-ranking Mafia figures during his tenure atop the Bureau of Narcotics. The FBI had not yet developed its interest in rooting out organized-crime syndicates. The Bureau of Narcotics alone had commenced linking the Mafia to the importation of vast quantities of heroin and other drugs into the United States and was among the first federal law-enforcement agents to develop significant intelligence about Mafia operations, including cultivating informants and sending in undercover agents in an effort to break open many early Mafia drug operations.

Three days after Moretti's killing, Fred Stengel, chief of police for Fort Lee, New Jersey, was found dead behind the town's Madonna Cemetery. He had shot himself with his service revolver. At the time of his death, Stengel had been under indictment for protecting the gambling operations of the Moretti brothers and Joe Adonis. Interestingly, Moretti had testified to the grand jury, which led to Stengel's indictment. Moretti also was expected to be called to testify at the upcoming trial. There was no evidence of foul play, and the chief had been acting noticeably nervous for months, according to Fort Lee police captain Carl Mains. "It was definitely suicide."[23]

The investigation into Moretti's killing did net a couple of potential suspects. On October 21, police brought in thirty-nine-year-old Joe Li Calsi for questioning, based on a nightclub singer's tip. The Tampa-born Li Calsi, denied any knowledge of the Moretti killing and was booked only on a vagrancy charge. He was held on a twenty-five thousand dollar bail and officially charged with Moretti's murder a couple of days later. But as it turned out Li Calsi was the singer's boyfriend, and the story of his involvement could not be confirmed. He was released.

Also arrested and charged with Moretti's killing was forty-eight-year-old John Robilotto, also known as Johnny Roberts, a soldier in the Anastasia crime family. Roberts was also an undertaker in Brooklyn. Information placed Roberts in the restaurant right before Moretti's murder. Johnny Roberts was officially charged with the murder on June 21, 1952, and arrested in Brooklyn. He was extradited to New Jersey on August 1. He was released on September 8 after posting a twenty-five thousand dollar bail.

A few years later, Chicago mobster Johnny Roselli told an FBI informant that Roberts had definitely murdered Willie Moretti. The charge was echoed by famed underworld turncoat Joe Valachi in 1963: "That's when Willie gets his, from Johnny and these other people."[24]

But Roberts himself had gotten caught up in an interfamily conflict brewing between Anastasia and the emerging power of Carlo Gambino. A year after the spectacular October 1957 daytime killing of Anastasia at the Park Sheraton in New York City, Roberts's bullet-riddled body had been found on a Brooklyn street corner after being dumped out of a car by three men.

The fallout from Moretti's killing reverberated throughout the Bergen County scene. Coupled with the Kefauver Committee's findings, the spotlight on the partnerships between the Mafia and law enforcement was fraying the already-delicate threads that tied things together. This placed some mobsters in unusual positions.

In early 1952, Bergen County chief of detectives Michael Orecchio was arrested and charged with involvement in gambling activities and for turning a blind eye to Mafia-run floating dice games. In a strange turn of events, Joe Adonis, along with Willie Moretti's brother Solly, testified before the jury during Orecchio's trial. Adonis admitted that he had been part of gambling operations from 1947 to 1950 in Bergen County and that he had seen Orec-chio out and about.

Though Willie had been outraged by his brother Solly's incarceration on gambling charges, which had prompted his Kefauver testimony, his brother was unable to avenge Willie's killing, save for his testimony during the Orecchio trial. Just a few months after he told the jury about the wide-open rackets in Bergen County, Solly died in prison from cerebral hemorrhage.

Now that Moretti was out of the picture, Adonis also faced expulsion not only from New Jersey, but from the United States entirely. After a protracted legal battle between Adonis and federal authorities, he was ordered deported back to Italy in 1956. In a few short years, Adonis, Anastasia, and the Moretti brothers were all gone. But, as was the case with most underworld power vacuums, there was no shortage of mobsters waiting in the wings to move in and fill the void.

And many of those mobsters attended the most infamous and ill-fated meeting in mob history.

Chapter Six

The DeCavalcantes

The hamlet of Apalachin is a small census-designated community in the town of Owego, part of Tioga County, New York. The small community is located on the Susquehanna River and boasts a population of just over one thousand, similar to what the population would have been in November 1957. The small, quiet town was home to Joseph Barbara Sr., a Sicilian immigrant and president of the Endicott Canada Dry Bottling Company of Endicott, New York, a perfect position for a man whose past included bootlegging during Prohibition. Twice arrested on suspicion of murder, Barbara lived away from prying eyes, on a fifty-eight-acre estate in an eleven-room stone house, with caretaker's cottage and a two-story horse barn. It was at this out-of-the-way locale that mobsters convened on November 14, 1957, for what they thought was to be a meeting of the minds, with all the major mob figures from across the country getting together to talk business. And, what with the spectacular gangland slaying of New York boss Albert Anastasia, the burgeoning casino business in Cuba, and the recent attempted assassination of the "Prime Minister of the Underworld," Frank Costello, there was no shortage of subjects to discuss.

The thinking that the Barbara house would be an ideal spot was based on its out-of-the-way location—up a hill on a dead-end street—and Barbara's good relationship with the locals. But when dozens of well-dressed men, many driving from out of state, started showing up in town, checking into local motels, it was apparent that something big was going on, and it caught the attention of a pair of New York State Troopers, Edgar D. Croswell and Vincent Vasisko. The two were checking on a complaint unrelated to the conference at the Parkway Motel when they observed Joe Barbara reserving rooms for out-of-town guests. The troopers knew Barbara's checkered history and decided to do a little digging. They staked out the motel and jotted down the license-plate numbers of guests arriving at the motel. The next day the two police officers made a trip up to the Barbara estate. When they pulled up the drive, they noticed a dozen men exiting the back of the house. The mobsters, seeing the troopers, panicked and started to leave all at once. Vasisko later recalled, "It was a misty day. We were in plainclothes, but one of the guys looked up at the road and hollered, 'It's the staties, it's the staties,' and they all started running into the fields and the woods. We had no reason to arrest anybody; they weren't doing anything wrong."[1]

The troopers called in for backup and set up roadbocks around the area. They also combed through the nearby woods, picking up some of the fleeing attendees. It must have been a sight to find men in camel-hair coats, spats, and dress shoes, trudging through the trees, woefully out of their element, uncertain where they were going. The troopers also canvassed Barbara's home and garage, finding a number of cars belonging to the attendees.

Fifty-eight men were detained, questioned, and ultimately released.[2] While follow-up subpoenas and obstruction-of-justice charges resulted in little more than nuisances for the rounded-up men, the revelation that Mafia figures from around the country were meeting to discuss underworld business at a remote home in upstate New York cemented the concept that there was a nationwide organized-crime syndicate in operation. Though the concept of a nationwide crime syndicate had been reported for decades and investigated by the Bureau of Narcotics, it was not much countenanced by the FBI under J. Edgar Hoover. Now, however, with the ensuing publicity and outright evidence that the attendees were tied together in a multitude of illegal business ventures, the FBI started to shift priorities and resources toward fighting the mob, adopting the Top Hoodlum Program and focusing efforts on gathering as much data and information as they could on the mob.

The reasons for the meeting at Barbara's Apalachin retreat were not made clear to police or investigators. "None of [the meeting invitees] suggested that they had been invited to a gathering for other than social purposes, and only three said that they had been invited at all. The most common explanation, given in one form or another by ten, was that the purpose of the visit was to call upon Barbara, a sick friend. Eleven gave other explanations for their visit to Barbara's."[3] In the ensuing years, theories about the real purpose of the meeting have focused on a few key areas. The first was the ascension of Vito Genovese to the head of the Luciano/Costello crime family; since his job promotion was hurried along by an attempted hit on a respected boss and influential Mafia member, a meeting to smooth things over was in order. There was also the Anastasia hit and its implications for the Mangano crime family; the new family boss, Carlo Gambino, had attended Apalachin. Other theories batted about included the importance of Cuba and all the ancillary action the mob was running on the island. Finally, drugs and narcotics trafficking was a major issue at that time in the mob's history; increased involvement by American and Sicilian mobsters in the "French Connection" heroin-smuggling operation was paralleled with increased scrutiny from the Bureau of Narcotics, along with stiffer penalties for convicted drug activity.

These thorny issues were likely, then, to be addressed at Apalachin by a mix of crime families, of various rankings, with bosses and underbosses, capos and consiglieres, from as far away as Dallas, Los Angeles, and Tampa. Of the mobsters netted in the New York State Police roundup were eight from New Jersey—next to New York, the most-represented state among the attendees.

One of the cars that was stopped was a 1957 Chrysler Imperial sedan, driven by Russell Bufalino, mob boss of the northeast Pennsylvania Mafia, Joe Barbara's crime family. Bufalino's car was crammed full of most of the New Jersey contingent. Though the Imperial sedan was over eighteen feet long, it must have been a cramped ride for the elite of the New Jersey underworld.

Jerry Catena was in Bufalino's car, along with Vito Genovese. Catena, at the time, was living in South Orange, a leafy suburb of Newark, while Genovese was living in Atlantic Highlands. Charles Salvatore Chiri, fellow crime family member, who lived in Palisades Park, New Jersey, had also wedged himself into the automobile. Two New Jersey–based representatives of the Philadelphia mob were also passengers in Bufalino's car: Dominick Oliveto was a Camden resident who had taken over the Camden-area rackets after the death of Philly mob underboss Marco Reginelli just the year prior; Oliveto's rap sheet included a series of arrests for gambling and bootlegging, and he was involved in a number of businesses in South Jersey. Joseph Ida, boss of the Philadelphia Mafia, lived in Highland Park.

The Bonanno crime family's New Jersey operations were represented by Anthony Riela of West Orange, another Newark suburb; Riela owned the Airport Motel outside what was then known as Newark Metropolitan Airport. Believed to have been a member of the Newark family under Gaspare D'Amico before it had broken up, Riela was also close with Illinois-based mobsters from Chicago and Rockford and remained active in the Bonanno crime family into the mid-1980s.

Two of the fleeing Apalachin attendees had stopped a local student driving home from school and asked him for a ride; the student later recounted, "It was an unusual day. My actual encounter with them was brief. They got in my car, and I took them down the road. Then they flagged down another car, a friend of mine."[4] After the two men got into the second car, they were stopped at one of the roadblocks the state troopers had set up. These two men—Lou Larasso and Frank Majuri—were officers in Local 394 of the International Hod Carriers' Building and Common Laborers' Union in Elizabeth, New Jersey.[5] Though not as well-known as some of the other attendees,

Larasso and Majuri were two well-regarded members of the small Elizabeth crime family that had, for the most part, flown under the radar of law enforcement up until that day in Apalachin. In fact, while individual Elizabeth family members had arrest records and were cross-listed in various documents as criminal associates, there was little indication law enforcement considered the men part of a crime family. In reading through FBI reports of the late 1950s and '60s, it's apparent that the FBI was, for the most part, unaware of this sixth family, though there were many who considered the Elizabeth family to be one of the oldest crime families in the United States.

The boss of the Elizabeth family at that time of the Apalachin fiasco was likely the longtime Zwillman associate who had been involved in the 1930 Rising Sun Brewery shooting, Nick Delmore. Although informants still named Phil Amari as Elizabeth boss until he retired to Italy in 1958, it is probable that Delmore was either actual boss or acting boss in 1957. His close circle included Emanuel Riggi and the two Apalachin attendees Majuri and Larasso, as well as Sal Caternicchio and Joseph Sferra. Delmore himself had led an interesting double life: he'd risen to become boss of a Mafia family while cultivating the image of businessman, farmer, and community benefactor.

During Prohibition, Delmore had owned a number of speakeasies and hotels, including one in Berkeley Heights, New Jersey, that had been robbed by two low-level gangsters back in 1926. But to residents of Berkeley Heights and nearby Plainfield, where he lived at the time, Delmore was a successful businessman and millionaire. Vacations he and his family took to their summer homes in Belmar and Long Branch on the Jersey Shore were featured in the society pages, and when his son needed an appendectomy, it appeared as an item of note in the local paper. There was even a curious mention in the paper on May 14, 1928: "Approximately 100 Plainfield Italians attended the annual outing of the Nick Delmore Association which was held yesterday at Kuntz's Grove on the Passaic River."[6] Delmore even donated a parcel of land in Berkeley Heights to the town so a volunteer fire station could be built, giving them $1,500 to start construction.

Not everyone thought so highly of Delmore, however. While many considered him "a fine, generous, and thrifty citizen . . . equal number describe him as a hoodlum, a racketeer, a braggart and the proprietor of questionable resorts."[7] This perception only increased after the Rising Sun Brewery incident. And while Delmore was ultimately acquitted of the slaying, his three years on the lam and negative exposure during the trial wore away at the veneer of an honest businessman. He was sought for questioning by the FBI in 1939, along with his old Prohibition compatriot Doc Stacher. By the early 1940s Delmore had relocated to Elizabeth, where he was involved with illegal gambling. He spent time in Florida in 1947, operating a craps game in

Miami, and then relocated back to New Jersey, settling in the town of Long Branch on the Shore.

In 1952 Delmore took a trip to the mobbed-up capital of vice in the Caribbean—Havana, Cuba—to visit with exiled mob boss Lucky Luciano. But upon his return to the United States, Delmore was detained by Immigration and charged with entering the country without a valid passport. The government contended that Delmore was not an American citizen and that this was the second time in five years the mobster had left the country and reentered without proper documentation, the first instance being in 1947 when Delmore had gone to Puerto Rico.

According to most sources, Delmore was born Nicola Amoruso in Nicosia, Italy, on December 23, 1891. But Delmore was equally adamant that he had been born the United States. In 1953 a reporter visited Delmore at his dairy farm, Delwake Farms, in Freehold, New Jersey, where the mob boss was photographed atop a tractor assisting a work crew cleaning out an irrigation ditch on his property. Delmore asserted to the reporter that he had been born in San Francisco in 1888 and that his birth record had been destroyed in the 1906 San Francisco earthquake. He said his father had come to the States to work on the Union Pacific Railroad in 1885 and that his sister had told him that he had been born there and the records destroyed. He also averred that in 1941 US Immigration had declared him native-born. Delmore also told the reporter he had spent thousands attempting to find his birth records but had come up empty.

Regardless, in 1953 the government moved ahead with deportation proceedings against Delmore, but he fought back in court, filing a suit to have himself declared a citizen. Over the course of the next two years, the court case brought by Delmore dragged on, as the government produced evidence supporting their contention that Delmore was in fact Nicola Amoruso from Italy. But the Italian family records that the government provided did not list the birth of Delmore's sister, Felicia. That, coupled with the 1941 letter from the former commissioner of the US Immigration and Naturalization Service, persuaded the judge to rule in October 1955 that Delmore was indeed a natural US citizen.

The seventy-five-year-old mob boss had avoided deportation and, despite his advancing age, still commanded respect in his *borgata* (branch of the Mafia) for his work ethic and golf game as much as anything else, as evidenced by a wiretapped conversation between Angelo "Gyp" DeCarlo (identified in the transcripts as Ray) and Delmore's underling Louis Larasso:

RAY: Does Nick [Delmore] hang around with youse at all any more?

LOUIS: No, he don't come in at all.

RAY: He's up early in the morning he told me; he goes to work.

LOUIS: Yeah, he's down in the office a lot.

RAY: What's that, heating systems?

LOUIS: Yeah.

. . .

RAY: He's smart; that will keep him young. He's about seventy-three or seventy-five and got all his wits.

LOUIS: Seventy-four. He golfs two or three days a week.

RAY: Yeah, he's good too—eighty-two or eighty-three. Where does he play? Old Orchard yet?

LOUIS: Yeah, well, he goes all around.[8]

Another Elizabeth family soldier was caught on another wiretap around the same time saying, "Nick Delmore could come in this room and give three of us a battle," with another adding, "Nick Delmore, at the age of seventy-five, went into a new business. He's in good shape."[9] Unfortunately, the wiseguy spoke too soon.

In the summer of 1963, the seventy-six-year-old Delmore suffered a heart attack. His fragile condition compounded with his advancing age forced Delmore to hand the family's day-to-day operations over to his nephew, Simone Rizzo "Sam the Plumber" DeCavalcante, son of an old-time Elizabeth family member. After Delmore's heart attack, DeCavalcante "announced to a group of Union County gamblers that he was taking over as boss in his uncle's absence."[10] DeCavalcante's ascension to the top spot became permanent when Nick Delmore died of pneumonia in the Monmouth Medical Center on February 3, 1964. DeCavalcante named longtime crime family member Frank Majuri as his underboss.

Sam DeCavalcante eschewed the Elizabeth neighborhood of Peterstown, favored by many of the crime family members, instead residing in the Princeton area in a decidedly suburban setting.[11] Sporting a salt-and-pepper moustache and combed-back, wavy hair, and always dressed in fine suits, Sam carried himself like a sophisticated mobster, always looking his best when the cameras caught him. His first arrest came when he was seventeen. He had been caught breaking into a store in Westfield, New Jersey. He was sentenced to time at the Rahway Reformatory and paroled in 1932. That following July, in 1933, DeCavalcante was chased by police for violating parole.

After jumping over some hedges and hiding out in an attic in Bound Brook, New Jersey, he was arrested by Westfield police. It's not clear whether or not he was sent back to prison for that run-in, but in 1938 he was arrested and charged with passing a bad check, again in Westfield.

It was soon after his check-cashing arrest that DeCavalcante was made into the Elizabeth family. He told one of his old cohorts, Anthony "Tony Boy" Boiardo, son of Richie the Boot, that he'd been made in the early 1940s, adding, "I was supposed to be made in Philadelphia," referring to the Philly crime family. "I've been in as long as Jerry Catena has. I could have been made with Albert's [Anastasia] outfit."[12]

By the time Sam DeCavalcante had been inducted into the Elizabeth family, Delmore and the mob had solidified their base of power with their control over Local 394 of the Hod Carriers' union. Hod carriers are skilled laborers that provide support to bricklayers. The union was established in 1903, and by the time the Elizabeth crime family—known from 1963 on as the DeCavalcante family—were in control of Local 394, the national head-quarters of the union was in Washington, DC. Delmore had started working the union from a number of angles. He was part of a scheme accepting payoffs from contractors who wanted to work on major developments with less than the full share of union employees—or, in some cases, none at all. Delmore was described as a "top-level mafioso, formerly a bootlegger, who has retired from violent crime to the quasi-legitimate field of labor unions. Obtains 'kickbacks' from Italian emigrants for whom he obtains employment through his power in the labor unions."[13]

The Elizabeth family's hold on the union was deep, with members like Louis "Fat Louie" Larasso and Frank Majuri holding offices in the local. They controlled the flow of work to members as well as how those members acted on job sites. The union also became a de facto employment office for members and associates of the crime family, supplying endless no-show jobs to mob guys who needed a way to show legitimate income on their tax returns.

Sam DeCavalcante's primary sources of revenue for the crime family were "gambling, some shylocking, control of labor unions, and he used the labor unions so that the construction people, the builders, had an agreement that they would pay so much per room to him so that they would not be obliged to use union labor at union scale."[14]

In addition to overseeing gambling in the Garden State, DeCavalcante's empire also extended up into Connecticut and west into Pennsylvania— specifically the town of Bristol, Pennsylvania, some twenty-three miles out-side Philadelphia. Starting back in the late 1940s DeCavalcante had become a regular at local craps games run by members of the Philly mob. When Philadelphia boss Joe Bruno retired in 1944 and leadership of that crime family passed to Joe Ida, DeCavalcante moved into Bristol. He "consolidated control over his [Bruno's] numbers operations in this area during the 1950s and caused the virtual elimination of the independents."[15] He took over the numbers game, and eventually dice and cards games, by aligning himself with two of the biggest independents, Charles Chillela and Augustus Montevino, and by financing a layoff back in Trenton run by the Philly family. His gambling in the Bristol area was expanding dramatically and often took place in some unusual locations. Case in point was a 1951 raid of a pig farm that resulted in the arrest of sixty-nine players at a floating dice game.

DeCavalcante also had some operations "down the Shore," as Jersey natives call it, primarily in Monmouth and Ocean counties. This didn't sit well with some of the other wiseguys, like Anthony Russo, who operated out of Long Branch, New Jersey, who was caught on FBI wiretaps complaining to Angelo "Gyp" DeCarlo about Sam's moves into his backyard.

> So he [Boiardo] started off about the mustached [DeCavalcante]. So I said, "Boot, let's straighten things out about that. Ninety percent of the Shore belongs to Ray [DeCarlo]. He gave me 50 percent to handle." He [Boiardo] didn't answer. I said, "Number two mustache is coming up with all this talk about Gene Catena and Jerry Catena over here, and when he goes to New York it's Carlo Gambino." I said, "Am I supposed to back away because of him?" Am I supposed to sit back and see him [DeCavalcante] take over the seashore? He's got Elizabeth tied up, closed, and he wants to push us out of the Shore.[16]

In the early 1960s, the FBI had started to target organized-crime figures in New Jersey using a variety of new methods, including wiretaps. One of their first operations was to wire the offices of DeCavalcante, who owned Kenilworth Heating and Air Conditioning on North Michigan Avenue in Kenilworth, New Jersey. The bugs, planted in 1961 through 1965, provided law-enforcement agents a compelling glimpse inside the world of organized crime in New Jersey.[17] Recorded conversations ranged from the mundane to the absurd, with enough nuggets of viable intel to allow agents to fill in many gaps about the organization of many of the mob families operating in the Garden State. Conversations of a personal nature came up as well, prying open the internal struggles of a mob boss with personnel issues with both his crime family and his own family.

But while the feds and local and state law enforcement had begun to infiltrate the mob in Jersey, for guys on the streets of the Garden State things couldn't have been better. And that was causing some issues. Because things were going so well for Jersey-based mobsters, wiseguys from New York were looking to move over and take part in the action. Anthony "Little Pussy" Russo was caught on FBI wiretaps talking to DeCavalcante about it.

> Do you know how many guys in Chicago are peeling [safecracking]? Do you know how many friends of ours in New York that made it peeling? What they

gonna do? Now there's a [Cosa Nostra] law that they can't touch it. They have no other way of making a living, so what can they do? All right, we're fortunate enough that we moved around and didn't have to resort to that stuff. We had legitimate things going on as well as horses, numbers, and everything. What are the other poor suckers going to do? Do you know how many dead-heads we take for them [New York bosses]? Two guys with Mike Sabella are running a ziginette game in New Jersey. Pretty soon we'll have all the mob here.[18]

DeCavalcante lamented that he was now on the radar of law enforcement after many years of not having really been known to them. He claimed his newfound conspicuity stemmed from a 1961 raid on a gambling house he was running in Trenton. And that, in addition to his having become boss of the family, meant he was involved with too many hangers-on and had to support too many people, including floating loans to customers with no means of repaying. But apparently his business sense sharpened, because by 1964 DeCavalcante was in solid financial shape. "Even his shylock loans have improved. He said he receives twenty-four thousand dollars per year from one person and ten thousand dollars from another person in interest alone."[19] Adding his extensive gambling operations, labor racketeering, and spoils from the proceeds of his underlings' criminal activities, DeCavalcante was doing quite well in his new position.

In 1964 DeCavalcante was drawn into a precarious situation with both the Commission—the Mafia's governing body—and one of his friends in the underworld, New York mob boss Joseph Bonanno. The Bonanno situation developed because Joe Bonanno and the Commission were at odds over a number of moves Bonanno had made in hopes of increasing his territory. There had also been dissention in the Bonanno family. Finally, Joe Bonanno left New York, claiming he'd been kidnapped—though that assertion was met with skepticism by members of the mob. In his place, the Commission appointed Gaspar DiGregorio, longtime capo, to be the new boss of the family. DeCavalcante took the side of the other bosses, telling his underlings that the Commission had no intention of hurting Bonanno and that Bonanno had better not retaliate in return. He also complained to Bayonne Joe Zicarelli that Bonanno knew the way the Commission operated, wondering why Joe would take issue with them when he himself was involved in other instances of the Commission's moving in to dictate terms to a family.

SAM: The Commission went in there and took the family over. When Profaci died, Joe Magliocco took over as boss. They threw him right out! "Who the hell are you to take over a *borgata*?" He's lucky they didn't kill him. And Signor Bonanno knows this. When we had trouble in our outfit, they came right in. "You people belong to the Commission until this is straightened out." They done the same thing in Pittsburgh. They made the boss John . . . uh. . . .

JOE: LaRocca.

SAM: LaRocca, step down.

Joe: He's no more boss?

SAM: Oh, it's straightened out now. But Joe Bonanno was in on that deal. They made LaRocca take orders from the Commission until everything was straightened out. So do you understand, Joe? If these people don't enforce what's right and what's wrong, what's the point of having the Commission?[20]

When the Commission voted to officially strip Bonanno of his status as boss, DeCavalcante sat down with Bayonne Joe Zicarelli to let him know and to warn him to watch out for any blowback from Bonanno—either against the Commission or back at his own family, saying, "the Commission doesn't recognize Joe Bonanno as the boss anymore . . . the Commission has nothing against any of you fellows. They respect all your people as friends of ours. But they will not recognize Joe, his son, and Johnny [John Morales]. Joe better not get any intention of hurting anybody either—that's the most important thing to tell you . . . he might try to hurt people in his own outfit to cover up the story—his story."[21]

Though the DeCavalcante family was much smaller in comparison to the five families of New York and the Bruno family in Philly, there was a level of respect offered Sam DeCavalcante that made some members of other crime families envious of his organization, even though their rackets may not have been as lucrative, or their influence as strong. Louis Larasso was told that "people from Carlo Gambino's family, people from Tommy Lucchese's family, and people from Gaspar DiGregorio's family wanted to join the DeCavalcante family because they know that DeCavalcante is a fair man and they have more chance to better themselves."[22] (Starting in the mid-1960s law enforcement and the press began naming the crime families after their bosses. From that point on, the Elizabeth crime family was known as the DeCavalcantes.)

Sam was also generous with his family, especially around the holidays, when he would throw them a Christmas party. He was recorded talking about it with his Connecticut capo, Joe LaSelva:

It's going to be over at Ange and Min's—down the cellar. Bring your brother down, too. I'm gonna have all the kids that are proposed down there, too. What we're gonna do—Carlo Gambino gave me two thousand dollars for that score we made over there in New York. So I was going to give everybody fifty dollars in the outfit. A Christmas present from us—which I think will be a nice thing. Give them a card from you, me, Frank, and the widows—we'll send them all fifty dollars. Give Mary Amari and Delmore a hundred dollars each— the rest fifty dollars each. If it's alright with you . . . at one o'clock we'll sit down and send for the other kids. So they'll be about forty of us. We'll blow the two thousand dollars.[23]

DeCavalcante was also loyal to the way the Mafia worked. He was steeped in protocol and respect for other made members, whether they were in his crime family or not.

There is no difference between you and our people. When you people are here, you are respected like our people. Respect for you belonging to another family; you don't have to tell me anything. If you need money, we will give it to you. We will respect you as *amico nostro* . . . Cosa Nostra is Cosa Nostra. I can only speak for my people but not for anyone else. When you call the family for your intention, an *amico nostro* is an *amico nostro*. If he belongs here or there, it doesn't mean a thing. If you give me preference, I will also give you preference.[24]

Sam DeCavalcante's outsized influence with the Commission may also have been influenced by his political savvy, both within the mob and without. He had a number of ties to elected officials, from state senators to local city councilmen. The bugs that caught much of the internal wranglings of the crime family also netted investigators tantalizing pieces of information about business dealings and "rainmaking" on DeCavalcante's part. Sam claimed to have a contact in the office of then-governor Richard J. Hughes. Sam claimed this person kept him abreast of law-enforcement efforts against the crime family. Obviously his contact was not privy to extensive wiretapping. Sam also boasted of contacts in the state beverage commission and of how he was able to straighten out issues ranging from associates who sold liquor on Sundays—which was against the law at the time—to getting liquor-license issues ironed out. Whether it was wishful boasting or an accurate representation of his prowess, DeCavalcante was still sought out by all kinds of people who needed help straightening out their problems.

Others in the family benefitted from his connections. One of those was Emmanuel Riggi, who was facing the prospect of deportation by the US Immigration and Naturalization Service; another of the family's political contacts was consulted about the case and assured Riggi that he would not be deported. Then, DeCavalcante told his underboss, Frank Majuri, that he was able to meet with a judge to iron out zoning problems that a DeCavalcante-associated developer was facing. And Majuri's son was arrested on gambling charges in 1965 and DeCavalcante pledged a payoff of five hundred dollars to the judge and a thousand dollars to the mayor of Elizabeth if the court decision came out favorably for the younger Majuri.

Other mobsters shared information with DeCavalcante when things were getting hot. Anthony "Jack Panels" Santoli, a Genovese solider in Ray De-Carlo's crew, came to Sam with some information about a pending federal raid:

PANELS: Unless you got a real good friend—we don't like to kick this around, because if it leaks out, these guys will come the following week and really catch everybody. But if you got any good friends, the feds are going in there this week.

DECAVALCANTE: Essex?

PANELS: Yeah. Anyway, they're definitely coming in next week—the feds—looking for stamps—bookmaking, horses, or numbers.[25]

One of the biggest connections with elected officials was the relationship DeCavalcante fostered with Thomas Dunn, longtime mayor of Elizabeth, New Jersey. In the months leading up to the election of 1964, Dunn, a former city councilman, was looking for a different result than the 1960 elections, where he'd lost his first bid for the mayoralty. He visited Sam at the Kenilworth Heating location, and the two discussed Dunn's chances, along with Larry Wolfson, DeCavalcante's attorney.

DECAVALCANTE: After November 3, you address him as Mayor.

DUNN: I been waiting for it for fifteen years.

DECAVALCANTE: Do you think we can get any city work?

DUNN: [laughing] Well, maybe.

Dunn then spoke of the difficulty he faced vote-wise in a primarily Jewish section of town. DeCavalcante promised that his "paesans" would do whatever they could to help out. Dunn then told DeCavalcante that at a debate Dunn's opponent, former mayor Nicholas LaCorte, had accused Dunn of having ties to gambling interests and to another individual named Mr. Magnolia.

DUNN: If you have any way of getting to Magnolia and LaCorte, tell them to keep their lousy mouths shut, because you know better than I do that I have no . . .

DECAVALCANTE: Oh, sure.

DUNN: Because this thing could cream me at the last minute. So, if you can in some way get to these two guys, tell them to keep this out of the papers.

DECAVALCANTE: It's a lot of talk. He couldn't come out with a thing like that with no proof.

DUNN: Well, just by association, Sam. So, if you have any way of getting to Magnolia.

DECAVALCANTE: I sure will.

DUNN: Well, that's good enough for me.

DECAVALCANTE: So, I wish you a lot of luck. Can you use this in your campaign?

DUNN: Thank you, Sam. You bet I can use it! Enjoy your trip to Florida. [26]

The last two lines were believed by investigators to refer to a campaign contribution Sam made to Dunn, who later admitted DeCavalcante had contributed around a hundred dollars to the campaign. Though this conversation was later made public, it did not do much damage to Dunn's success. He was elected Elizabeth's mayor in 1964 and served in the office twenty-eight years. He later claimed in 1969 that he'd found out that his buddy Sam was a Mafia boss through a book he'd read—but he'd learned this, he insisted, only after their recorded meeting had taken place.

When the DeCavalcante wiretaps were released to the public, they became the subject of a number of books. These wiretappings were one of the first major efforts by law enforcement to gather intel for the sake of intel. Other similar efforts were occurring in Chicago and other cities. Though some of the wiretaps were not authorized, and others barely legal, they started to reveal the depth of the mob's influence in the United States. In fact, it's safe to say that the heyday of the mob in America ran form the 1940s through the 1960s, and it was the efforts of law enforcement and the new tools it had at its disposal—both at a state and federal level—that enabled them to start gaining ground against a criminal organization that had for decades been entrenching itself.

Managing risk was an important part of being a mobster—whether soldier, capo, underboss, or boss. It was also about balancing reward with risk, the chance that the police might arrest you. As the years went on, it became increasingly difficult for street guys to get away from the myriad of eyes looking at them. Not only were there police, but reporters, both print and TV, scrutinized their every move. But at least they could find some level of comfort in knowing that their own compatriots would never turn against them. The code of *omertà*—or, basically, keeping one's mouth shut about all things Costa Nostra—was still strong. To be sure, there have always been guys who fed the cops information on potential rivals or gave them threads of intel, enough to whet their appetites but not enough to do any real damage. It was a dance between cop and robber, both playing the other in an attempt to keep one step ahead in the game. But real damage was about to be done. Even with sensational reports of wiretaps, confidential informants, and the revelations of the Kefauver Committee, it would be a live witness, testifying before Congress, who would captivate the country and lay bare the inner secrets of the mob in America.

Chapter Seven

On the Wire

By the early 1960s, the FBI had started to catch up with state and local authorities with regard to understanding the extent of the mob's influence on crime and legitimate businesses. In the early part of the twentieth century the Federal Bureau of Narcotics was the dominant federal agency recognizing that there was a structured organized-crime syndicate responsible for a variety of criminal enterprises—among those narcotics trafficking, which is what first brought the mob to the attention of the Bureau of Narcotics, even before the FBI. But after the Apalachin fiasco, and years of reports from local and state agencies, the FBI field offices turned their attention from Communists to gangsters and within a few short years started to develop a broad understanding of the form and function of traditional organized-crime syndicates across the United States. But the early years of intelligence gathering were still hit or miss.

A two hundred–page report by the FBI in 1963 outlined the activities of la Cosa Nostra in the United States, with a significant section dedicated to New Jersey, under the guidance of the FBI's Newark field office. The list of mobsters that called the Garden State home was extensive. The Genovese family list had forty-two names, from the boss and the power players— Ruggerio Boiardo, Gerardo Catena, Charlie "the Blade" Tourine, and Anthony "Tony Pro" Provenzano—as well as lesser-known members—Joe "the Indian" Polverino, Anthony "Tony Ambrose" D'Ambrosio, Nicholas "Joe Bones" Bufania, and Peter "Andy Gump" Costello. The Bruno list had over a dozen members in both South Jersey and Newark, while the four other New York families' lists were skimpy at best.

In the fall of 1963, Congress held a series of hearings on organized crime in America. What set this set of hearings apart was the explosive testimony provided by of a mob insider, which helped elevate the Mafia even further into the public consciousness and give law enforcement a real glimpse into the inner working of the mob. The informant was Joseph Valachi, and the window he provided on the history of the Mafia in America to that point was the most informative in terms of outlining how the mob operated and the various linkages between crime families in different cities. He also introduced America to the term *la Cosa Nostra* ("this thing of ours," used to describe the Mafia internally), *amico nostro* (a fellow member of Cosa Nostra), and *borgata* (one's crime family).

In his testimony before Congress, "Valachi said that the 'Cosa Nostra' was a highly organized unit with a strict code of fealty, which was guaranteed by blood ties and arranged marriages within the tightly controlled framework of the organization. He told authorities that the organization had been responsible for numerous gangland deaths throughout the country, including the slayings of gangster Albert Anastasia and Frank Scalise, and an attempt on the life of Frank Costello."[1]

But the testimony of one mob soldier wasn't enough to generate cases against mobsters. The FBI also began an aggressive campaign of wiretapping crime bosses—as had amassed the DeCavalcante tapes. From Chicago to Miami, the FBI started listening in on numerous conversation between mobsters, their associates, and often their political contacts. In New Jersey, DeCavalcante was not the only mobster under the microphone.

In the early 1960s the FBI illegally wiretapped the "barn," a building behind the La Martinique Tavern on Route 22 in Mountainside, New Jersey, a small borough in Union County, just to the west of Elizabeth. The barn was the headquarters and everyday hang out of Angelo "Gyp" DeCarlo, a member of the Boot Boiardo's Genovese family crew. Though the tapes were not released until the latter part of the 1960s, they provided a similar glimpse into the inner workings of the Mafia as had the DeCavalcante tapes.

The wiretaps were in place to catch a good deal of conversation between Ray "Gyp" DeCarlo and other mob members as they watched the Valachi hearings on television. On October 1, 1963, DeCarlo asked an unidentified wiseguy, "How can they get to him?" The unknown male replied that "they'll take him [Valachi] out of the country," adding that "Joe and twenty-one other guys are in on it . . . they can get twenty-five years"—possibly talking about potential fallout from Valachi's testimony. DeCarlo replied, "That's right— the innocent go with the guilty." Ray also told the men that "the New York Prosecutor's office knew all the information [Valachi was giving them] before the hearings started," adding that Congress and the hearings were "glorifying Valachi, who is a convicted narcotics user and a murderer."[2]

DeCarlo was always on the lookout for "stoolies"—a derogatory term for informants. One wiretapped conversation in June of 1964 had DeCarlo talking about a possible stool pigeon named Benedetto Indiviglio. "Certainly,

Lucky Luciano sent the word over a long time ago—before he did—that he [Indiviglio] is a stool pigeon. He'll get killed if they let him out."[3]

A lot of the DeCarlo tapes are snippets of day-to-day drudgery, from what they wanted to eat for dinner to watching the news. It quickly became apparent that the "glamorous life of the gangster" was in reality many times as mundane as the average Joe they so often mocked for working a regular job. DeCarlo and his crew did often engage in one of the pleasures of late-night New York City–area television of the era: *The Joe Franklin Show*, a longtime fixture on WWOR-TV, broadcast out of Secaucus, New Jersey.

Some snippets of conversation from both the DeCarlo and DeCavalcante tapes related to how the crime families were set up and how they inducted new members. To officially be a Mafia member—or be "made" in the Mafia—you had to be formally inducted into the crime family. The requirements varied by crime group but generally maintained that the inductee must be of full Italian lineage and, at least according to some sources, that he had to have "made his bones"—or killed someone. Other sources say that big earners who brought in sizable amounts of money were also let in. But the Mafia's governing Commission in New York kept a lid on how many members were allowed into a crime family and when the "book were open"— when new members were allowed to be inducted.

According to FBI informants, the "books" were closed to new Mafia members in the early to mid-1960s. While the edict originated out of New York—supposedly due to the Gallo-Profaci war in Brooklyn, as well as the Apalachin conference—the prohibition extended across the border to New Jersey, with capable up-and-coming gangsters waiting patiently for their turn to become fully fledged members of the mob. This was backed up in recorded conversations and in tips from informants. In October 1962, Gyp DeCarlo was recorded at a meeting with other gangsters, stating that the books had been closed and would probably stay that way for a few more years. He did make a point of complaining that the Philly family was not following the rules and had recently inducted three new members to replace three that died. Louis Larasso—the DeCavalcante capo also at the meeting— agreed with DeCarlo, saying, "I'm going to tell you how we make guys. We were the only family, going back now five, no, four years, who could have made anybody. We had an okay for seven guys. You know we didn't make anybody. Then after that big ——— in upstate New York, everybody got pinched and we couldn't make anybody after that. I don't know how the hell these guys do it."[4] Larasso went on to point out to DeCarlo that the Elizabeth family was "very discreet and that only a few were known to outsiders."[5]

Louis Cocchiaro, then an associate of the DeCavalcante family, was training a crew of younger wiseguys in a program with "hit assignments and other dirty jobs that bind the mob together testing each individual mob member's ability to stand up under pressure." The FBI noted that this program may have been effective because "one of the problems with the hoodlum element today is that there are too many 'leisure' guys, those individuals who want the money from gambling and other activities but who do not want to murder anyone."[6]

Among the mobsters identified as part of Cocchiaro's crew at the time were Gaetano "Corky" Vastola and Robert DiBernardo. While Vastola would become a made member of the DeCavalcante family, DiBernardo, who was living in Brooklyn at the time he was mentoring under Cocchiaro, became a made member of the Gambino family. His claim to fame was his vast influence in the porn industry in the seventies and eighties, before he was killed in June of 1986 on orders from John Gotti. Interestingly, Vastola also ran afoul of Gotti while they shared a cell together in the mid-1980s. Gotti believed Vastola could become a government witness and tried to recruit the leaders of the DeCavalcante family to go along with having Vastola killed. The FBI were bugging this conversation (among others), and the murder plot never got off the ground.

Throughout the sixties, the feds were in deep on surveillance of suspected Mafia members. With the implementation of various wiretapping laws, enhanced budgets, and a willingness to cultivate a wide array of informants, the FBI spent a good part of the decade playing catch-up. But it was apparent to the wiseguys on the streets that their every move was now subject to surveillance and that even small gatherings of gangsters were now on law-enforcement radar. One example was when the FBI got wind of an important sit-down in Miami in January of 1968. The intel emerged from a group of mobsters and their wives that had chartered planes to Freeport in the Bahamas. Included in the group was Santo Trafficante Jr., Angelo Bruno, and mobsters Carl Samuel Ippolito and John James Simone. Bruno was returning to Miami, with Trafficante to follow suit on a another flight, where they were going to meet up with other mob figures in the Miami area, including capo Peter LaPlaca and a New Jersey mobster named Danny Polidori.[7]

One area of particular concern for federal investigators listening to mobster conversations was finding the links between the underworld and the political world. In order for any organized-crime group to really gain a foothold in power there needed to be a level of political corruption. Early Jersey bosses like Longy Zwillman and Nucky Johnson knew how to straddle both sides of the political fence: neither side would get any favorable treatment unless it meant a seat at the table. Generally mobsters looked unfavorably on elected officials unless they provided something to further the goals of the gangsters. Gyp DeCarlo firmly believed that "The most degenerate people in the world come from Washington."[8]

Unfortunately for the image of the Garden State, New Jersey has long been associated with political corruption. One study of the subject says that "New Jersey was and remains an ideal laboratory to study political and public corruption and its corrosive effects on the body politics of govern-ment . . . what makes New Jersey unique and well suited for corruption to flourish is the fact that 521 municipalities populate the state, most with their own political structures and police departments. These fiefdoms of home rule are in and of themselves quite powerful in ensuring that the 'good old boy' network remains in place decade after decade."[9]

On the Gyp DeCarlo tapes, DeCarlo was caught in a number of conversa-tions discussing ways to help certain candidates get elected and have others removed from their posts. This fascinating glimpse into how much power was concentrated into the hands of a few key mafiosi would be a boon to federal law-enforcement agents, who then used this information to go after many of the public officials named on the tapes. DeCarlo also bragged about a number of other political appointments and posts that he was able to con-trol. One of their big pet projects was John V. Kenny, mayor of Jersey City, and long-term, powerful figure in Hudson County politics. DeCarlo told Jack Panels Santoli that he was with John Kenny on April 25, 1964, and he was pushing for the removal of Brendan Byrne from the position of Essex County prosecutor. Kenny had an in with the governor and told DeCarlo that Byrne was a favorite of the administration. DeCarlo told Kenny that he controlled two open judge positions and that he could get Byrne appointed to one if he were removed, or stepped down, from the prosecutor position.

DeCarlo also talked about putting police on the payroll, comparing two cities in Middlesex County, New Jersey. "Perth Amboy is too big. You'd have fifty cops and all the detectives coming by to get on the payroll. You got to have a little town like Carteret with ten to fifteen cops. You put about ten of them on for a sawbuck a week, a fin a week, you can handle them."[10]

Richie the Boot and Gyp DeCarlo had their claws sunk into the mayor of Newark, Hugh Addonizio. The relationship between the mayor and the mob had been a long and fruitful partnership that allowed Boiardo, DeCarlo, Catena, and the rest of the crews in Newark to operate almost out in the open, especially since they also had deep ties to and a corrupting influence on the police department. An indication of how deeply entrenched the mob was with Mayor Addonizio was in evidence on November of 1964 when Boiardo took a vacation to Puerto Rico and stayed at the Americana Hotel in San Juan. Accompanying Boiardo were some of his crew, including Joe "Joe Beans" Bianco, owner of Valentine Electric Company in Newark; Joe Rizzo-lo, Boiardo's bodyguard; and Andy Gerardo, who would later take over Boiardo's crew after the Boot's death. Staying at the nearby Caribe Hilton Hotel was Mayor Addonizio. On November 9, Boiardo held a cocktail party with a gambling session at the Americana casino for thirty guests, and Ad-donizio was among them. To summarize, the mayor of the largest city in New Jersey was drinking, gambling, and socializing with the biggest crimi-nal in the city, at a resort hotel in Puerto Rico. To even Addonizio's staunchest defenders, this was indefensible. But in Newark in the 1960s it was how the mob was still able to control vast swaths of the city's criminal landscape, some forty years after Longy and Ritchie the Boot had started carving up the city for their own profit.

Addonizio later testified in court that he'd met with Boiardo in Puerto Rico. "I met him at a dinner for Saint Anthony's Orphanage. . . . I also had occasion to meet him at the Pope Pius [XII] humanitarian-award dinner. . . . I also met him once in New York. . . . I also had an occasion to bump into him once on an airplane. . . . I also had occasion to see him in Puerto Rico on several occasions."[11]

A conversation indicating the depth of corruption in Newark was recorded on February 23, 1963, between Boiardo, DeCarlo, Louis Larasso, and Sam DeCavalcante.

> BOIARDO: I don't want to see Tony Bananas anymore. I told Louis, "You go back and tell Bananas that 'Ham' Dolasco has got a beef. That Dolasco still wants a piece of the monte game like it was originally set up."

> DECARLO: Is Tony Bananas still going with the money game yet?

> BOIARDO: No, Dick Spina told him to stop. You know Dick Spina asked me, "Why don't you and Ray DeCarlo get together and open up?" I said, "What is there to open up?" You know, Hughie Addonizio got hold of me; he said, "Look, tell Ray DeCarlo that the FBI knows about Irving Berlin. I'll tell you how much the FBI knows."[12]

This short snippet reflects how comfortable Newark police director Dominick Spina was with Boiardo and DeCarlo. Also Boiardo's relationship with Addonizio and his bagman Irving Berlin. Another conversation has Boiardo flat out telling his mob cohorts that Spina is on the take.

> DECARLO: Today, if you don't meet them and pay them, you can't operate.

> BOIARDO: The only guy I handle is Dick Spina. Gino Farnia and them guys handle the rest of the law. About seven or eight years ago I used to handle them all.[13]

DeCarlo was also caught another time bragging, "Spina, the mayor, Irving Berlin. Any of us guys can put any politician we want anywhere."[14] He further relayed a conversation he'd had with Dominick Spina regarding how Spina felt like all he did was take orders from people, like Mayor Addonizio. "And then I gotta take orders from Jerry Catena—but you [DeCarlo] and Jerry never ask me to make a move. I gotta admit it. You never ask me for a favor. But Bananas [Anthony Caponigro] and Tony Boy [Anthony Boiardo]! I feel like telling them to go to hell!"[15]

Addonizio's downfall began on July 12, 1967, when the Central Ward of Newark became engulfed in a major race riot that lasted for six days, triggered by the arrest and beating of a black cab driver by two Newark policemen. It's beyond the scope of this book to discuss in much detail all the factors that led to the riots, the events that transpired over the course of those six days, or the twenty-six people who were killed and the hundreds injured, including civilians, police, and firefighters. But how organized crime played a part in fomenting the conditions that led to the riots can be traced back to the levels of corruption and forces that were at play in the city. After the riot, the Governor's Select Committee on Civil Disorder (known as the Lilley Commission) heard from over a hundred witnesses and reviewed an additional seven hundred staff reports. The causes, they found, were endemic poverty, lack of economic opportunity, and dissatisfaction in the black community of Newark. One underlying theme that also emerged was a pervasive culture of corruption in Newark municipal government from lower-level employees straight up to Spina and Addonizio. And the catalyst for that corruption was the influence of organized crime.

In the wake of the riots and the Lilley Commission report, a series of hearings and investigations were undertaken. The staff director of the President's Commission on Law Enforcement declared that "Official corruption in New Jersey is so bad that organized crime can get almost anything it desires."[16] A new US attorney, Frederick Lacey, was brought in to lead the charge as evidence was unveiled and indictments were prepared against a who's who of organized crime and elected officials.

Hugh Addonizio was tarnished by the fallout from the race riots and subsequent investigations. Indictments were leveled against Addonizio and other elected officials from Newark to Jersey City. The Newark mayor was still trying to run his upcoming 1970 mayoral campaign while dealing with an upcoming trial on extortion charges as a result of a kickback scheme netting over a million dollars from contractors working on city projects. Addonizio went to trial in the summer of 1970 with four other defendants, and on July 22, 1970, the jury returned a verdict of guilty on sixty-four counts of extortion. He also, not surprisingly, lost his reelection bid. The twice-defeated mayor slumped in his chair in court as the verdict was read. He remained free on bail while appeals were lodged. Once those were exhausted, the disgraced mayor reported to federal prison in 1972. He was released in 1977 under unusual circumstances and fought the parole board through 1979 to keep himself from going back to prison. He died in 1981 of cardiac arrest, no longer a force in New Jersey politics but to this day a reminder to many of how power corrupts, especially in New Jersey municipal politics.

One of US Attorney Lacey's first cases against organized crime featured Gyp DeCarlo, who was indicted in 1969 for loan-sharking as part of a complicated financial scheme. In 1967 a financial analyst named Gerald Zelmanowitz had approached a labor racketeer he knew, Lou Saperstein, to invest fifty thousand dollars in a Swiss bank so Zelmanowitz could use the money for financial transactions, with a guaranteed profit to Saperstein. The two men then approached DeCarlo to lend them additional funds. DeCarlo had them to talk with one of his associates, Daniel Cecere. Saperstein already owed DeCarlo money as a result of a prior loan-sharking transaction. However, Cecere decided to invest on behalf of himself, DeCarlo, and Joe "the Indian" Polverino. Though the initial returns had been good, trouble with the IRS cut into the profits. To add further fuel to the fire, Saperstein was falling behind on vig payments. Cecere took him to the barn, and they worked him over. When Zelmanowitz came looking for his friend, he found him in a state. "There was a group of people in the first room as I entered, and I heard my name called, and there is another room attached to this room, which I entered, and when I got in there, Mr. Saperstein was laying on the floor. He was purple. He was bloody. His tongue was hanging out of his mouth. I thought he was dead."[17]

The day before he was found dead, the result of an acute ingestion of arsenic, Saperstein wrote a letter to the FBI asking for their help:

> Gentlemen: I am writing you, maybe others can be helped by my plight. On September 13, 1968, I was severely beaten at a place in the rear of Weiland's Restaurant, Route 22, DeCarlo's headquarters. I was then told and given three months until December 13, 1968, to pay the entire accumulated amount under threat of death. Cecere, DeCarlo, and Polverino also stated many times my wife and son would be maimed or killed. Please protect my family—I am sure they mean to carry out this threat. Last night from my home I called DeCarlo and pleaded for time but to no avail. Over the phone DeCarlo stated unless further monies was paid the threats would be carried out.
>
> Louis B. Saperstein[18]

With the information at hand the FBI started investigating and charged DeCarlo and Cecere with loansharking. Their trial began in early 1970. DeCarlo, then sixty-seven years old, was described at the trial as "silver-haired, short and stocky, with an impressive paunch . . . heavy face, a long, sharp nose and shelving chin" who didn't walk as much as "waddle into the courtroom."[19] DeCarlo and Cecere were found guilty on three charges each of making extortionate loans to Saperstein. His death was never determined to be either murder or suicide, though it was brought up at trial, resulting in DeCarlo and Cecere's unsuccessful appeal. However, DeCarlo did not spend long in prison. In December 1972 his sentence was commuted by President

Richard Nixon. The Justice Department told the press that it was done on compassionate grounds due to DeCarlo's serious illness. DeCarlo died on October 20, 1973, from cancer. He had been living at his home in Mountainside, New Jersey.

After DeCarlo's clemency, there were rumblings of mob influence. One theory held that Frank Sinatra reached out to Spiro Agnew to personally make the plea to Nixon that DeCarlo needed to be released. The FBI and Justice Department both said that the pardon followed all the proper protocols and reiterated it had been given on account of health reasons. They said an investigation "failed to turn up 'one iota' of evidence suggesting official impropriety in DeCarlo's release from prison."[20] And some sources say that Jerry Catena reached out through Walter Annenberg to intervene on DeCarlo's behalf, citing Catena's ties to Walter's father, Moses Annenberg. Catena's involvement is an interesting theory with little substance to back it up. But the fact that Catena's name was thrown around as having the clout to influence a decision by the president is a testament to how far Catena had come since his days working for Longy Zwillman. Catena had moved up through the ranks of the Genovese family and emerged as one of the most understated yet powerful mobsters in New Jersey.

Chapter Eight

Bayonne Joe

Ellis Island, the entry point into the United States of America for millions of immigrants at the turn of the twentieth century, today is often a day trip for tourists visiting New York City. With the Statue of Liberty, Ellis Island is often seen as the epicenter of the American immigrant experience, where so many came to find their way in a strange and unfamiliar country. And the entry to this country was through the bustling metropolis of New York City. For that reason, the Statue of Liberty is one of the most ubiquitous images associated with the largest city in the United States. But while the image of Ellis Island as a wholly unique New York City experience remains strong, in 1998 the Supreme Court of the United States, after years of legal wrangling, declared that 90 percent of the island actually belongs to New Jersey—in Hudson County, to be exact.

The Hudson River stretches along Hudson County's east side, Newark Bay on its west. At the southern tip of the peninsula, the city of Bayonne borders Staten Island before turning north, looking across the lower Hudson River to Brooklyn, before paralleling the West Side of Manhattan, all the way up to West One Hundredth Street. The county in many ways is the nexus between New Jersey and New York City. Cities like Hoboken and Jersey City, now bedroom communities for commuters, dot its landscape.

Before the Mafia planted its flag in the county, the kingpin of the gambling scene was an old-school Irish mobster, Joseph "Newsboy" Moriarty. Born in Jersey City in 1910, Moriarty acquired the Newsboy moniker when delivering newspapers in Jersey City as a kid. Accounts say that by the time he was a teenager he was running a successful bookmaking operation. It was as a teen that Moriarty became friendly with the most powerful elected official in Jersey City at the time, Mayor Frank Hague, who ran Jersey City—and by default Hudson County—from 1917 to 1947. Hague was an old-school political boss whose power went unquestioned. A friendship with him served Newsboy Moriarty through the formative years of his gambling career. Newsboy found many wiling customers in the blue-collar bars and taverns of Jersey City and Bayonne, filled with longshoremen and factory workers. With Hague watching over him, Moriarty was able to grow and expand his business throughout the county.

Moriarty did not play the part of a traditional gangster. For one, though he did business with mobsters, he was basically a one-man operation, with little interference from the wiseguys who also roamed the streets of Jersey City. This was in part due to Newsboy's relationship with Hague and the Jersey City Police. As one detective said, "Joe just took bets. No muscle, no violence, no dirty stuff. He didn't mix with narcotics, prostitution, or syndicates." Another added, "Moriarty was essentially an honest, industrious man in an illegal business." [1] By sticking to gambling and eschewing the violence associated with the Mafia, Moriarty made it easier to keep relationships with police and avoid press coverage of his activities.

Also, Newsboy's sartorial choices were not what one would consider high fashion, and he never spent money lavishly, like so many other gangsters did. He "lived frugally, dressed shabbily, drove a string of shabby-looking cars that were capable of high speeds, and made most of his collections alone." [2] At the height of his success, his bookmaking and gambling operations were said to bring in millions of dollars a year, and whenever police picked him up they'd find wads of cash in his pockets, upward of seven thousand dollars in one instance. But he only owned a few pairs of trousers and lived for many years with his sister in a cramped apartment.

Newsboy also managed to stay largely under the radar when it came to the press. But though his name had cropped up from time to time in local newspapers, he finally made headlines across the country in July of 1962 when workers were removing some old garages from an industrial area in Jersey City. They came upon an old 1947 Plymouth sedan. When they opened the car they found a cache of $2.4 million. Along with the cash was some paperwork tying the money to Moriarty. Police started searching in other nearby garages and found an additional $168,000 and paper bags filled with numbers and gambling slips. Moriarty must have been fuming about the find. There was no way he could get to any additional stashes he had hidden around Jersey City. At the time of the discovery of what the press dubbed "Moriarty's Millions," Newsboy was in prison, serving a two- to three-year sentence for numbers running and illegal gambling. The ensuing battle for control of the money pitted Newsboy against the IRS, the police, Jersey City, and the two workmen who'd found the money. Ultimately a judge awarded the IRS the cash in 1965.

The discovery of the money wasn't the only hit that Moriarty took that summer of 1962. A few weeks before the millions were discovered, Hudson

County police arrested over seventy people in a massive effort against illegal gambling in Jersey City and Bayonne. Many of those arrested were part of Newsboy's extensive network of operatives. While Newsboy kept his action mainly concentrated in Jersey City, he did make a move to expand into Newark. In 1967 he arranged to buy a numbers operation from Richie the Boot. Boiardo, however, had seller's remorse and convened a meeting at Gus's Cozy Inn on Bloomfield Avenue with Newsboy and Jerry Catena. Moriarty agreed to sell back the numbers to Boiardo, averting a possible showdown.

Though Moriarty's money stash was gone, there were some who thought he was still flush with readily available case. In 1971 Moriarty was kidnapped, handcuffed with a hood over his head, and driven down the Jersey Shore. He was beaten, and his hands and face were burned with a blowtorch. The kidnappers wanted to find out where Newsboy was keeping his money. But it was clear that Newsboy didn't have any stashes of millions left for them. Still, they kept at it. When his captors tired themselves out and fell asleep, Newsboy took the opportunity to free himself from the handcuffs and sneak way. He walked through some woods to a motel where he called the police. He claimed to not have seen his kidnappers and had no idea why they would want to do this to him. "Newsboy told us he was not sure he could identify the three men, and he didn't even know where the house was. He only said 'These were real tough guys.'"[3]

Though the newspapers at the time described Moriarty as retired from his operations, he was actually still at it, taking bets from his loyal customers. But the times had changed. The jovial local bookmaker was now engaged in activity that violated federal rules. The FBI was on Moriarty now, and even his relationship with local police wasn't enough to stop them from arresting him in 1973 for gambling conspiracy. He was convicted on those charges and sent to prison. Suffering from prostate cancer, his sentence was commuted by Governor Brendan Byrne in 1976. Newsboy died in February of 1979.

Part of the power that gangsters like Newsboy enjoyed stemmed from the deep level of corruption in some of the municipalities in Hudson County. When John V. Kenny was elected mayor of Jersey City in 1949, his administration inherited a police racket squad that was highly effective in combatting illegal gambling and other vice activity in the city. When Kenny suggested to the police commissioner, Charles Witkowski, that he change the makeup of the squad, arrests plummeted. Witkowski, sensing that Kenny was trying to sabotage the squad, put some of his own men back. "In the sixteen months of the squad's operation, over 325 arrests for gambling, numbers, etc., were made, the highest per capita percentage in the United States." To which Kenny told Witkowski, "between the gambling squad and the waterfront squad, you're hurting our friends."[4]

And while Newsboy had a large chunk of the gambling action, there was plenty of money to be made in the county. Along with Newsboy Moriarty there was another dominant crime figure in Hudson. His name said it all: Bayonne Joe Zicarelli was born in Bayonne in 1912 and rose through the ranks of the Bonanno crime family to become the county's underworld king. He was "reportedly the head man in the numbers, lottery, and gambling operations in Hudson County, New Jersey, with its headquarters in Bayonne."[5]

Though he was born to a Calabrian family, not Sicilian, and had no known ties to the Mafia, Zicarelli was nonetheless introduced to organized crime by neighborhood associates. He earned a reputation as a tough street hood who was not afraid to stand up and fight. This reputation remained with him throughout his life. Bayonne Joe had a soft side as well. According to local residents, on Thanksgiving and Christmas he would "send five- or six thousand turkeys to needy people" and on Easter would "send one thousand hams."[6]

Zicarelli had a long list of run-ins with the law, starting back in the post-Prohibition late 1930s when he was sentenced to three years' probation for violating liquor laws. In February of 1949 he was indicted for running a gambling house in Bayonne. He pled no contest and was fined a thousand dollars, a mere portion of the take from his gambling operations. The following year he was charged with conspiracy to defraud and possessing a still. That case was dismissed. Zicarelli was rising in the ranks of the mob, with few convictions to his name. And he looked to expand his empire outside the neighborhood.

In the late 1940s and early '50s, Zicarelli was following other northern mobsters in looking for gambling opportunities overseas, the main target being Cuba. Zicarelli explored options to establish gambling operations in Caracas, Venezuela, as well. He was an entrepreneur of the Mafia and a big earner. That caught the eye of various mob families who were always on the lookout for guys who could line their coffers.

According to mob hitman Harold "Kayo" Konigsberg, Zicarelli was the subject of an intense feud between Angelo "Gyp" DeCarlo, Charlie Tourine, and Carmine Galante. Each of the mobsters wanted Zicarelli to be part of their respective crews. DeCarlo and Tourine were Genovese guys, while Galante was a Bonanno. Galante won out, and Zicarelli became a made member of the Mafia in 1955. Zicarelli and Galante became business partners as well in a number of legitimate business endeavors.

Joe's notoriety eventually garnered the attention of federal authorities, and his name became associated with international events in 1959. An FBI report of that year suggested that Zicarelli might be "active in purchasing guns for a Cuban revolution, gambling activity in Mexico, kickback contracts in Venezuela, possible assassination of a Venezuelan political leader, and a possible link in the disappearance of Jesús de Galíndez-Suárez. Another government agency has furnished information that Zicarelli has been authorized to purchase one million dollars' worth of rockets and machine guns for the Dominican Republic."[7]

The next year Zicarelli came up on the feds' radar again. He was running part of his gambling empire out of the Park Royal hotel on West Seventy-Third Street in Manhattan. Zicarelli was getting concerned the police in Bayonne were putting too much heat on his gambling enterprise in Hudson County. So, while the FBI listened, Zicarelli called Cornelius "Neil" Gallagher. Neil was of particular interest to the eavesdropping feds, not because of his criminal connections, but because of his political ones. Gallagher was a US congressman from New Jersey. A war hero in both World War II and Korea, he also served on the House Committee on Foreign Affairs and the Operations Committee. He was so well respected in Washington that there was talk that Senator Lyndon Johnson, who was running for the presidency, was looking at Gallagher as a possible running mate.

The phone call to Gallagher went through, and Zicarelli laid out his concerns, especially about a top police official. Gallagher assured him that he would take care of it. A few days later, Zicarelli reached back out to Gallagher. "I got hold of those Bayonne police, and there will be no further problem." The congressman told Bayonne Joe. Joe replied, "I hope so, because they're ruining me." Gallagher then added, "They damn well better not."[8]

Gallagher was also supposed to assist Zicarelli in his plans to get involved with a Dominican airline, Compañía Dominicana de Aviación. For years Zicarelli had been involved in running guns to the Dominican Republic during the reign of Rafael Trujillo. When Trujillo was assassinated on May 30, 1961, Zicarelli saw opportunity in the ensuing chaos: an opening to gain control of the Dominican airline, a chance to invest in a legitimate business. Zicarelli thought that Gallagher's pull in the Committee on Foreign Affairs could be of help, but the deal fell through even after Gallagher had personally flown to the Dominican Republic to advocate for Zicarelli's bid for the airline with Trujillo's successor.

One of the most bizarre alleged ties between Gallagher and Zicarelli was revealed in a 1968 *Life* magazine article. This story came from the confessions of Kayo Konigsberg. Kayo, who was serving time in prison, started talking to authorities about some of the murders that he had committed both in the employment of the Mafia and on his own. One of the stories he told involved not murder but the disposal of a dead body.

Konigsberg said that he had been called to the house of Congressman Gallagher one night back in October 1962. Gallagher and Konigsberg had both grown up in Bayonne. Gallagher had brought Kayo down to the basement and showed him the body of a local shylock named Barney O'Brien. When later relating this to police, Kayo said he didn't think Barney had been murdered by the congressman, but he wasn't sure how he had died. What Kayo did know was that Gallagher had asked him to remove and dispose of the body. Unsure whether he wanted to get himself involved in anything, Kayo insisted on calling Zicarelli, who told Kayo to do the favor. Kayo then loaded the body in his car and drove it to a remote area where he buried it. Gallagher adamantly refuted the story, claiming Kayo had never been in his house and that there were no phone calls made to Zicarelli on the night in question. He further told the reporter for *Life* that O'Brien did occasionally come to his house but hadn't that night.

Gallagher distanced himself from the Zicarelli connection. A recording of Zicarelli and Emmanuel Riggi, a DeCavalcante solder the government was looking to deport, had the Bonanno capo telling Riggi that if things came down to the wire Zicarelli could reach out to a few judges he had in his pocket but that the best option was for Riggi to contact "Neil the Congressman."[9] It was Bayonne Joe's opinion that, if all else failed, Gallagher could step in on Riggi's behalf and halt the deportation process.

In the mid-1960s, during the Bonanno family internecine war, Zicarelli was among thirty Bonanno family members and associates subpoenaed to appear before a federal grand jury investigating the internal warfare.

As internal confrontations strained the Bonanno family to its breaking point, Zicarelli was alleged to have held a number of positions within the family that was constantly in flux. In 1967 a top echelon informant told the FBI that Zicarelli was the New Jersey underboss to Angelo Caruso.[10] A few weeks after that report, another said that Zicarelli was part of a reshuffling that saw the top spot go to Paul Sciacca and that Zicarelli had been dropped from the underboss position. By 1968 Zicarelli was seen as a "type of referee and advisor in the continuing problems."[11] In late 1968 Zicarelli was approached by the leadership of the family and offered the position of consigliere, which he turned down.

All the constantly shifting alliances and positions were draining Zicarelli mentally and physically. Bayonne Joe told Sam DeCavalcante on June 11, 1965, that he was actively seeking to move into another family and wanted DeCavalcante to take him into the Elizabeth group. He saw the DeCavalcantes as stable and small, not partial to the bickering that was driving such a wedge between so many Bonanno mobsters. DeCavalcante was in favor of the move and floated the idea to Carlo Gambino to see if the Commission would approve; but ultimately it was determined that Zicarelli should remain in the Bonanno family.

During the Bonanno family turmoil, one of Zicarelli' s top associates started looking around for other opportunities as well. John DiGilio started spending a great deal of time with members of the Genovese family—namely, Patty Mack Macchiarole, a Jersey City–based mobster with close ties to the longshoremen's union. DiGilio saw more opportunity at the port than

Zicarelli. The Bonannos didn't have much of a presence at all on the New Jersey waterfront. Since that's the direction DiGilio was moving in, a decision was made to allow him to switch sides, and he went with the Genovese, eventually becoming a made member. Gyp DeCarlo was heard on a wiretap telling a colleague that DiGilio was his man on the piers and that he was only allowing Zicarelli to operate there are as a favor but that now DiGilio would be talking over all operations on the docks. It was unclear whether DeCarlo was talking about union-related activities or mainly gambling.

Adding to his issues, Bayonne Joe was indicted in November of 1970 with conspiracy to corrupt the mayor of West New York, John Armellino. It was alleged that Zicarelli and his associates had been paying Armellino a thousand dollars a week to protect their gambling operations. The mayor and his brother were also indicted and charged with accepting the payoffs and facilitating the gambling operation through failure to enforce the laws of the State of New Jersey. Bayonne Joe was sentenced to twelve to fifteen years in prison. The indictment was another illustration of how deep corruption went in Hudson County and how Zicarelli was such a pivotal player in how politics was run in county, for the most part.

While Zicarelli was dealing with legal and Mafia-related issues, a new player was emerging in the Hudson County underworld. The main competition in Hudson County for both political corruption and illegal gambling was the Corporation, a Cuban organized-crime syndicate led by José Miguel Battle, a hardened Bay of Pigs veteran and former police officer under Fulgencio Batista, the president of Cuba who had been overthrown by Fidel Castro. Batista was also close to mob figures like Meyer Lansky and Santo Trafficante Jr. due to the mob's hotel and casino operations in Cuba. Battle's bases of operations were Miami and Union City, New Jersey, which is in Hudson County. Battle was close to Santo Trafficante Jr. in Miami, but his relationships with mobsters in New Jersey and New York City ran the gamut from mutual cooperation to turf battles. There are sources that maintain Joe Zicarelli assisted Battle in his early efforts to set up multi-million-dollar-policy and bolita networks in Union City and other areas in Hudson County. But the Corporation would become a major crime syndicate on its own, and close ties with Mafia families diminished over the ensuing years.

After Zicarelli was released from prison in 1977, he was remanded to state prison to finish a sentence for contempt. His lawyers argued that he needed a medical furlough to address a host of health issues, including hypertension, kidney problems, and ulcers. He was released at the end of 1977 for medical reasons. Bayonne Joe died in 1982.

Figure 8.1. Enoch "Nucky" Johnson at his tax-evasion trial. Source: Avi Bash.

Figure 8.2.   The Blue Mirror, Longy Zwillman's hangout in the 1930s and 1940s.
Source: Author's collection.

Figure 8.3.   Site of the Casablanca Club in Newark, a major underworld hangout owned by Longy Zwillman. Source: Author's collection.

Figure 8.4. The Riviera Hotel, Longy Zwillman's base of operations. Source: Author's collection.

Figure 8.5.   Abner "Longy" Zwillman (smiling at camera). Source: Myron Sugerman.

Figure 8.6.   Joseph "Doc" Stacher. Source: Myron Sugerman.

Figure 8.7.   Max "Puddy" Hinkes, associate of Longy Zwillman. Source: Myron
Sugerman.

ELIZABETH CARTERET HOTEL, ELIZABETH, N. J.

Figure 8.8. Elizabeth Carteret Hotel, site of Max Hassel and Max Greenberg's murders. Source: Author's collection.

Figure 8.9.   Gene Catena, brother of Jerry Catena. Source: Avi Bash.

Figure 8.10.　Gerardo "Jerry" Catena. Source: Myron Sugerman.

Figure 8.11.   Ruggiero "Richie the Boot" Boiardo, longtime New Jersey Mafia figure. Source: Author's collection (UPI photo; author owns original).

Figure 8.12. Willie Moretti murder scene. Source: Avi Bash.

Figure 8.13.   Simone "Sam the Plumber" DeCavalcante. Source: Author's collection (UPI photo; author owns original).

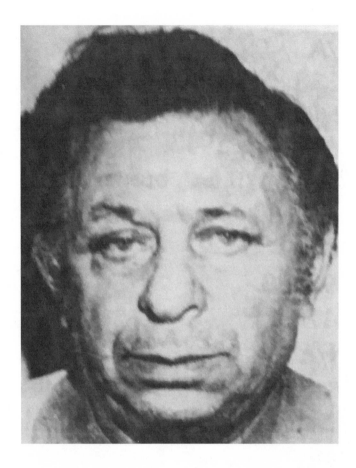

Figure 8.14. Joseph "Happy" Bellina, Newark-based mobster. Source: Author's collection.

Figure 8.15. Angelo "Gyp" DeCarlo. Source: Author's collection (UPI photo; author owns original).

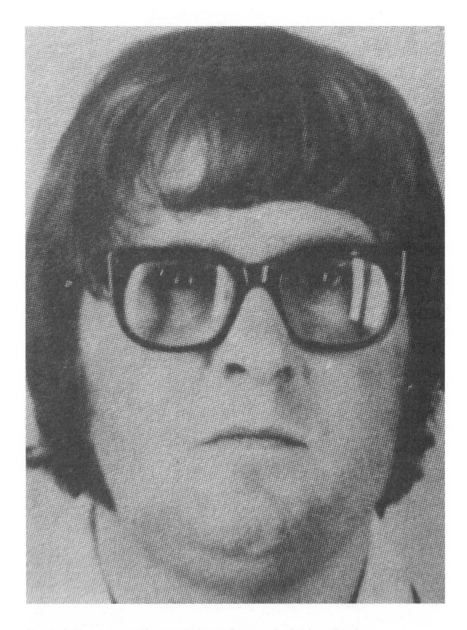

Figure 8.16.   Joseph "Scoops" Licata. Source: Author's collection.

Figure 8.17.   Mafia boss and Atlantic Highlands resident Vito Genovese. Source: Author's collection (UPI photo; author owns original).

Figure 8.18.   Thomas "Tommy Ryan" Eboli. Source: Author's collection (UPI photo; author owns original).

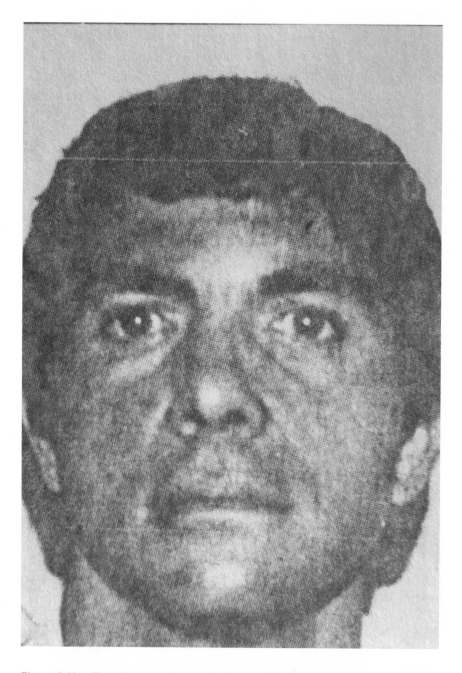

Figure 8.19.   Tino Fiumara. Source: Author's collection.

Figure 8.20. Anthony "Little Pussy" Russo. Source: New Jersey State Commission of Investigation.

Figure 8.21. Albert "Reds" Pontani. Source: Author's collection.

Figure 8.22.   Louis "Streaky" Gatto, Genovese capo of the Lodi crew. Source:
Author's collection.

Figure 8.23.   Joe Sodano. Source: Author's collection.

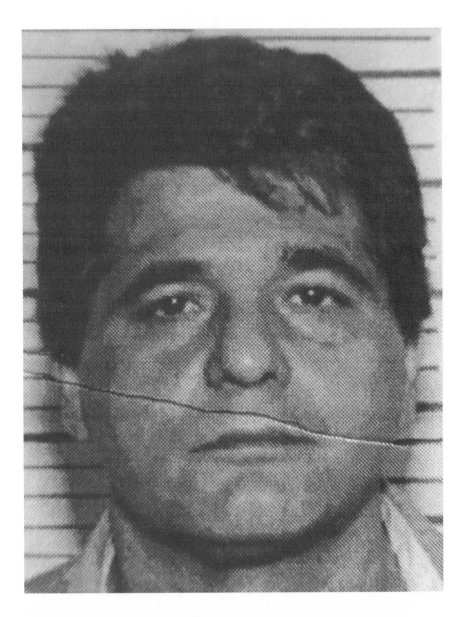

Figure 8.24.   Michael Taccetta, 1992 mug shot. Source: Author's collection.

Figure 8.25. Surveillance photo of John DiGilio. Source: New Jersey State Commission of Investigation.

Figure 8.26.   Myron Sugerman giving a talk on the history of the Jewish mob.
Source: Myron Sugerman.

Chapter Nine

Bruno and the Down Neck Mob

In the city of Newark is a neighborhood that stands out as an ethnic enclave that has stood the test of time through the city's turbulent twentieth-century history. It's more commonly known as the Ironbound, so named because it's bordered on all sides by railroads and major highways. The Ironbound district is a thriving blue-collar immigrant community, shaped in recent decades by a large Portuguese population with Brazilian and Ecuadorian influence. The narrow streets are lined with well-kept homes, and the main commercial strips, including Ferry Street, are known statewide for their Portuguese, Spanish, and Brazilian restaurants, markets, and bakeries. When Portugal won the Euro 2016 championship, the streets of the Ironbound were jam-packed with throngs of the soccer team's supporters sporting Ronaldo shirts.

The Ironbound is also known colloquially as Down Neck. The moniker refers to the neighborhood unique geographic location where the Passaic River 'droops', though some also say it referred to an older name of Dutch Neck. It was here in the narrow streets and corner taverns that many New Jersey mobsters were born and raised. The social clubs that dotted the landscape provided a meeting place to discuss gambling and loansharking over coffee and *pastéis de nata*. Gangsters from the Genovese and Gambino families grew up Down Neck. Cut off from the other heavily mobbed-up neighborhoods of the First Ward, Vailsburg, and Silver Lake, Down Neck guys tended to stick together. According to one former wiseguy, "the Down Neck mob was a mob unto itself."[1] And their loyalties and alliances stood the test of time. There was a real camaraderie with the Down Neck guys, and the area was, and is still, a ripe spot for mob activity.

While the neighborhood spawned mob figures that belonged to many different families, it became a New Jersey outpost for an unlikely Newark-based crew from the Philadelphia crime family. How that happened is an artifact of a choice made by one of the early bosses of the Philadelphia crime family, Joseph Bruno. When the Castellammarese War was winding down in New York, Salvatore Sabella was the boss of the Philadelphia Mafia family. He stepped down at the end of the war, around 1931, and leadership was passed to John Avena, who was murdered in 1936. The mantle was then passed to Joseph "Bruno" Dovi. Joe Bruno, as he came to be known, ran the family for the next decade. The Philadelphia family's presence in Newark dated back to the 1940s and featured two main events: The first was the relocation of Joseph Bruno from Bristol, Pennsylvania, where he had been living, to New Brunswick, New Jersey, a city of about thirty-five thousand, forty-five minutes south of Newark. The second was the arrival to Newark of one of Bruno's men—Tony "Bananas" Caponigro.

Joe Bruno's relocation to New Brunswick put him into contact with more New Jersey–based mobsters. When he died in October 1946 of natural causes, his successor, Joseph Ida, maintained these connections, also living in New Brunswick, before he moved to Italy, abdicating the throne and letting Angelo Bruno (no relation to Joe Bruno) take over. Of the move one wiseguy commented, "He [Ida] used to stay home under the grapevine and read a book. He must love it in Italy, 'cause all he ever did in New Brunswick until they made him the boss was to read books. He never went no place until they made him the boss. And then he didn't want to go to them meetings and all. He was a quiet man. His pleasure was reading books. Now in Italy he must feel right at home."[2]

It was at this time that an enterprising young Philly mobster, Anthony "Tony Bananas" Caponigro, made a move up to the City of Newark to find opportunity. Tony Bananas was made in Philadelphia in 1947 during Ida's reign. Upon arriving in Newark, Caponigro first went to set up shop in the First Ward, then starting its decline as the premier Italian neighborhood of North New Jersey. However there was still money to be made there, and by 1947 it was firmly under the control of Richie Boiardo, who was having none of what Caponigro was trying to do. Rather than come in and try to work with Boiardo, Caponigro was looking to set up his own shop and own operations. After all, he wasn't beholden to Boiardo's family. But there was a lot of money to be made in the Newark area, so, wanting to remain in the area, Caponigro went a couple miles away to the neighborhood of Down Neck, where he felt there would be less in the way of competition.

At that time, Down Neck was run by Anthony "Tee Vee" Verniero. Born in the First Ward of Newark in 1901, Tee Vee wasn't a made guy, because he was half-Jewish, but he held considerable sway over numbers operations in the neighborhood. Caponigro saw an opportunity to team up with Verniero to expand their numbers and other rackets. He approached Verniero with a proposition to share costs and open up joint monte and craps games. To Tee Vee, this was a win-win proposition. Down Neck was still pretty open at the time, and having a made guy as a partner was a good bet against interference from other wiseguys looking to take a piece of Tee Vee's action. But Tee Vee made a mistake: He turned around for one minute, and when he looked back, Bananas had taken over everything Tee Vee owned. Instead of being the boss of a vast gambling enterprise, Verniero was now a member of Caponigro's crew. With that, the Philadelphia Mafia had a crew operating in Newark. Tee Vee was referred to as one of Caponigro's principal operators when he was arrested in 1963 in a clothing store at 118 1/2 Mulberry Street in Newark and charged with possession of lottery slips and bookmaking.

Tony "Bananas" Caponigro was a born leader in the mob. He cultivated and grew the Bruno operation in North Jersey with little support or oversight from his superiors in Philadelphia. George Anastasia, author and journalist, said of Caponigro, "I think he benefited from Bruno's laissez-faire management style. Most guys either liked him or feared him, and they all knew they could make money with him, which is always the most important thing anyway."[3] The location of Down Neck was not always conducive to favorable relationships between the crime family's base of operations in South Philly and their far-north satellite operation. As a Philly mob source told a reporter in 2001, "Newark has always been an aggravation for Philly. All of North Jersey has. There's so much money to make there, but it's a big fuckin' headache. Newark is so far from South Philly, and so close to New York. And you know what that means. Trouble!"[4]

Tony Bananas was the man about town—at least in Down Neck—often visiting his games and making sure he looked the part to impress fellow mobsters and the women who often hung around his casino-style gaming rooms. "He was a real ladies man, this Tony."[5] He owned the 311 Club on Ferry Street and often hung out at the Ironbound Republican Club at 113 Delancey Street, the Luso-American Bar at 71 Ferry Street, the Plaza Lounge on Commerce Street, and various social clubs around the neighborhood. Caponigro was known as a benevolent dictator among his crew, which he rapidly expanded after he took over Tee Vee Verniero's gambling interests. "Bananas was vicious. He ran a tough crew, and he was a tough leader. He was very ambitious."[6]

Tony had a system for keeping his crew in line, financially. "He has several people on his payroll at 'a yard and a half ($150.00) just to hang around.' He said that even if he gets twenty-five thousand dollars in the kitty nobody gets a five thousand dollar score. Bananas stated that he felt it more practical to see that his men get a payroll each week rather than cutting up large sums at irregular intervals."[7]

In the early years, many in the Down Neck mob were lesser-known crime figures who avoided both the media and, for the most part, law-enforcement attention. They were guys like Louis Luciano and Jerry Fusella. "Bananas got all these guys made in 1954—Patty Specs (young), Jerry Fusella, Blackie

Napoli, Louis Luciano."[8] The guys that Caponigro made became loyal to him more than they were loyal to the Philadelphia leadership. That would get some of them into trouble in the years ahead. But back when Tony was starting out, it seemed like an easy way for the Philly family to stake a lucrative claim with a satellite operation. As long as the money kept getting sent back to South Philly, things worked.

Joseph Anthony Bellina, aka Happy Bellina, was a longtime member of Caponigro's crew in Newark. Born in 1909, Bellina was a longshoreman by trade and a burglar by skillset.[9] In 1936, Bellina was arrested in Massachusetts for a jewel robbery. He broke into the home of a Boston clothing-store owner, tying up the man's wife and maid before leaving with over $125,000 worth of jewels. Sentenced to fifteen to twenty years in prison, Bellina was paroled in February of 1946. However, his penchant for crime returned with a vengeance. Though he was a Newark resident, the Boston area was fertile ground for his activities.

In late October 1947, right before Halloween, along with five other crew members, Bellina and five other men, all wearing masks, stormed into the Westinghouse Electric Sturtevant plant in Boston, armed with sawed-off shotguns, and grabbed over a hundred thousand dollars in cash from the company's payroll. The next day the crew hit a sugar refinery in South Boston for another payroll score of twenty-nine thousand. Police described the Westinghouse robbery as "the biggest and boldest in Boston police records."[10] Bellina was arrested by FBI agents and Newark detectives and arraigned in Newark before being shipped up to Boston. Bellina was proposed for membership in 1954 into the Mafia, and some sources say that was when he was made. But an informant report from 1963 says that Thomas Pecora was approached by Louis Luciano and asked if they would support Happy Bellina's membership in the Mafia. Luciano further stated that Bellina had just been released from prison. The report doesn't say whether or not Happy was made, but at that time the books were still closed for New York families. But, as discussed in an earlier chapter, Philadelphia was still making new members, so it can be construed that Happy was looking to get made into the Angelo Bruno family, under his crew leader, Tony Caponigro. Certainly by the early 1980s, as stated in police reports, Bellina was considered a solider in the Philly Newark crew.

Gerardo Carmine "Jerry" Fusella first appeared on the radar of Newark police when he was arrested and convicted for robbery. He then killed another man in a street fight in Newark on April 9, 1939. Only twenty-three at the time, Fusella skipped town and became a fugitive from the FBI. Over the next seven years, he stayed under the radar, evading capture. His wanted poster had this to say about his "peculiarities": "wears mustache occasionally, frequents poolrooms, tries to look tough."[11] Of course, just below that it said he carries two guns and was to be considered dangerous, so maybe looking tough was more than false bravado. The FBI caught up with Fusella in 1946 in Staten Island. He next showed up as a longshoreman in 1954 at the Port of Newark. He was denied his registration as a longshoreman by the Waterfront Commission who were investigating organized-crime ties in both unions and hiring practices at the various ports in New York and New Jersey. By that time, Fusella was a made member of Caponigro's crew.

Another Down Neck mob member who is never really regarded as a Newark mobster, mainly because of his activities elsewhere, was Charlie "the Blade" Tourine. Born in Matawan, New Jersey, Charlie owned Zappia's Tavern at 186 Oliver Street in Down Neck, a noted hangout for crime figures in the neighborhood. It was noted that "during the 1930s and 1940s Tourine had a very vicious reputation and was known as a killer."[12] Tourine was never affiliated with the Caponigro crew. Like another Down Neck native, Jerry Catena, Tourine became a made member in the Genovese crime family. His arrest record dated back to 1926 when he was arrested for murder. Those charges were eventually dropped, but his run-ins with the law continued throughout his life, with over thirty arrests ranging from gambling to intimidating witnesses, robbery, tax evasion, and bribery, all before he was forty years old. In the 1950s Tourine left the confines of Newark, moved out to Manhattan, and started investing in casinos in Cuba, where he worked with Santo Trafficante Jr., the mob boss of Tampa, in some of his casinos—namely, the Sans Souci. Tourine remained active in the New Jersey rackets, overseeing gambling operations in the Newark area, especially after Castro took over Cuba in 1959 and kicked all the mobsters out. Tourine was considered by fellow mobsters to be tight fisted with a nickel, but his extensive array of crimes afforded him a lifestyle a lot of street-level guys were never able to achieve. He relocated to Miami in the sixties and became a senior Genovese figure for their South Florida operations.

Other members of the Down Neck mob included Ralph Albert "Blackie" Napoli, born in Newark in 1914, was a solider in Caponigro's crew. He had a long arrest sheet for loan-sharking, assault, and illegal gambling. In later years, he would step up and become a captain of his own crew when he relocated out of Down Neck. Nicholas Alfred "Turk" Cifelli was a gambling figure who ran bookmaking out of Francesca's Restaurant in Down Neck and hung out at the Italian-American War Veterans in Newark. Pasquale "Patty Specs" Martirano, a younger member of the original Caponigro crew, would rise to capo in the mid-1980s, overseeing the Down Neck mob.

Joseph "Scoops" Licata was another younger member of Caponigro's crew who started in the late 1960s. He was a bookmaker and loan shark in Down Neck. It was said that "Scoops appeared to be very close to Tony Bananas, and he liked to brag it was because he was such a big earner."[13] A former wiseguy who was around the Down Neck Bruno crew originally felt the same but changed his opinion over the years: "In the past, I spoke about

Joe Scoops in a very unflattering way. In retrospect I wish I could take it back. The guy has always done his time. He worked hard both in the 'life' and in the legit world. I have redefined my understanding of 'tough guy.' He was a good family man and a survivor. My assessment stands corrected."[14]

The thing that set the Down Neck crew apart was that, with the exception of some moves Caponigro made into neighboring cities, they tended to run card games and gambling in their own neighborhood. From the 1950s through the 1990s they kept their activities very local. This may have been to ensure that the games would run smoothly, as well as to keep a close eye on the operators and bettors. One of the card games that was a popular mob-run racket in Down Neck was monte. As explained by one of the crew, in monte, which was similar to the game of baccarat, "one of the players acts as the 'bank,' betting against the other players. This means that, as the house, we were not betting against the bettors the way a casino does in craps or black-jack; instead, for holding the game and providing food, drinks, and other services, we took a 'cut' of every pot . . . our cut of the pot could add up to fifty thousand dollars or more per night."[15] Bananas had "long been known to control gambling in Essex County" and operated the "largest monte game in the metropolitan New Jersey area, which gets very heavy play, particularly on weekends."[16]

Another popular card game was ziginette, a popular Sicilian card game that features a fifty-two-card deck—the eights, nines, and tens removed— and a metal card box from which one card is removed at a time. The basic idea is that the player bets on a table card to not be matched before the dealers. But it's a little more complicated than that. The game's popularity stems from its fast pace and the house's ability to win regardless by taking a 10 percent cut of all player winnings. The FBI recorded Carl "Leash" Silesia and Gyp DeCarlo talking about the game:

LEASH: Do you want to open a joint?

DECARLO: Ah, well, let's see.

LEASH: 'Cause I think I can get a spot Down Neck.

DECARLO: Oh, is that what you want to do? What can you open?

LEASH: Anything I want to. Ziginette.[17]

Though the Down Neck mob was the main Philadelphia presence in New Jersey, there were guys throughout South Jersey. Many of them merely lived in the bedroom communities of Philadelphia, but there were some who had their own territories and were put in charge of their own crews that operated in the southern swath of Camden, Cumberland, Gloucester, Salem, Cape May, and Atlantic counties of New Jersey.

Joe Scafidi and John "Keys" Simone lived in Trenton, New Jersey. Simone had been sent to Trenton in 1956 by Angelo Bruno to oversee the burgeoning operations in the state capital. Simone worked for a vending company but also ran a sizeable bookmaking operation. At that time he worked under Charles "Pinky" Costello, called the "boss of Trenton numbers and gambling."[18] Though the state capital, Trenton was not nearly as lucrative a spot to run rackets as other New Jersey towns, including Newark, but it would be a base of operations for a Philly crew for decades. Interestingly, though the Philly family had the run of the state capital, there was very little in the way of political corruption at a state level being orchestrated by Angelo Bruno or any of his crime family capos or soldiers. The statewide corrupting influence was definitely directed more by the New York family crews in Jersey. Perhaps that's because of the relative size of the Philadelphia Mafia compared to the five New York families, or compared to the older, and deeper, well of presence that the other crime families had that enabled them to gain more of a foothold through the political process than had the relative newcomers to the state. Part of it may also have stemmed from an aptness to Angelo Bruno's moniker, the Docile Don, with his not wanting to rock the boat, being perfectly okay to keep his empire small and avoid unnecessary risk.

As the Down Neck mob grew in size and influence, so did Caponigro. He was regularly meeting with higher-ups in the New York Mafia as well as the DeCavalcante family. An informant told the FBI in early 1967 that Bananas was "becoming more and more powerful in LCN [la Cosa Nostra] and that his activities are becoming more widespread."[19] Kayo Konigsberg told the FBI that Caponigro had ten to twelve soldiers under him. He was looking to expand outside his backyard when he purchased a pizzeria in Wayne, in Morris County, New Jersey. He set up a network of numbers operators throughout the area, which included Parsippany and Caldwell.

Louis Luciano was as close to a right-hand man as Caponigro had in the sixties. Luciano ran most of the gambling for Tony out of the Plaza Bar. Luciano also had his own small crew of men that assisted him in running the day-to-day of the Down Neck mob's operations. Luciano was well respected by Caponigro but fell out of favor at some point.

In the late 1960s Luciano moved out of Down Neck to suburban Roseland, west of Newark. On February 12, 1971, according to news reports, he arrived home and was getting out of his car, carrying a box of pastries. An associate was in the car as well. A car pulled up to the house with three men inside who were wearing ski masks. They opened fire. One of the gunmen jumped out of the car and "from about fifteen feet hits him with one blast right in the back. He goes down, the pastry box goes up in the air." Then the gunman "moves to within about five feet of him and lets off two more blast in the back. There wasn't much of Louis left."[20] The bodyguard had dived under the car but was hit by stray bullets. The gunmen were using shotguns and a .38. After Luciano was killed, the assailants sped away in the car, tossing the weapons out as they left the scene. Police recovered the car a few miles away in a ShopRite parking lot, but the gunmen were long gone.

Within a year the police knew the whole story of the Luciano murder, from a turncoat. Luciano had been murdered by members of a violent crew, the Campisi mob. The core group was comprised of brothers and cousins, with a few nonrelatives as strong-arm men. They were not tied to any crime family (though two would be made in later years to different families). The Campisis ran gambling and a robbery crew across Central Jersey. They were known for their proclivity for violence and dealing with situations by force instead of reason. Lou Luciano had committed a few crimes that had brought him between the Campisis' crosshairs. First, he had been moving in on some of their gambling operations, trying to poach independent gamblers who paid tribute to the Campisi. Second, he had tried to convince the son of the titular head of the crew, Anthony "Na-Na," to join him instead of staying with the Campisis. Luciano told the young man, "You know you're young yet. You're a fool for sticking with you father and your cousins. They're all gonna go some day. Come in with me, and you can do good with me—before it's too late."[21] The Campisis took this as a sign that Luciano might also have been plotting a move against them, angering Na-Na even further. Finally, there were stories that the tall, silver-haired, well-dressed Luciano had been sleeping with the wife of another Campisi, Tommy, who had been given the information by a local police officer, who showed him evidence of all the times Luciano and his wife had been meeting.

The Luciano murder angered one of his young protégés, Tino Fiumara. Tino was from Down Neck and started as a Bruno guy with Louie Luciano. When Luciano was killed, Tino knew that the order had to come from above. The Campisis told other members in their group that Carlo Gambino had given the order. But it was apparent to Fiumara that Tony Bananas Caponigro had to have been consulted. Luciano was a made guy and in his crew. There was no way that Caponigro would have allowed this to happen, in his backyard, without at least being consulted. Tino made his frustration felt. He went over to the Vesuvius Restaurant on Bloomfield Avenue and complained. Everyone knew there was going to be a problem between Fiumara and Caponigro if this continued. A move was made on Tino's behalf to bring him over to the Genovese family. He was "straightened out" with the Genovese and put in the crew of Pete LaPlaca, which kept the Brunos from going after him. But it also put Tino in a crime family that was bigger and more influential than the Brunos, a crime family that was the largest and most powerful in New Jersey.

Chapter Ten

The Genovese Family

The Horizon House co-op in Fort Lee, New Jersey, sits atop the Palisades overlooking the Hudson River, just south of the George Washington Bridge. Building four is a seven-story mid-rise in the center of the complex. In 1972, the rent on an apartment was eight hundred dollars, an easily affordable sum for Genovese boss Thomas Eboli and his common-law wife, Mary. But the gangster, who had suffered some recent health setbacks, was looking to relocate and purchased a home in Passaic, New Jersey, fifteen miles away.

Thomas "Tommy Ryan" Eboli was born in Italy and lived for many years in various New Jersey towns—Ridgefield, Teaneck, and Englewood Cliffs— before moving to Fort Lee. But it was during a formative year living in Greenwich Village in New York City that he became friends with Vito Genovese and Anthony "Tony Bender" Strollo and started on his life of involvement with the Genovese family, eventually working his way up to acting underboss by the mid-1960s. When Vito Genovese died in 1969, Eboli became part of a family ruling panel that also included Mike Miranda and Jerry Catena. Though described by fellow underworld denizens as a hothead, Eboli kept a low profile during his time at the top.

On the night of Saturday, July 15, 1972, his driver, Joseph Sternfeld, drove Eboli to New York, through Manhattan and into Brooklyn. He dropped Tommy Ryan off at 388 Lefferts Avenue in the Prospect-Lefferts Gardens neighborhood of Brooklyn, next to Crown Heights. It was allegedly the home of Eboli's mistress. According to police, Sternfeld told them he had been directed by Eboli to drive around for a bit and come back to pick up the mob boss around 1 a.m. on the 16th. Sternfeld did as he was instructed and pulled back up to the building at Lefferts Avenue just after 1 a.m. Eboli was waiting it the lobby, and when he saw the car pull up he walked outside.

When Eboli emerged from the building, a yellow truck that had been parked just up the street started up and drove toward him. As Eboli walked toward the blue 1971 Cadillac, the truck passed by, from which rained a fusillade of shots at him and the Cadillac. The driver, Sternfeld, later told police that he ducked under the dashboard when the shooting started. "I didn't see anything, I don't know what happened, I just heard the shots fired."[1] Five bullets ripped through Eboli's body, hitting him in the face and neck, from a .38 caliber pistol and a machine gun. Eboli fell to the ground, dead, and the truck with its shooters tore away from the scene, the gunshots awaking neighbors. Police rushed to the scene and found the truck with its engine still running, abandoned a few blocks away. They also found a stolen car nearby with an M3 machine gun. It was obvious that two cars had been used in the hit.

Police found two thousand dollars in hundred-dollar bills in Eboli's coat pocket. His trademark hat was nowhere to be found. The funeral home where Eboli was laid out, Romanelli F. and Sons in Ozone Park, Queens, was awash with local, state, and federal law enforcement, but few mob guys showed up. Neither did many come to Eboli's resting place, a cemetery back across the bridge in Paramus, New Jersey. This lack of respect paid to the fallen mob boss may have hinted at one of the reasons for his demise. To some on the street, the reason for Eboli's death had been pretty simple: he wasn't well liked. Some sources said that his murder had been orchestrated by Jerry Catena and Phil Lombardo after Eboli had disrespected Catena. Lombardo at the time was just a soldier, but a well-connected one who was close to the powerful Catena.

Joseph Sternfeld gave police the names of some suspected underworld figures who may have played a part in the killing. The police didn't reveal the names at the time, but among those that they were looking at were Vincent Mauro and Vincent Gigante, the one-time boxer who'd shot Frank Costello in the head in 1957 and would come to play a prominent role in the Genovese family in the 1980s.

In April of 1972, a few months prior to his murder, Eboli was supposed to have flown to Florida for a meeting with Vincent Aloi of the Colombo family and Santo Trafficante Jr. but had been held up in New York. There was talk that Eboli's death was linked to fifteen other gangland murders that had started with the shooting of mob boss Joe Colombo on June 28, 1971. Authorities speculated that the Gallo-Colombo war then raging in the streets of Brooklyn may have played a part in Eboli's death. But the message was clear from the other leaders in the Genovese family: Eboli was no longer of use to them and was even considered an impediment to the family's growth and prosperity.

The Genovese family has the largest New Jersey operations of any of the New York crime families. The West Side mob, as they are often colloquially known, has long been considered one of the most secretive, and successful, mob families in the United States. And the vagueness of their exact leadership structure was one way they maintained that secrecy. Even their own mob guys on the street were often a little cloudy as to who exactly was running things and when. Sources describe the Genovese family operation like General Motors; it was one company with different divisions. The Genovesi had a whole different corporate structure than did other mob families. As they trusted each other, they let each crew do what it wanted, which had the added benefit of shielding the boss from the prying eyes of law enforcement who might be investigating a crew at any given time.

In reality, while Eboli was thought to be part of the ruling panels that oversaw the family's business concerns, the real power lay with Jerry Catena. From his early years as a driver and partner of Longy Zwillman, Catena had moved up the ladder of influence in New Jersey through the 1960s and had become a major mediator in disputes as well as a ready source of consultation and advice for other mob bosses. Along with Gyp DeCarlo, Catena was the most prominent Genovese family representative in Jersey. But Catena held far more sway than DeCarlo.

Catena, according to one former wiseguy, "wanted to rule with no rule. His power was undisputed. He was one of the most underrated mob bosses in history."[2] Others echoed those sentiments. "The most underrated, without a doubt. My father said he could run either the Pentagon or General Electric. He was that qualified. He had extreme executive skills and ability."[3]

In 1959, Jerry Catena appeared before the Senate Select Committee on Improper Practices in Labor and Management—or the McClellan Committee, as it was also known. There Catena was grilled about his criminal activities and his interest in jukebox companies. True to form, the mobster, his eyes hidden behind sunglasses, refused to answer any questions, invoking the Fifth Amendment some seventy times. Catena's influence extended to Vegas, as did other Genovese members', who were more forthcoming with the committee on their Vegas activity. Gyp DeCarlo, for example, outlined his position in the Desert Inn and the Stardust: He said that the Cleveland mob held fifty-five points in the Desert Inn and sixty points in the Stardust and that they received about $120,000 from all their points combined, as their take from the skim. He calculated the value of each point as being worth $1,800 in the skim. He admitted he had points in both hotels as well.

Upon Eboli's death, many thought the Genovese family mantle would naturally be taken up by Jerry Catena; but, according to some sources, Catena—who at the time of Eboli's shooting was serving time at Yardville Youth Reception and Correctional Facility, in a section specially set aside for mob figures—did not want the position. Catena had been boss since early 1969 and did not want the additional exposure and headaches that came with heading the family. He'd already amassed a sizeable fortune and was looking forward to stepping out of the limelight and enjoying himself. He saw another candidate who would be a better choice than he.

Funzi Tieri, a Naples-born mobster of slight stature, was sixty-eight at the time of Eboli's death and mentioned as a likely successor to the throne. According to some sources, Tieri was approached by Carlo Gambino, Philip "Benny Squint" Lombardo, and Catena to take the top spot. He initially didn't want it but eventually agreed. Part of his reluctance was based in the common perception that Carlo Gambino wanted to have some influence over the Genovese family and, with the appointment of Tieri, would be able to do just that. Tieri, however, was adamant that he was going to rule the family without interference. Tieri also wanted his friend Frankie Casina to take over as capo of his crew. Fat Tony Salerno was appointed consigliere.

However, the generally accepted hierarchy of the Genovese family has Benny Squint Lombardo taking the top spot post-Eboli. He remained in the leadership role throughout the 1970s until 1982 when Fat Tony Salerno took over. Part of the confusion with developing an accurate hierarchy of the family has to do with how the Genovese family was set up and how they often used front bosses and acting bosses in place of the real power. The Lombardo/Tieri boss situation is a perfect example of the type of obfuscation that allowed the Genovese family to shield the bosses from law enforcement for so many years. Another reason the Genovese inner workings remain shrouded in such secrecy is that, after Joe Valachi's explosive federal testimony, the Genovese family did not have another major turncoat for decades. The family kept things running tight.

There was a Genovese crew based in Bergen County, in Northern New Jersey, in the borough of Lodi. Home to Satin Dolls—the strip club featured on HBO TV series *The Sopranos* as Bada Bing!, main character Tony Soprano's headquarters—Lodi is a blue-collar town with long-standing ties to the Genovese family. For years the crew operating there was led by Peter "Lodi Pete" LaPlaca. Lodi Pete was known for his aptitude in dealing with stolen securities and bank fraud. He was considered "one of the strongest criminal bosses in New Jersey and one of the most feared and dangerous men in organized crime."[4] That may have been a bit of hyperbole, but LaPlaca had significant influence in a number of criminal rackets, one of which was refuse disposal.

One of the men under LaPlaca was Ernest Palmieri, head of Local 945 of the International Brotherhood of Teamsters, in which LaPlaca also had an interest. The local was in West Paterson, New Jersey, right in the heart of Genovese territory. Palmieri "controlled garbage in New Jersey during his reign."[5] He became a centerpiece of the mob's control of waste handling in the New Jersey/New York area starting in the 1970s. And one of the mob's more lucrative ventures was the handling and disposal of chemicals and other toxic refuse.

Prior to the establishment of the Resource Conservation and Recovery Act and the Toxic Substances Control Act, both signed into law in 1976, there had been little effort to split toxic materials from regular garbage. All materials were often comingled in landfills. But around the time of the passage of the two acts, coupled with increased attention paid to the environmental consequences of improper disposal, a market emerged for handling this material. By 1983 the market had expanded to "between four billion and five billion dollars a year to manage the regulated portion of hazardous waste."[6]

With the regulations, the cost of disposal of chemicals increased. To maintain tight cost control and ensure that waste companies under the mob's ownership controlled the marketplace, a meeting took place in the mid-1970s to form a waste-haulers association in New Jersey. The representatives at the meeting, according to insider Harold Kaufman, included Pete LaPlaca, James "Jimmy Brown" Failla, a Gambino capo, and Tino Fiumara.

Fiumara, by the early seventies, was firmly in the crew of capo Pete LaPlaca. He also dealt with another up-and-coming Genovese crime-family member who was making waves in New Jersey—John DiGilio. John was described as "cruel and heartless, a bearded man in his mid-forties who often wore a poor boy's cap over his brown hair and was built like a small bull, packing 180 pounds into his 5' 7" frame. He was not someone you wanted to spend a lot of time around."[7] When he switched over from the Bonanno family crew of Bayonne Joe Zicarelli, DiGilio made his move onto the waterfront, becoming secretary-treasurer of Local 1588 of the International Longshoremen's Association, which base he used to expanded his criminal empire across the Jersey docks.

By comparison, Tino Fiumara had "a reputation for being particularly vicious. Waterfront executives were terrified of him, and many wiseguys lower down on the Genovese ladder were scared to refer to him by his real name, instead simply calling him 'T' or 'the Good-Looking Guy.'"[8] Already entrenched with the Down Neck mob and Genovese family, Fiumara also had good relationships with members of the Lucchese and Colombo families.

The New Jersey State Police were keeping an eye on the activities of Fiumara, DiGilio, and Bruno family member Jackie DiNorscio. While surveillance was a good way to gain valuable intel, the state police felt they needed a better angle, an undercover operation set up to allow the mobsters to hang themselves. The plan was to dangle a legitimate business in front of them and let them infiltrate, take it over, and use it as a base of operations. It was by no means a guaranteed success, however; guys like Fiumara were cautious and not readily open to new people in their sphere.

Future New Jersey State Police superintendent Clinton Pagano set the operation into motion with the help of an inside source, Pat Kelly, a businessman with ties to the mob. When it came time to pick the undercover operatives, Pagano chose among them Robert Weisert, Ralph Buono, and Bob Delaney. Best known as a longtime referee for the NBA, Delaney got his start as a New Jersey state trooper and was the pivotal agent in the undercover operation, codenamed Project Alpha. In a bold move, Delaney chose as his undercover name "Bobby Covert." Not too subtle.

Alpha got underway in the summer of 1975 when the state police opened a trucking company, Mid-Atlantic Air-Sea Transport, in Elizabeth. The building was completely wired for sound and video. The setup was nondescript—and that was the point. Even the keenest mob eye wouldn't notice the hidden monitoring equipment, which, for 1975-era technology, was a feat. Working at the trucking company by day, Bobby Covert hung out at mob bars, like the Sting Lounge in Bayonne, at night. He eventually gained the trust of members of DiGilio's crew. "For me," Delaney recounted, "this early period was all about being seen, being around, trying to make some breakthroughs for the operation . . . I could talk like they talked, exude the same Jersey attitude, and come across as real."[9]

Mid-Atlantic was not attracting the big fish, so the state police decided to move operations up to Jersey City and expand the trucking firm. They renamed it Alamo Trucking and increased the size of their truck fleet. The mob starting coming by. In addition to members from the Genovese family, members of the Lucchese family and Bruno Newark crew started nosing about. The Alamo building, like Mid-Atlantic before it, was wired extensively, leaving Weisert worried that a mobster would find the hidden microphones under the planters and sundries about the office. "We were always under the constant fear that someone would pick up a wine bucket and that the tape would fall out or that it would malfunction and start beeping."[10]

The Alamo operation started spinning into ancillary avenues, and the three main targets, John DiGilio, Tino Fiumara, and Jackie DiNorscio, were all taking a piece of the business, as well as billing personal items to the business accounts—from soil tests of Fiumara's lawn to a Disney vacation for DiNorscio's family. But the success of the operation was also drawing attention from other law-enforcement agencies, both local and federal. That, coupled with the amount of information the operation gathered and the time it would take to develop that raw intel into cases, caused the state police to pull the plug on the operation in 1977.

Two hundred FBI agents and state troopers fanned out across New Jersey early on the morning of September 28, arresting thirty-five wiseguys, including Fiumara and DiGilio. Bob Delaney's undercover operation was one of the most successful in state history. Fiumara was convicted and sentenced to fifteen years in prison in 1979. It wasn't a death knell by any means to the Genovese New Jersey operations but was a significant obstacle for them to overcome. Fiumara was, among other things, a good earner, and that trumped everything else.

Project Alpha and other efforts by law enforcement in New Jersey to infiltrate organized crime and disrupt the mob's control of unions and legitimate businesses was helped by the passage of the Racketeer Influenced and Corrupt Organizations Act, better known as RICO. With this new tool, passed in October 1970, law enforcement now had the ability to target the mob, and other organized crime syndicates, with patterns of criminal activity and the threat of longer prison sentences. It became one of the most valuable tools for prosecutors. But in order to apply the law, there needed to be strong intelligence and in-depth investigations of criminal activity. And New Jersey formed one of the country's most effective investigative bodies to delve deep into the underworld.

Chapter Eleven

The State Commission of Investigation

By the late 1960s the spotlight on organized crime had spread beyond the Garden State stage. National media had begun reporting on the in-depth penetration of the mob into labor unions, the garbage industry, and other legitimate industries. But when *Life* magazine reported on the levels of municipal corruption in the state, the legislature decided to take action. Not that there hadn't been efforts in the past, but this time they sent a clear message that the corruption and municipal strife that had been plaguing the state would no longer be business as usual.

The specially convened Forsythe Committee was tasked with figuring out how to adequately address the rise of organized crime in New Jersey. The committee studied various methods and came up with a creation of two separate entities, with a system of checks and balances to ensure that the entities would be free of corruption and mob influence. These were the Division of Criminal Justice and the State Commission of Investigation.

The Division of Criminal Justice was a prosecutorial body, while the State Commission of Investigation (SCI) was designed to be the intelligence-gathering arm of law enforcement. The SCI was slated to begin their work on January 1, 1969, their initial investigation focusing on the intrusion of organized crime into the solid-waste industry, a subject the SCI would revisit numerous times over the next many decades years.

The SCI's initial investigative staff was comprised of three individuals who had come out of the NYPD organized-crime squad. They had expertise in organized crime and had worked with both the Kefauver Committee and the McClellan Commission. SCI staff later recalled, "There was a climate in the late sixties where a couple of things came together in a perfect storm to rip the lid off organized-crime involvement in business. There was that series of articles in *Life* magazine—about organized crime in the public sector in

New Jersey—state police, legislature, and municipal corruption. There were federal corruption investigations that were underway in New Jersey. And Assistant Attorney General William Brennan III gave a speech to the state chapter of Sigma Delta Chi in December of 1968 where he echoed these themes."[1]

Brennan's speech zeroed in on members of the New Jersey Legislature whom he felt were too closely associated with crime figures. As assistant state's attorney, Brennan was overseeing a grand jury in Mercer County empaneled to investigate ties between the mob and local government. He told the journalists of Sigma Delta Chi, "Too many local governments are responsive more to the mob than to the electorate that put them in office."[2]

The three main politicians he was referring to were David Friedland, minority leader of the New Jersey General Assembly in the late 1960s, State Senator Sido Ridolfi from Mercer County, and Mercer County Assemblyman John Selecky. All three vehemently denied the allegations, saying they were victims of character assassination. They even spoke at a special session of the legislature in late December 1968 to call for disciplinary actions against Brennan.

But the special legislative session asked the Supreme Court of New Jersey to look into the allegations. They found evidence that Selecky and Ridolfi had committed ethics violations. Selecky had once testified as a character witness for Sal Profaci, nephew of one-time New York–family boss Joe Profaci. Salvatore himself was a capo in his uncle's crime family—which was to become known as the Colombo family after Joe Colombo took control, following Joe Profaci's death. Sal Profaci was also married to Emilie Danzo, daughter of Joseph "Whitey" Danzo, a New Jersey labor leader and organized-crime associate. Ridolfi's suspected ties to organized crime stemmed from his admission that he had helped Philadelphia mob member "Johnny Keys" Simone, purchase a home in New Jersey.

The court held their opinion about David Friedland pending a grand jury investigation into Freidland's handling of a case involving his client, Genovese mobster John DiGilio, who at that time had been a soldier under Bayonne Joe Zicarelli.

A few weeks after the Brennan speech, the SCI was launched, on January 1, 1969, and wasted no time in delving into its investigation of organized crime and solid waste. In fact, the SCI would go back three times in the ensuing years to look at the status of the industry. The initial investigation, however, was set up to develop a framework for laws and regulations and oversight for the industry. The SCI found that "organized crime rooted in New York was spreading into commercial garbage collection in New Jersey and warned that the industry was at dire risk of becoming rife with bribery, extortion, price-fixing, collusive bidding, and other forms of corruption."[3] Solid waste was the first but by no means last legitimate business enterprise that the SCI investigated. Over the ensuing decades, the SCI investigated the role of the mob in boxing, the liquor and bar industry, official corruption throughout the state, and even the recycling and medical industries.

The impetus for the investigation was found from a variety of sources: information gleaned from previous investigations, requests by the legislature, and even citizen complaints via a hotline.

SCI staff were allowed to conduct their own surveillance. They were authorized to undertake wiretaps in conjunction with other law-enforcement agencies, and, if they found any wrongdoing, it was referred to prosecutors. The SCI was (and still is) as close as you can get to independent: its four appointed commissioners, two appointed by the governor, and two by the legislature, served staggered terms so there were checks and balances and overlap.

The SCI also had the power to subpoena witnesses. Starting in 1969 they issued twenty-five subpoenas to major New Jersey organized-crime figures in hopes of gathering information on the structure of the mob in the Garden State—but also it didn't hurt that the SCI had the power to offer limited immunity and that, if the witnesses refused to talk or plead the Fifth, the SCI could take them to the court and get a contempt judgment.

This proved an important investigative tool, allowing the SCI to not only flesh out its picture of the underworld but also rattle some cages—and, in the case of nine mobsters, send them away for a while for contempt. The subpoenas also had the unintended consequence of displacing mob figures. Some of the men who were subpoenaed simply left town, reluctant to return until the SCI probe was complete. But if they were under the impression that the investigation was short-term, they underestimated the intent of the commission; some of the mobsters remained outside New Jersey for years, in some cases throwing their business interests and operations in to disarray. "The commission's confrontations with organized criminals has been credited by law-enforcement authorities with having a major disruptive effect on the structure and operations of organized crime in New Jersey due to the prolonged incarcerations and the flight from this state of several underworld operatives to avoid being served commission subpoenas."[4]

One of the first people subpoenaed by the commission was not an organized crime figure but, rather, one of the most popular entertainers of all time and a New Jersey icon—Frank Sinatra. Rumors of Sinatra's ties to the mob had dogged the entertainer for years, all the way back to his earliest days in Hoboken (and the allegations would stick to him, later reemerging after an infamous picture surfaced of the crooner backstage at his 1976 Westchester Premier Theater concert, his arms thrown around Carlo Gambino, Paul "Big Paul" Castellano, Jimmy "the Weasel" Fratianno, and Greg DePalma). The FBI amassed a voluminous file on the singer, who was tied to mobsters from

Lucky Luciano and Charlie "the Blade" Tourine to Angelo Bruno and Sam Giancana.

Sinatra was first subpoenaed to appear before the commission on June 25, 1969. He was scheduled to appear on September 19 but was opening a string of shows at Caesars Palace in Las Vegas. Shortly after that, Sinatra left for the Caribbean, unaware that, when he failed to appear in September, a warrant was issued for his arrest on October 14, 1969. Though the warrant was enforceable only in New Jersey, his lawyers started filing a series of motions. They convincingly argued that the singer should not be forced to appear before the commission and won a restraining order, which prevented the commission from forcing Sinatra to return to New Jersey. "The complaint in this case seeks to restrain the New Jersey State Commission of Investigation from 'taking any further action against or with respect to plaintiff.' It appears that the commission is attempting to compel the plaintiff to appear before it and to supply information in connection with an investigation now in progress."[5]

In a statement to the press, Sinatra said, "For many years every time some Italian names are involved in any inquiry I get a subpoena. I appear. I am asked questions about scores of people unknown to me. I am asked questions based on rumors and events which never happened. I am subjected to the type of publicity I do not desire and do not seek. I am not willing to become part of any three-ring circus which will necessarily take place if I appear before the state commission of investigation in New Jersey whether the hearings be public or private."[6]

Sinatra's lawyers tried one last motion, appealing to the US Supreme Court to reverse the commission's decree. But the Court ruled four to three against Sinatra. Reluctantly, he agreed to testify. On February 17, 1970, he traveled to Trenton to appear before the commission. This appearance was sandwiched between two others of an entirely different sort—an appearance a week earlier at a Democratic National Committee event for Harry Truman in Miami Beach, and one the following week in Tucson, where he filmed scenes for one of his last films, *Dirty Dingus Magee*. The commission questioned Sinatra for just over an hour and, at the time, found him cooperative, though the actual transcript of his testimony was kept secret. After Sinatra's death in 1998 a former SCI member told a reporter that Sinatra had actually been evasive and uncooperative, though he had not been called back to appear again in front of the commission.

One of the first mobsters to appear in front of the commission to testify was Jerry Catena. He appeared in two private hearings—once on November 18, 1969, and again on February 17, 1970—but refused to answer over eighty questions about his involvement in organized crime. On March 4, 1970, Catena was found in contempt of court and "committed until such time as he purged himself of contempt."[7] That purge was a long time coming; Catena was kept out of the rackets for over five years while his lawyers fought for his release from Yardville State Prison. Finally, on August 19, 1975, after a series of court rulings and legal arguments about his continued incarceration, Catena was freed.

But while Catena was in Yardville, concerns about his status arose among some of his old business partners who were involved with the Vegas skim operations. One former mobster recollected the mood at the time.

When I was in Israel, Doc Stacher, who was living in Israel at the Old Shera-ton, ordered me to show up at the hotel for Shabbat lunch. I had no idea why Doc suddenly was turning religious. I found out why. When we were seated, Meyer Lansky walked in and took the empty seat reserved for him next to me. He was a real gentleman who engaged me in lengthy conversations about his affection and admiration for my father, and then we talked about the law, history, politics, et cetera. At the end of the long Shabbat lunch, after all the guests left, Messiers Lansky and Stacher took me to the end of the lobby where nobody was seated and couldn't listen to the conversation, and they proceeded to ask me to give them an update on Jerry Catena concerning his incarceration together with the others who refused to testify and were held in contempt of court. Over a period of time, and because of situations which I was involved in, I realized myself that both Meyer Lansky and Doc Stacher were concerned for their flow of funds coming out of Las Vegas casinos (the rake) and that, since Mr. Lansky was no longer in control since he fled to Israel to avoid prosecution, it was now Mr. Catena who ruled. It was my own conclusion at the time that this was the purpose of the Shabbat lunch. It wasn't intended to enhance the Sabbath with spirituality and prayer and the singing of Shabbat songs. I understood clearly that the order came from Mr. Catena to Abe Green to use me as the carrier pigeon to send the message to Doc Stacher that the faucet had been turned off. Years later, on September 13, 1991, I went down to Fort Lauderdale at the behest of Al Miniaci, who was a close associate of Frank Costello. He was hosting a party for his wife on her seventieth birthday. He told me that Mr. Catena had specifically asked if I was going to be at the party. I sat with him at his table all night, and he shared intimate history with me, so I knew for sure that he in fact never turned off any faucet on Meyer Lansky because he held Meyer in such high regard.[8]

The Genovese family was also represented by Funzi Tieri, who fled to Brooklyn to avoid his subpoena, making only occasional forays back into Jersey for business. Despite Tieri's reluctance to appear in front of the com-mission, there was enough evidence presented during the hearings for a grand jury to indicted him on February of 1973, though it would be a number of years before he would be arrested and tried.

Louis Anthony "Bobby" Manna, Hoboken-based Genovese capo, was called before the commission in 1972 and imprisoned in Yardville from 1972 until April 1977, while John DiGilio also fled to Brooklyn to avoid his subpoena. DiGilio was indicted in 1979 by a state grand jury for loan-sharking conspiracy based on evidence presented at public commission hearings. Two other Genovese mobsters sought by the SCI, Emilio "the Count" Delio and Pasquale "Patty Mack" Macchiarole, relocated to Florida.

Another rising Mafia figure who appeared before the commission yet refused to testify was Nicodemo Scarfo. The young mobster was a member of the Philadelphia crime family, but his base of operations was Atlantic City, by then a run-down resort town whose best days were behind it. Scarfo was making waves in the South Jersey underworld and deemed important enough at the time for the commission to make him one of their top targets. But Scarfo followed in the footsteps of his boss and refused to testify, landing in Yardville from 1971 to 1973, sprung only briefly between November 22 and 25 of 1972 to spend Thanksgiving with his family.

For Scarfo, being together in Yardville with other high-ranking Mafioso was a career boon. Nicky Scarfo's nephew, Phil Leonetti, who would later turn on the Philly family and become a government informant, said of his uncle, "While my uncle was in Yardville it allowed him to get closer to Angelo Bruno, which was a good thing . . . my uncle also started getting real close to guys like Jerry Catena, Nick Russo, Blackie Napoli, and Bobby Manna . . . my uncle and Bobby Manna became extremely close in Yardville. They were the same age and spent a lot of time together."[9]

Tony Bananas Caponigro fled for the warmer climes of Florida in 1970 when he received word that he was going to be called to appear. He spent most of the next four years out of New Jersey, staying for a time in Manhattan and covertly driving back into Newark to keep tabs on his crew, as well as his home in Milburn, New Jersey. On New Year's Eve,1974, Bananas was at his home when he saw a car parked outside. The short-tempered Caponigro assumed it was a process server. He got into his car and took off down the street, sideswiping the other car as he drove off. It wasn't a process server in the vehicle but an FBI agent, staking out the house. Bananas was arrested and booked into Milburn Jail and soon after arrested by the FBI. He was also presented with a subpoena. Caponigro's ramming of the FBI car did not sit well with Angelo Bruno and other New Jersey mobsters. Law-enforcement officers were considered off-limits and immune from reprisal. The thinking was that, if police and FBI agents were harassed or attacked, they would bring even more heat down on mob operations. It had been a long-standing Mafia rule, and Bananas broke it. His transgression stained his reputation.

Another member of Caponigro's Down Neck crew, Ralph "Blackie" Napoli, was called before the commission in 1971 and refused to testify. After two years, he experienced a change of heart and told the SCI that he was ready to talk. But after changing his mind once again, he was sent back to Yardville, where he remained through 1977, serving six years in total.

Trenton-based Bruno-family member Carl "Pappy" Ippolito crossed the border into Bristol, Pennsylvania, to avoid being called. He neglected to change his dentist, though. One afternoon, while sitting in the dentist's chair in Trenton, Ippolito was served. He appeared, and "Some 182 questions were put to him at the SCI hearing. He refused to answer ninety-eight of them, claiming his Fifth Amendment privilege against self-incrimination."[10] The SCI challenged his right to take the Fifth, and the court battle dragged on until 1978 when the Supreme Court of New Jersey ruled that he did not have to answer questions without immunity. Ippolito was asked to appear again but refused. He was arrested and convicted in 1980 for contempt, drawing a fine of five thousand dollars. Ippolito's fellow Trenton mobster Johnny Keys Simone avoided the probe altogether by moving first to Florida and then Yardley, Pennsylvania.

The DeCavalcante crime family was also represented in the commission's first batch of subpoenas. Crime-family boss Sam the Plumber DeCavalcante was asked to testify on December 29, 1973. Over the next couple years, he was ordered an additional seventeen times to appear but only showed up for seven appearances, citing various health conditions. It should be noted that DeCavalcante lived another twenty years, though from his lawyers' pleas to the SCI it sounded as the don was at death's door. He moved to Florida and tried in 1979 to have the subpoena quashed once and for all. He was denied. "The court noted the record does not demonstrate harassment or oppression. The continuances over the years have been requested by the commission, DeCavalcante, and by counsel. DeCavalcante's poor health has been a factor in the prolonged proceedings."[11]

Frank Condi Cocchiaro, referred to by DeCavalcante as a "rough guy I have to watch,"[12] actually fled the hearing room rather than be compelled to testify, as did another DeCavalcante solider, Robert "Basile" Occhipinti. Like others, Cocchiaro fled to Florida, living under the nom de guerre Frank Fagnotta. Unfortunately for Cocchiaro, a 1972 traffic accident gave up the ruse, and he was set back to New Jersey in June of that year. He pled guilty to criminal contempt and appeared before the commission after serving a six-month term.

Three Gambino mobsters fled to Florida to avoid the SCI. Joseph "Demus" Covello—a mobster based in Belleville, New Jersey—took off for South Florida and ran illegal gambling operations with members of other crime families. Newark-based Frankie "the Bear" Basto's time in the sun was cut short when he was arrested in Florida for a jewelry robbery in 1974. He was returned to New Jersey where he was indicted on a series of home break-ins that had occurred in Essex County. Gambino capo Joseph Paterno relocated to Florida in 1974. On a trip back to New Jersey in 1978 he was caught by a process server and testified in front of the commission in 1979.

For the mobsters who did not skip town and ended up being sentenced for contempt, time in Yardville was nothing like time in maximum security. If anything, it was more like the prison scene from the movie *Goodfellas*.

"Their quarters on the second floor of the Clinton building consist of a common living room, which has a color television set, a refrigerator for foods of their special liking, and a hot plate for warming snacks . . . Mr. Catena has been seen swinging a golf club and practicing his chip shots on the lawns."[13] The wiseguys socialized with each other, and some even received weekend and holiday furloughs. But even with such amenable accommodations, being locked up in close proximity with other wiseguys sometimes led to temper flare-ups and to lapses in judgment and protocol.

Johnny "Coca-Cola" Lardiere was not unknown to law enforcement. He had been interviewed by the FBI in 1959 about the Apalachin conference and the attendees from New Jersey, already part of their Top Hoodlum Program. Throughout the early 1960s Lardiere was a frequent companion of Jerry and Eugene Catena, as well as of Anthony "Tony Pro" Provenzano, top labor racketeer in New Jersey. In 1964 Lardiere was hired by Local 945 of the Teamsters as a business representative, earning a salary of just over ten thousand dollars. But he was also supplementing his income with gambling activities in Paterson, New Jersey, as part of Catena's crew.

Lardiere was jailed for contempt in August of 1971. While the time with other mobsters in Yardville was a boon to the careers of some—like Nicky Scarfo—it didn't do much to help others. Some time during the stay, according to sources, Johnny Coca-Cola said something that offended Blackie Napoli as well as Jerry Catena. One source said that Coca-Cola told Catena to fuck off. Mouthing off to Catena, the most powerful mobster in New Jersey, was a death warrant.

In April of 1977, Lardiere was still in custody, having been moved to the Clinton Correctional Facility in New York, when he received a weekend furlough for Easter, along with Napoli and Bobby Manna. They were released from the facility at 7 p.m. on Saturday, April 9, with orders to return by 9 p.m. the following day, Easter Sunday. Lardiere ended up at the Red Bull Inn, a motel in Bridgewater, New Jersey, at 2 a.m. early Sunday morning. He went into the hotel lobby to get the keys for his room. When he went back out to his car to get a suitcase, a gunman emerged and shot Lardiere with a .22, which jammed. Lardiere entered mob legend when he supposedly asked the gunman, "What are you gonna do now, tough guy?"[14] The gunman then pulled out a .38 and shot Lardiere three times, in the head, neck, and stomach. The sixty-eight-year-old Lardiere was dead.

After the shooting, the gunman left the .38 and a hat, which authorities kept as evidence. Though they knew it had been a mob hit, the case went cold and over time seemed destined to become another unsolved underworld hit. Then in the mid-1990s, Tommy Ricciardi, a New Jersey Lucchese mobster, decided to flip and become a government witness. He told the FBI that he knew who had killed Johnny Coca-Cola, fingering a Genovese soldier named Michael "Mikey Cigars" Coppola.

With this new information, the FBI retrieved their long-held evidence, which included a hair they had found on the .38, and were now able to test it for DNA evidence. The FBI visited Coppola at his home in the Shore town of Spring Lake in August of 1996 and asked for a DNA sample. Though the mobster obliged, the feds did not detain him. When they left, so did Coppola and his wife. Over the next thirteen years, the FBI focused on finding the fugitive. Coppola was even featured on the popular television program *America's Most Wanted*, and reports of sightings of the mobster all across the globe poured into the FBI. But one tip said that Coppola was close to home, nesting on the Upper West Side of Manhattan. Sure enough, it was there that on March 9, 2007, police found Coppola, bringing to end a long manhunt, and, they hoped, closure in the Lardiere case. Coppola went to trial for racketeering, including the Lardiere murder, in 2009. Though he was convicted of racketeering, he was acquitted of killing Johnny Coca-Cola.

The SCI continued its investigations through the 1970s, receiving an extension to its mission from the governor. The initial probe into mob activities started winding down by 1979, but the organization has kept its mission active through the present day. The work they did in first exposing the citizens of New Jersey to the range of Mafia activities in the state brought a lot of law-enforcement pressure on the seven mob families there. But even time in prison was not enough to dissuade some from a life of crime.

Genovese soldier Anthony "Little Pussy" Russo had a rough start to the 1970s. The State Commission of Investigation called him in January 1970 and gave him limited immunity to testify. He refused and was sent to Yardville, like so many others. He also had a perjury conviction from the state, which resulted in his transfer to a second state facility in late 1970. But the commission intelligence on Russo and his operations gave prosecutors enough evidence to charge him with tax evasion for his involvement with a construction company in Monmouth County. Russo pled guilty to those charges and was fined fifty thousand dollars and sentenced to eighteen months in federal prison. While in prison he was sitting down for lunch in the mess hall when another inmate stabbed him in the neck. Russo unsuccessfully tried to sue the state for ten thousand dollars in damages. He was released from federal prison in 1973 and sent right back to Yardville.

Russo finally agreed to testify in front of the commission in 1974. His lawyer said the mobster "could no longer bear the pressure of incarceration."[15] Plagued by circulatory problems in his legs, Russo had been in and out of prison medical facilities though much of his time behind bars. Russo testified before the commission in a closed-door session in late April 1974, but his testimony was not made public. Now back on the streets, Russo made for his home in Long Branch, New Jersey, where he went right back to work, scheming for ways to make money. His vision turned westward to the gambling and entertainment mecca of the United States, Las Vegas. Russo was going to own a casino.

Chapter Twelve

The Big Bets

The Jolly Trolley casino was not one of the higher-class casinos on the Vegas Strip. Located at the corner of South Las Vegas Boulevard and West Sahara Avenue[1] on the North Strip, the Trolley had borne other names before its rechristening in 1977—the Big Wheel, the Centerfold Club. Though the name changed, the casino always managed to retain its somewhat-unsavory reputation. When it was the Centerfold, it was known for its topless dancers. The Trolley advertised, "Burlesque is Back—Naked but Nice." The casino had good deals in addition to the strippers: one-dollar, single-deck blackjack and a breakfast special of eggs, bacon, toast, and coffee for sixty-nine cents.

The Jolley Trolley was also renowned for serving "steak by the ounce," where the servers would bring out a full piece of meat and diners could choose how much they want cut off and cooked. It was one of a few gimmicks the Trolley employed to bring in customers, and it became a successful operation, drawing crowds from politicians to locals. It also drew local underworld figures like Anthony "Tony the Ant" Spilotro, Chicago's man on the ground in Las Vegas. In 1978, Spilotro was a regular diner at the Trolley, much to the chagrin of local law enforcement.[2]

The Trolley had no hotel rooms, unlike larger resort-style casinos further south on the Strip, but with any gambling in Las Vegas there was money to be made. And back then Vegas was truly a mob town. When the casino became the Jolly Trolley in 1977, the new owners from New Jersey had a hidden partner in the mob. And for the next five years the mob attempted to skim away as much of the profit as they could. Most of that money went back east and up the chain of the Genovese crime family, through Anthony "Little Pussy" Russo.

Russo was well-respected, though not necessarily well-liked, in the underworld and, though only a soldier, regularly rubbed elbows with significant mob figures from across the country. He spent a good deal of time in South Florida in the 1960s. He was regularly spotted in the company of mob bosses like Santo Trafficante Jr., of the Tampa crime family. Russo was overheard by the FBI counseling Trafficante on how to avoid law-enforcement surveillance:

> You live here, you're a native. Where are they going to chase you? The only thing you can do, if it was me—I can't advise you—but if it was me, get a couple of goodfellows [sic], let them run, let them handle everything, so your name is going to be thrown around, let them throw it, but the right people you gotta sit down with, you sit down with . . . but you're not in any of these spots, like they say about me, Pussy got this, Pussy got that. Yeah, I got it, but prove it, sure I got it.[3]

Russo's main base of operations was at the Jersey Shore, specifically the town of Long Branch. Originally a beach resort town, Long Branch, by the 1960s, had become a growing residential community, one that was ripe for corruption and easy for one man to significantly influence. Starting in 1967, a series of high-profile investigations targeted public corruption in the town. Law enforcement suspected that Russo "controlled the mayor and city council," and "official reports indicated mob figures were operating in an atmosphere relatively secure from law enforcement."[4]

All aspects of the town were under Russo's control. When a city manager started looking into the gambling establishments, he was removed from his position by the city council. Russo approached the fired manager and told him that if he wanted his job back he would have to look the other way while Russo expanded his illegal gambling. The police department was not that effective in tackling the organized-crime issue either. A police chief in the mid-1960s was thwarted in his attempts to raid Russo's gambling establishments when news of the impending raids was leaked from within the department. After his death in 1968, the new police chief "lacked the integrity and the will to investigate organized crime and attempt to stem its influence."[5]

After he was released from prison as a result of the SCI investigation and after his convictions for tax evasion and perjury, Russo ran into the three men who were looking to buy into the Jolly Trolley. He saw this as an opportunity to make some serious money far away from New Jersey law enforcement and the SCI. First he needed to convince the three investors that they needed a fourth partner for the casino venture. Through first persuasion and then overt pressure, Russo managed to squeeze his way into 25 percent ownership of the casino.

Now that Russo was in, he set out to skim as much money from the casino's profits as he could. After all, the skim was the quickest way to make money in the casino industry. For the mob, it became their main source of income in Las Vegas. The skim was a simple concept: In the back counting rooms, mob associates would merely take piles of cash out before they were entered into the books. The money simply walked out the door, either going right into the pockets of local gangsters or being shipped out to cities like Chicago or Kansas City, where the bosses got their piece of the action.

Though he never actually entered the casino himself, so he wouldn't tip off law enforcement that he had an interest in the property, Russo had his guys keep an eye on things and, of course, move as much money as they could out of the casino. "The only way we get money out is when they go to the room to count the money. 'Paulie' grabs what he could to put it on the side."[6] The skimmed money was split up between Anthony and his brother John, with a chunk being "kicked up" to their capo, Richie the Boot Boiardo. The Boot netted up to three thousand dollars a month just from his portion of the skim from the Trolley when business was good.

But Little Pussy Russo wasn't quite happy with the money coming out of the Trolley. He complained to his brother John that they were not involved with a higher-class operation. "We know we're getting clipped, John . . . you gotta remember we got a pit joint . . . everyone's scared to work in the joint."[7] Russo knew that he was not in the best position in Vegas. Some of his Jersey mob compatriots like Tony Pro Provenzano were involved in higher-end properties like the Dunes. But still, the Trolley was a source of income far removed from the heat that was trained on him in New Jersey.

The deal that Russo struck with the three owners would have stayed hidden but for the copy of the contract Russo kept hidden on the back of a painting hung in his New Jersey office. And since Russo was considered one of the top racketeers in New Jersey, the police were working on a case against him. So when law enforcement raided his office in 1979, they found the contract, spurring the investigation of the casino. And less than two years after branching out to Vegas, Russo's dream of hitting the jackpot came to an end.

Late on April 26, 1979, Russo, who had recently returned to his home at the Harbor Island Spa in Long Branch from a trip to Florida, was visited by three of his underlings, Thomas "Pee Wee" DePhillips, Joe Zarro, and Anthony DeVingo. Russo let the three men into his home. When Russo turned to get a drink, he was shot in the head three times, a fourth bullet hitting a nearby sliding glass door. The gunmen left, locking the door behind them. The next day, one of Russo's other associates, Louis Ferraro, found the feared mobster lying dead among a collection of stuffed cats.[8] Though no one was ever charged with the killing, police eventually closed the case, naming the three gunmen in the late 1990s. According to sources, the Russo hit was where Pee Wee made his bones and became a fully inducted member of the Genovese family.

Russo's killing was not wholly unexpected. He was very talkative and often viewed as someone who would cooperate with police if ever arrested.

That fear was felt down the line of his organizations as well. It turns out that they were right about Russo's big mouth; it would get them all into trouble.

There were also some sources who indicated that Russo may have been holding back money from his superiors in the Genovese family. A recording of Little Pussy and his brother John underscored that Russo's capo, Ritchie the Boot Boiardo, was not happy about the wait time for his portion of the Trolley's skim. This piece of tape also shows the respect the elderly gangster, in his late eighties, still commanded and Boiardo's never-ending chase after another dollar.

JOHN: Now the Old Man, he started going with me the other day, Vegas and everything else. It's three, you know.

ANTHONY: What's three?

JOHN: Three months [since Boiardo was paid]. He says, tell your brother I'm eighty-seven years old. Tomorrow I may die." He says, "I want it now."[9]

Upon hearing this, Little Pussy confided that he was in deep financial trouble because the casino was not as profitable as he had hoped. He also said that he had to take out a fifty thousand dollar loan from a loan shark just to keep things going. The payback on the fifty thousand dollar vig was a thousand dollars a week. This was indication that the money coming in from this particular Vegas venture was a far cry from what the crime family expected. Later in the tape it came out that the skim from the Jolley Trolley casino was sometimes as low as only a hundred dollars a week.

But there is also another rumor about the real reason for the Russo killing, and it had to do with the Jolly Trolley itself. Though Russo supposedly never went to the actual casino property, he was often out in Las Vegas. On one trip he met with Anthony Spilotro, who, in addition to being Chicago's point man in Las Vegas, was also a frequent customer at the Trolley. Spilotro wanted a piece of the Trolley profits, reasoning that Vegas, though an open city where mobsters from around the country could operate, was his territory. Russo answered Spilotro's request by offering him 10 percent, to which Spilotro reportedly told Russo that Chicago wasn't a 10 percent outfit. This soured the relationship between Spilotro and Russo, but, since Russo was already unpopular and on the outs with the Genovese family, the story goes that the Russo hit was done as a favor to Chicago.

Regardless of the reasons for his murder, five months after Russo was gunned down, an indictment naming Richie Boiardo, James V. Montemarano, and the Trolley's three owners—Paul Bendetti, Dennis Mastro, and Peter DeLamos—was handed down. Montemarano, like Russo, lived in Long

Branch. He had an arrest record for larceny, auto theft, stolen property, weapons, extortion, and armed robbery. They were all accused of skimming the profits from the Jolly Trolley casino. The centerpiece of the case was the collection of tapes law enforcement had made of Russo's musings on underworld business, including the Trolley.

The Russo tapes were about sixty hours of conversations that the state police had collected using wiretaps, body mikes, and other listening devices. The original probe had been directed at the Genovese family and its operatives, including not only Russo but also Pee Wee DePhillips and Richie Boiardo—in his late eighties at the time but with still enough juice to dress Russo down in a restaurant, reminding Russo who was still boss and excoriating him for losing control of operations.

The Jolly Trolley was not even a focus of the initial probe, but Russo's big mouth allowed investigators to start piecing together information about what was going on in Las Vegas only a couple of years after the mobsters had set up operations there. Russo even outed fellow Genovese mobsters Tony Provenzano and Matty the Horse Ianniello and their Vegas connections.

The Trolley's three owners, whom Russo had muscled in on, were as much victims as anyone in the case, and their lawyer, Oscar Goodman, made a case to prosecutors for a lenient plea deal of a fine and probation. But the judge did not allow the plea deal, insisting the case go to trial. The three owners chose another lawyer and were found guilty on thirteen counts of conspiracy and sentenced to three years in prison and a hefty fine.

James V. Montemarano was cleared of his role in the skimming operation, though he was in prison for a separate conviction with other members of the Genovese family's Jersey operations. Boiardo, who cut a striking figure at the trial daily, wearing a green velour suit, was found guilty of RICO conspiracy, as were John Russo and the late Pussy. It was big win for the government and started closing the door on the Genovese operations in Vegas. With Jerry Catena more or less retired in Florida and the aging Boiardo squarely in law-enforcement's crosshairs, New Jersey's influence in Vegas began to wane.

But purging the mob's overall influence in Vegas was still a few years away. The Midwest crime families still had their hand in many of the casinos, running the skim through Chicago, Kansas City, and Detroit. Smaller crime families in Saint Louis, Denver, and Milwaukee also had a seat at the table. Though the era of Howard Hughes ended mob ownership of the casinos and the Nevada Gaming Control Board's Black Book kept many wiseguys out of the casinos, there was still money to be made both illegally and legitimately. In Vegas, law enforcement had already started on their all-out assault on mob control of the casino skim as well as ancillary services to casinos, like infiltration of the service and workers unions, not to mention

Spilotro's Hole in the Wall Gang, which was committing all kinds of street-level crimes in the tourist mecca. But for all of the crime and vice, or perhaps because of that allure, Vegas was continuing to expand not only its gambling resorts but its population as well. With that in mind, New Jersey began looking at ways to reinvigorate one of their tourist towns, which by the mid-seventies had become a fading shadow of itself—former stronghold of Enoch Johnson, Atlantic City.

In the aftermath of Prohibition, the perception of Atlantic City as an epicenter of organized crime had diminished, as had the former resort town itself. The old hotels and their fading facades were becoming vestiges of a bygone era. But in the neighborhood on the south side of the boardwalk, economic despair was buffered by a thriving illegal-gambling scene. Law enforcement found at the time that "The city is riddled with rackets, including every known type of gambling operation. Its famous boardwalk is lined with stands operating devices purporting to be games of skill but looked upon by their customers as games of chance. It contains two substantial numbers syndicates, and nearly every cigar store is a front for a bookmaker."[10]

Enoch Johnson himself had fallen out of power when indicted in 1941 for income tax evasion and served four years in prison. When he was released in 1945, the political winds had changed, Frank S. Farley was the new political power broker, and Johnson found himself having to take a backseat to Farley, though he supported the politician and his machine. Unlike the TV version of Nucky Johnson portrayed in *Boardwalk Empire*, Johnson was not killed on the boardwalk by a boy seeking revenge. In real life Johnson spent the rest of his years working as a salesman before dying on December 9, 1968.

The one remnant of the old days that still stood strong through the mid-century blues of Atlantic City was the 500 Club. Located at 6 Missouri Avenue, the 500 Club was the premiere entertainment establishment on the South Shore for decades. An iconic presence in the city, the 500 was owned and operated by Paul Emilio "Skinny" D'Amato, a larger-than-life Atlantic City legend. Today a historical marker in Atlantic City commemorates D'Amato, along with a 500 Club Lane. His zeal for entertainment was matched only by his style, which made him stand out even in a room of celebrities. D'Amato knew better than anyone what would bring people to Atlantic City. "By mid-century, he had created an environment where anyone could temporarily jettison his conscience, thereby enabling the average guy to be in possession, if only for a night, of a sense of self-importance, special-ness, power—even fame. The average guy could be . . . *cool*."[11]

The 500 Club was where Dean Martin and Jerry Lewis developed their stage banter and comedy routines that led to their huge successes. Another of Skinny D'Amato's friends was Frank Sinatra. During Sinatra's early years, D'Amato offered his help and a place to perform. When his star rose again,

Sinatra did not forget D'Amato's outreach and often returned for performances at the 500 Club, sometimes with the whole Rat Pack in tow. Sinatra was even pallbearer at D'Amato's funeral when the club owner died in 1984. Entertainment was not an afterthought at the 500. All the top stars of the mid-twentieth century played there. It was also the epicenter for gambling in Atlantic City before gambling became legal. The club would open up at 5 p.m. and stay open, through the night, 'til 10 a.m. the next day. The backrooms drew hundreds of people eager to try their luck at gambling. Police and federal law enforcement were sure that D'Amato was involved with the mob. The FBI referred to the 500 Club as a "notorious Atlantic City hoodlum hangout."[12]

D'Amato was not a made member of the mob himself, and according to people who knew him always maintained that he was a legitimate businessman who was merely looking to show people a good time. However, in the business of operating a nightclub that was a major gambling establishment it was inevitable that not only would the 500 become a big hangout for wiseguys but that D'Amato would also find his business interests entangled with them.

Philly boss Angelo Bruno was a regular at the 500 Club, spending many of his summer evenings there. He attended many shows—like Sammy Davis Jr.'s residency at the club in the summer of 1958. Bruno was also reportedly close to Skinny D'Amato. Some sources say that Skinny's son Angelo had been named after Bruno. There are other connections between Bruno and the 500 Club that may indicate Bruno had more than a passing interest in the club's entertainment roster.

Two Bruno family soldiers, Alfred Iezzi and Felix "Skinny Razor" DiTullio, worked at the 500 Club in the early 1960s and, according to the FBI, may have held a proprietary interest in the venue. Iezzi, in fact, was overheard discussing with Angelo Bruno in 1962 his desire to sell his shares of the club because he was having troubles keeping things in order while he ran his other establishments back in Philadelphia and that the 500 itself was not making a profit. He also discussed getting Nicky Scarfo a job at the 500 Club. The young Scarfo, at that time, had recently moved to Atlantic City and needed some income. Iezzi had first gotten involved with the club "to look after a couple hundred thousand dollar loan from the Philadelphia LCN [la Cosa Nostra] to aid D'Amato in a financial crisis."[13]

D'Amato, when pressed about this by the FBI in 1961, "denied that he has ever had any type of business transaction with Bruno and has never been approached in any way by Bruno or any members of his family in respect to any business transactions. He stated that he never loaned or borrowed money form Bruno or members of his family at any time."[14] D'Amato did admit to knowing Bruno and said their association dated back to 1946, but he declined any further comment. He later told a newspaper, "Why shouldn't I be friendly with them? They were good guys to me. But I never made a penny from them."[15] Accusations of mob involvement in the 500 Club continued until the club itself was consumed by a fire on the afternoon of Sunday June 10, 1973.

To reinvigorate Atlantic City, New Jersey put a referendum to the citizens to allow legalized gambling, but restricting it to Atlantic City. The vote came in on November 2, 1976, and gambling was legalized in Atlantic City. The New Jersey Casino Control Commission was immediately formed to oversee the hiring of casino personnel and the operation of games and to handle any recommendations made by the Division of Gaming Enforcement, a branch of the state attorney general's office. Law enforcement as well as some elected officials had some concerns that organized crime might make a move to infiltrate the casinos and the myriad of ancillary services attached to them. The Atlantic City police chief at the time assured the public and press that there was no indication of widespread organized-crime involvement in their city. Others were not so sure. Some resorted to outright histrionics, declaring that "hand-in-hand with gambling, whether it be legal or illegal, comes organized crime and corruption. Gambling fosters crime, attracts crime, breeds crime, and finances crime."[16]

Though the heyday of the 500 Club and the era of Enoch Johnson were gone by the time Atlantic City gambling was legalized, organized-crime figures in the area had been operating on the fringes for years, overseeing illegal gambling operations and making a living off the dying city. One of the crime figures still active in the area was Herman "Stumpy" Orman, a gambling kingpin of Atlantic City, who traced his tutelage back to the days of Nucky Johnson. He was active into the late 1970s and considered by the State of New Jersey to be one of the big racket kings in Atlantic City. Even Gyp DeCarlo was caught on tape calling Orman the man to see in Atlantic City. By the time gambling was legalized, Orman was brokering commercial real estate. He was involved with negotiations between Resorts International and MGM Grand for a casino in Atlantic City and brokered a number of commercial deals, including the sale of the Mayflower Hotel to *Penthouse* magazine. Resorts International had previously been linked to Meyer Lansky and Dino Cellini, a top crime figure active in casinos in Havana and London and throughout the Caribbean.

Even Little Pussy Russo was looking to get into Atlantic City, to supplement his Vegas "empire"—prior to getting clipped. He was talking about insinuating himself before the casinos and resorts under construction opened to the public. And likely before law enforcement had a chance to nip his incursion in the bud. Russo looked at getting into the parking business and floated the idea of involvement in residential high-rise construction. He was also looking to set up a deal with Jerry Catena, who, after serving his five-and-a-half-year bid in Yardville, had decided to pack up and "retire" to Boca

Raton, though he was still very much sought after for advice and business deals. And in that deal, as wiretaps revealed, Russo turned to Catena's partner and old Zwillman associate, Abe Green.

"I'm waiting for a guy to call me, guy with Jerry—Abe Green. This is with the machines. There's a new guy they chased, they're getting rid of, and Jerry's behind the guy here, Jerry and Abe Green. I'm supposed to call Abe Green; Jerry is supposed to be there, to try and straighten them out in Vegas with the joint's machines. In other words, a couple of joints that are down in Vegas wanna come to Atlantic City. So Jerry's gonna find out if I can throw them the machines."[17]

But the biggest beneficiary of legalized gambling in Atlantic City was the Bruno family—specifically, Nicky Scarfo, who had been forced to make do with low-level rackets. Now, with the advent of legalized gambling, the associated surge in real estate development, and the promise of increased economic opportunity and population growth, Atlantic City was the place to be, and the Bruno family had a grip on the town. Or so that's what Nicky and many rank-and-file soldiers thought. They believed that Angelo Bruno, named the Gentle Don, would show at least enough strength to keep the New York families from staking a claim in Atlantic City. After all, Nicky had been sticking it out during the lean times. Now, with riches on the horizon, why shouldn't the Philly mob take Atlantic City all for themselves?

But Bruno was not as adamant that the legalized casinos be beneficial to the organization. He was a cautious boss who kept the made members in the crime family to a manageable number and retained a tight rein on what his soldiers were involved with, making sure it wasn't too high profile to attract law-enforcement attention. Bruno could dish out violence if needed, but killings only brought additional heat from the law, a lesson his successor had failed to heed. We know what Bruno's feelings about Atlantic City were because he testified about it before the State Commission of Investigation. He was compelled to do so because, had he continued to refuse cooperation with the SCI's investigation, he would have been returned to Yardville. He had previously been released in 1973, after spending three years there for contempt and refusing to testify before the grand jury. Now, faced with additional time, Bruno capitulated.

In June of 1977, Bruno started testimony in front of the commission, with a public hearing held on August 8. With four lawyers at his side, Bruno started by telling the commission of his job, working for a vending operation run by Long John Martorano, a crime-family associate who also was a major methamphetamine dealer.[18] Investigators asked him about a meeting with Gambino boss Paul Castellano in Valentino's Restaurant in Cherry Hill, New Jersey, and whether it pertained to doing business in Atlantic City:

Q: Did You discuss in Valentino's doing business separately in Atlantic City?

A: I don't know what you mean by "separately."

Q: Well, did he tell you what business he was going to go in, perhaps, and you tell him what business you were going to go in?

A: I don't recall it, but I don't know what his intentions are. I have a pretty good feeling about what my intentions are with Atlantic City. Would you want me to tell you that?

Q: What are your intentions with Atlantic City, Mr. Bruno?

A: Stay away from it. That's my intentions . . . I got nothing to do with Atlantic City as far as gambling's concerned. I'm not interested in any hotels; I'm not interested in any casinos, directly or indirectly. [19]

Though it could be argued that Bruno was merely placating the commission with his protestations that he had no intention of moving into Atlantic City, it seemed like that was indeed his plan, apart from expanding the vending business that he was involved in with Martorano. Reports started coming in of Gambino family members staking claim to businesses in Atlantic City and investing in properties. Bruno's dismissal of Atlantic City fed the growing dissatisfaction other members in the crime family already had about the way he was running things. There was a feeling among them that he was really only out for himself and that his reluctance to declare Atlantic City Bruno territory would cost them all. That, and other factors, ultimately sealed his fate.

Bruno was called before the SCI to testify several more times, the final occasion being on March 20, 1980. The next evening, on March 21, Bruno was eating at Cous' Little Italy, a well-known Italian restaurant in South Philadelphia, owned by another crime-family member, Thomas DelGiorno. After a meal of Chicken Sicilian and a few cups of coffee, Bruno gave word for Long John Martorano to drive him home; but Martorano was unavailable. Instead, a young Sicilian named John Stanfa drove the boss back to his house, a few miles from the restaurant. As the car pulled up in front of Bruno's house, Stanfa used his controls to lower the passenger-side window, and a gunman walked out of the shadows and up to the car. The man had a shotgun in his hand and blasted away at Bruno's head, taking out the don who had ruled the Philly mob, and South Jersey, for decades.

Bruno's murder set in motion a chain of events that would both decimate and reshape the New Jersey–underworld landscape and lead to a war for control of the Philadelphia mob that left a trail of bodies and scores of convictions of the top leaders of the Philly mob. In the immediate aftermath of Bruno's hit, the top spot was quickly filled by Bruno's underboss, Phil Testa. And he was about to step into pop-culture history, Jersey style.

Chapter Thirteen

South Jersey War

New Jersey's favorite son, Bruce Springsteen, opens "Atlantic City," a song off his album *Nebraska*, in a way that may be enigmatic to casual listeners unaware of their historical context.

> Well they blew up the Chicken Man in Philly last night
> Now they blew up his house too
> Down on the boardwalk they're getting ready for a fight
> Gonna see what them racket boys can do. [1]

But for those who were around the Philadelphia/South Jersey area in 1981, the meaning is crystal clear. The Chicken Man was Philip Testa, boss of the Philadelphia Mafia. And they did blow him up one night. Testa was killed when a bomb went off as he walked up to his house at 3 a.m., the morning of March 15, 1981. Testa was coming home late, and, as he walked through the door, a bomb made of nails was detonated, sending literal shockwaves through the neighborhood. The device had been set off remotely from a van parked across the street, which was driven by Rocco Marinucci, driver for Testa's underboss, Pete Casella.

Testa's demise was a pivotal point in a series of events that had started almost exactly one year prior and for the next decade would envelop not only the streets of South Philadelphia but also South Jersey and Atlantic City. The 1980 killing of Angelo Bruno was the incident that really set the wheels in motion, and the planning for the hit had taken place in New Jersey. Bruno's death had been the result of simmering resentments shared by his underboss, Testa, and consigliere, Tony Caponigro. Much of their frustration had to do with Bruno's allowing the Gambino family into Atlantic City, a territory many in the Bruno family—including Nicky Scarfo, who had operated in the city for years before gambling had been legalized—thought was rightfully theirs and not up for sharing, especially with a New York family. But a bigger reason Testa and Caponigro stewed may have been the drug business.

Angelo Bruno had stood adamantly against drug dealing and trafficking in his own family. But many on the street felt this injunction was both holding them back from earning as well as hypocritical. The charges of hypocrisy stemmed from activity taking place just a stone's throw from Bruno's territory. While the Philly family was embroiled in an internecine war for control of the organization, the Gambinos, through their Sicilian wing, were quietly working in one of the largest heroin-distribution operations ever uncovered in the United States. And they were parked right across the Delaware River, in the township of Cherry Hill, New Jersey, an upscale bedroom community located less than ten miles from Philadelphia. They had moved there when Bruno was still alive, prompting many to speculate that the Philly Boss had been taking a cut from their operations. "The supposition in the organization was that they were giving him money that was drug money."[2] Bruno even "allowed" Gambino operatives to open a disco and restaurant in Atlantic City, Casanova Disco. The Gambinos in Cherry Hill— Rosario, Joseph, and John Gambino—were essentially their own Gambino-family mini-crew. Distantly related to Carlo Gambino and his sons, the Cherry Hill Gambinos had been born in Sicily and were members of the Sicilian Mafia before they relocated to the United States.

While the disagreement between Bruno and his administration could have been taken care of in a more diplomatic fashion, Caponigro believed that he had received proper guidance from the Genovese family as to how to properly resolve the internal dispute. What is generally known is that Caponigro drove into New York City and met with the Genovese family and told them of the problems with Bruno. They told Caponigro to take care of it. Construing that as a tacit go-ahead to murder his Boss, Caponigro set the wheels in motion that led to just that. Another version of the story deals with a two million dollar bookmaking operation Caponigro was running in Hudson County that had been coming up against members of the Genovese family. Caponigro had disputed with the Genovese in the mid-1970s; the story was that Funzi Tieri wanted to take over the bookmaking operation, and that had led to friction with Caponigro. So, later, when it came time to put into motion his power play against Bruno, Caponigro, not wanting to further ruffle any Genovese feathers, went to the family, and Tieri, to get their okay for a hit, telling them he was having trouble with Bruno. Again, he was supposedly told to "take care of the problem," which he interpreted as a blessing to carry out the hit.

Regardless of how it went down, after the Bruno murder the whole Philly underworld was on edge. Nick Caramandi saw Caponigro at a club a few weeks after the murder. Caponigro told him, "When I come back Monday, everything's going to be under control. You're gonna get down."[3] The last part Caramandi took as referring to his possibly being formally inducted into the crime family. To Caramandi, and others around Caponigro, there was a sense that, whatever had happened with Bruno, Caponigro had been involved and that he was getting ready to make a play for a bigger role in the organization. But first Caponigro wanted to get with the Genovese in New York for a debriefing.

April 17, 1980, was a Thursday. Tony Bananas Caponigro drove into Manhattan with his brother-in-law, and former bootlegger, Alfred Salerno, who owned a jewelry store there. Bananas and Salerno were picked up in Midtown by members of the Genovese family, where Bananas likely expected to be inducted as new boss of the Philly mob. But that didn't happen. Some say it was a double cross by the Genovesi; others saw it as another internal power play. But what was clear was that Bananas hadn't really had the Commission's backing to kill Bruno. And killing a boss without permission is a cardinal sin in the Mafia. Despite his longevity with the organization, his earning power, and the respect in which crime families throughout the northeast held him, Caponigro's unforgivable mistake meant a certain outcome.

Early the next morning, on April 18, police discovered the nude body of Tony Bananas Caponigro, wrapped in a body bag and covered with cash, a sign of excessive greed. "He had been shot three times behind the right ear and once behind the left ear. Rope was tied around his neck, and most of the bones in his face were broken."[4] Five hours after Caponigro's broken body was found, a kid walking his dog found Salerno's body, just a few miles away. Salerno was also wrapped in a body bag. His hands had been tied behind his back, and "he was shot eleven times, and a rope was tied around his neck."[5] It was said that "Bananas had been shot so many times, his body was almost not identifiable. Then they had stuffed money into his mouth and other body cavities."[6]

The word spread quickly through the bars and social clubs of Newark and South Philadelphia. One associate recalled, "Joey Sodano came to my house and said, 'Nobody has heard from Bananas in twenty-four hours.' I said, 'What does that mean?' He said, 'It means he's gone.'"[7] Rumors also began emerging that Caponigro's brother-in-law and companion on the fateful trip to New York, Alfred Salerno, had also been involved in the Bruno hit. It was a message from the Genovese—but also likely had been approved by Phil Testa, who, as Bruno's underboss, moved in as boss.

Fast-forward a year, and, after Phil Testa is blown up, Nicky Scarfo takes over the Philly family, seeking to gain complete control of all the family's operations and quash any rebellion in the ranks. What followed was a bloody mob war that left over two dozen bodies on the streets of Philadelphia and South Jersey over the ensuing decade. The double-crosses, backstabbing, and out-and-out revenge killings were so bad that a number of high-level mobsters chose to defect to the government. While Scarfo and his crew mugged for the camera from his yacht in Fort Lauderdale, the FBI with state and local authorities were dismantling his enterprise from the inside out. Their focus was mainly on the Philly street rackets that Scarfo was bringing under his control, which included drug dealing, the racket Bruno had once prohibited that was now emerging as a major money earner, especially with the trafficking of methamphetamines and their key ingredient, P2P.

The casino industry was on police radar along with Nicky Scarfo. Joe Salerno—a plumber who became embroiled in the (newly rechristened) Bruno-Scarfo family's South Jersey operations—testified before the New Jersey Casino Control Commission that Scarfo "boasted that he 'owned' the union representing Atlantic City's fourteen thousand casino workers, Local 54 of the Hotel [Employees] and Restaurant Employees and Bartenders International Union."[8]

Prosecutors at the time tried to downplay organized crime's involvement in the casinos. It was after all, less than ten years after politicians and officials had assured their constituents that organized crime would have no involvement in any legalized casino industry in Atlantic City. It was alleged that in the early 1980s Scarfo controlled the union through the president, Frank Gerace. By 1982, the Casino Control Commission was actively trying to remove Gerace from the post. They produced a seventy-two-page opinion tying Gerace to Scarfo, alleging that Gerace had donated ten thousand dollars to a "pool of money that Scarfo and his defendants used to post bail"[9] when they were on trial for the murder of Vincent Falcone.

In addition to his involvement in Atlantic City's casinos, Scarfo reached out to elected city officials. His years in the town during its desolate days had given him a sizable network of contacts and associates he could turn to his benefit. And now that he was the big boss, his cache had grown far greater than what he had enjoyed as a mere street-level gambling boss. The boon in casinos and resorts in Atlantic City made even the most "moral" of public officials susceptible to graft. In an undercover FBI operation, Atlantic City's mayor from 1982 to 1984, Michael Matthews, was caught taking a ten thousand dollar bribe from an undercover operative posing as a Mafia member. Matthews was sentenced to five years in prison.

During the Bruno-Scarfo family purge, the bodies were piling up, but there was still a need to make money, and the guys were out on the street, busy hustling, working the deals while always looking over their shoulder, waiting for the other shoe to drop. One of Scarfo's South Jersey soldiers, Albert "Reds" Pontani, was long known to law enforcement, though he had kept a low profile through the early eighties, avoiding many of the internal family conflicts. In fact, many South Jersey soldiers were seemingly immune to Scarfo's temper and subsequent hit-list designation. It may have been because they were out of his line of sight for the most part or could have been because they were earners. Reds was based out of Hamilton Township, just outside of Trenton, where he owned a trucking company. Pontani's name first shows up on police radar in the early 1960s when he's listed as part of Angelo Bruno's family. Described then as a "rising young star" who "will try anything from robbery to rubouts at a price,"[10] by the eighties Pontani had amassed a criminal history that included kidnapping, burglary, assault, weapons offenses, and robbery. Pontani also inherited John Simone's bookmaking operation after Simone's death in 1980, and "The Pontani sports and numbers operation is active in Southeastern Pennsylvania and Southern New Jersey."[11]

South Jersey became as important during the Scarfo era as the streets of South Philadelphia. Though much of the business was centered on Atlantic City, there was a wide area to operate where the New York families had little to no representation. "If you're not from this area, it's hard to understand, but South Jersey is in large part a Philadelphia suburb. Guys move back and forth. And the Jersey Shore is their summertime place."[12]

Other South Jersey operatives in the Scarfo organization were Salvatore Frank Sparacio, who operated out of Gloucester Township in New Jersey and was "involved in sports bookmaking, loan-sharking, and drug trafficking."[13] Lawrence Merino lived in the seaside town of Margate, New Jersey, long a popular summertime vacation spot for the Philly family. Soldier Tommy DelGiorno lived in Ocean City, New Jersey, in a rented condo, which state police eventually bugged, leading to DelGiorno's eventually turning state's evidence and becoming a protected witness.

Sal "Blizzard" Passalacqua, who lived in Pennsauken, New Jersey, was a longtime gambling operative in South New Jersey. Born in 1909, his active years with the Philly family spanned back to the pre–Angelo Bruno days, though he had chosen to keep a low profile, and title, never rising above a soldier. By 1990, he was partnered with Frank Iannarella and hung out at the Medford Village Country Club on Golfview Drive in Medford, New Jersey. Blizzard also hung out with Salvatore Sparacio as part of his crew. Sam Scafidi was out of Bridgeton, New Jersey. Born in 1922, Scafidi's uncle Gaetano and cousin Rocco were longtime Bruno-family soldiers.

Post-Scarfo South Jersey guys included John Stanfa—the driver for Bruno the night of his murder—who lived in Medford when he took over as boss following his release from prison in 1991. Ray Esposito lived in South Jersey. He was a Stanfa loyalist and hit man for the mob. Ralph Natale, another former boss, lived in an apartment on the Cooper River in Pennsauken, near Camden, when he was in charge. Anthony Staino lived near Swedesboro, New Jersey. And Ron Previte, who later became a federal witness against the family, lived and operated in Hammonton, New Jersey.

With Scarfo's paranoia increasing and the number of men wiling to testify against him growing, it was only a matter of time before his bloody throne was toppled. Scarfo and fifteen members of the crime family were indicted on a variety of racketeering charges in 1987 and in 1988 were convicted of a host of crimes, ranging from murder to extortion. Scarfo's reign at the top was one of the most bloody and destructive to any crime family and was fairly short, compared to his predecessor's.

But there was one region that was overlooked by Scarfo during that time, the Down Neck Newark crew. Even though the seeds of the ultimate destruction of the crime family emanated from the streets of the Ironbound, the mob war never hit the shores of the Passaic River. Rather, the Newark family kept their heads down and their ears open for potential trouble. They also kept earning, running the monte and ziginette games that were such a big part of their revenue stream. But trouble was coming for the Down Neck crew, from one of their own.

After Tony Bananas Caponigro had been killed, leadership of the crew had gone to Blackie Napoli. Fresh out of prison for the SCI investigation, Blackie Napoli was the natural choice, having been a loyal soldier under Caponigro but also enjoying connections and ties back to Philly. He ran the crew for five years before stepping down in 1985 to allow Pasquale "Patty Specs" Martirano to take over. Napoli had had enough of the boss job, and with the Philly mob war in full swing at that point he may have felt it wise to lay low. Patty Specs took over in 1985 and brought some new blood into the crew.

One of the associates particularly close to Martirano was George Fresolone. The two men grew up together in Newark and ran in the same crowds, though they were separated in age. Fresolone looked up to Specs as almost a father figure. Specs was well respected across Newark. Members of all the other crime families knew who he was and worked well with him on joint operations. Fresolone and Martirano were arrested in the late eighties and charged with a variety of crimes, including gambling. After his arrest, Fresolone was approached by the New Jersey State Police, who wanted him to cooperate with their investigations. Fresolone at first refused but then, in order to protect Patty Specs, decided to become an informant. Fresolone felt that by controlling the pieces of information he fed to the State Police he could keep investigations away from Specs, if not outright ask the troopers to shield him from their inquiries. Fresolone still felt loyalty to Specs and some of the guys he was around. But one time the State Police came to George and played him a tape that shattered Fresolone's image of his so-called friends. They played Fresolone a recording of "Slicker" Attanasio and Turk Cifelli talking about him: "Who the fuck does he think he is? He ain't straightened out. In fact, he ain't shit. It's time we put him in his place."[14] That sealed the deal for Fresolone. He decided that he wanted to get out once and for all. He wore a wire on all the members of the Newark crew. Fresolone's fateful decision happened to coincide with Patty Specs's move to make new members into the Newark Crew.

The average crew member was getting a little long in the tooth. Old-timers like Happy Bellina and Jerry Fusella were still around, and, though there were a few younger made guys like Scoops Licata, Patty Specs wanted to get approval to make a new batch of loyal soldiers One of those he tapped was Fresolone. For the state police, this was a potential gold mine. It would be one of the first times that a making ceremony would be recorded.

The making ceremony that Patty Specs and Anthony Piccolo oversaw took place on July 29, 1990. It was at the Bronx home of John Praino. The soldiers who were to be formally inducted that day included Praino, Turk Cifelli, Vincent "Beeps" Centorino, Nicky Oliveri, and Fresolone. Cifelli was a longtime Down Neck crew member, and at sixty-eight years old the eldest of the inductees. Fresolone was wired and recorded the entire ceremony. Afterward, the police pulled the plug on his informant status, spiriting him away into the Witness Protection Program. [15]

The Fresolone tapes recorded at the induction ceremony called into question the real status of the men made by Patty Specs. Because the ceremony had been infiltrated, the soldiers were not recognized on the street as legitimate. It further cast a cloud over the Newark crew. But Patty Specs wasn't around long enough to see how much damage Fresolone had done to the organization; he passed away soon after the ceremony, late in 1990. Speculation ran rampant that Fresolone's protecting Patty Specs meant Specs had also been an informant, passing his own information on to authorities; but that was not the case. "After his death, people whispered that Patty Specs was 'bad.' Tommy Adams said so on a tape I made. For the record, the first question I asked the New Jersey State Police and the FBI at the time of my arrest was, 'Was Patty bad?' The answer is no. He was unaware of George Fresolone's defection. I'm sure George protected him." [16]

When Fresolone was pulled off the streets and the police swept in, it was the latest blow to the beleaguered Philly crime family. Scarfo had decimated the ranks on the street through the many killings and making many of the rest so miserable with the life that they turned to the government to get out. His mismanagement began to take down his entire administration, leaving a power vacuum that other, younger Philly guys looked to move into. The Philly family would never totally recover, plagued by internal warfare throughout most of the nineties as well as by additional turncoats, including their one-time boss Ralph Natale, who decide to cooperate with the feds after his short stint at the head of the table.

But the Philly family wasn't the only crime group in the 1980s that was feeling the force of law enforcement's concerted efforts against organized crime. Since the passage of the RICO Act in the early seventies, the FBI had eaten away at the mob's power base, virtually eliminating many smaller families in cities like Denver and Saint Louis. But even in major mob strong-holds like New Jersey it had become almost impossible to keep track of all the trials, arrests, and convictions through the 1980s. A front-page headline the *New York Times* in 1988 asked if a battered and ailing Mafia was losing its grip on America. While that may have signaled the eventual demise of the mob in the Northeast and Chicago, it was the death knell for Cleveland, San Francisco, Los Angeles, and a dozen other cities where the combined forces of immigrant assimilation, enhanced law-enforcement techniques, the RICO Act, and the passage of time collaborated to eliminate once-powerful mob families. The FBI was making up for lost time, and the mob was so thrown off course that everywhere they looked was either a secret microphone, video surveillance, a trusted member waiting to inform, or another waiting to kill them. In New Jersey the homegrown DeCavalcantes were sailing through the morass relatively unscathed, but that was about to change, even with their dynamic leader at the helm.

Chapter Fourteen

The Eagle and Video Gambling

John "the Eagle" Riggi first appears in FBI documents in the early 1960s with his father, Emanuel Riggi. Emanuel was a business agent of Local 394 of the Hod Carriers' Building and Common Laborers' Union in Elizabeth and a close confidant and friend of Nick Delmore, then-boss of the Elizabeth crime family. Emanuel was sentenced to two years on a racketeering conviction in 1957. Around that time, John Riggi was brought under the wing of Sam DeCavalcante and appeared on a number of recordings that made a part of the FBI's surveillance of DeCavalcante's Kenilworth Plumbing.

Initially a soldier, John Riggi was elevated to the position of capo in the early 1960s after Sam DeCavalcante had grown unhappy with labor decisions made by a capo at the time, Joe Sferra. As a member of the Hod Carriers' Union, Sferra's job had been to make sure that family men were taken care of first when it came to getting jobs and keeping them on the payroll; but he had been unable to do his job properly.

SAM: You see, Joe, over here I'm trying to build up a good relationship with everybody in the Commission. Our *brigata* [brigade] is small, but we can do things as good as anybody else. And I told you—as long as they are *amico nostri* [sic], I don't want them to go to the hall. I want them to keep working before everybody else.

And so, after Sferra failed to make an impact after repeated warnings, Sam DeCavalcante brought John Riggi in to take Sferra's place. Sferra was taken out of the union and demoted from his capo position in the crime family.

SAM: I'm going to let you take over this *decina* [branch]. Now this fellow is supposed to be treated with the utmost respect [Joe Sferra]. He's still an *amico nostro*. What he done, stays with him, understand? This is your future, John, but you have to take care of these men.

RIGGI: The least of your worries will be our people. I can tell you that.

SAM: I've always said I like Joe Sferra. But more than I like Joe Sferra, I like our people.[1]

Sam next brought Riggi into a position as treasurer at St. Joseph's Orphanage of Ribera, Sicily. DeCavalcante was the third boss to serve as head of the charity, succeeding Amari and Delmore before him. His choice of Riggi as treasurer showed that he was grooming the young capo for a bigger role. By 1969, John Riggi appeared on the FBI's org charts of mob families as a capo in the DeCavalcante family, following in his father's footsteps. When Sam DeCavalcante went away to prison in March of 1971 for his role in a massive gambling conspiracy, Riggi's star was on the rise, and he was named acting boss, bypassing older, more-seasoned soldiers like Frank Majuri. And when DeCavalcante was released on December 20, 1973, he decided to take a step back from his leadership role. It's unclear exactly when Riggi became DeCavalcante boss, if it was immediately after Sam the Plumber's release or not, but by the mid-seventies Sam was living in Miami Beach and Riggi was the man to see in New Jersey.

Unlike many mob guys who never finished high school, John Riggi had graduated from Linden High School in 1942 as a lettered athlete and class president. The following year, he enlisted in the US Army. Among the residents of the Peterstown neighborhood of Elizabeth, Riggi was highly regarded. "He answered the call of the churches, organizations, and government when buildings needed repair or when parks and ballfields were needed."[2] Though he lived in Linden, New Jersey, he was a regular presence in the Peterstown, stronghold of the DeCavalcantes. Viewed by neighbors as a generous benefactor to the community, Riggi made a point of keeping crime-family business out of sight, eschewing violence in his early years—though later events changed that policy.

Riggi exuded power to those around him. "I visited Riggi when he was in prison in Cumberland, Maryland. This was the mid-nineties. Even in that environment he was a man familiar with the use of power. He was a war hero. The impact of the Greatest Generation even affected members of Cosa Nostra. They had a pride in the immigrant community at that time. I don't think that was ever lost on him."[3]

John Riggi's influence even extended outside New Jersey, which for the small DeCavalcante family was a feat. Here they were, a crime family of less than fifty, in the shadow of the Five Families of New York City, and even still, Riggi commanded respect. "The minute you said to anyone in Jersey or

New York, you said the name Riggi, it was an automatic. It was incredible, the power he had."[4] And Riggi knew it. He was overheard on a wiretap enjoining an associate to "Learn how to use the power."[5]

One contemporary says of him,

> John Riggi mentored me in a lot of aspects of life. We remained in contact until his passing a few years ago. Riggi was a great man. Not a great mob guy. A great man. In fact, he aborted my induction into the Colombo family while I was in prison. John Pate, who was my captain at the time, offered to "straighten me out" in the bathroom at Otisville Federal [Correctional Institute]. Riggi put the kibosh on it. He was looking down the road. He saw clearly that I could be "more." and I will always view him with great affection and appreciation as well. A month later, Pate was removed in the middle of the night and cooperated.[6]

A large part of that power base came from Riggi's control of labor not only in the Hod Carriers' Union but also in Local 394, where Riggi held a position for thirty years. "What made him powerful was that in the summertime the building trade was biggest source of summer jobs. Having the ability to put people to work, giving out labor contract to contractors."[7] This labor control was one of the main DeCavalcante rackets since the days of Nick Delmore. Despite all the government crackdowns on their activities, the small Elizabeth family was able to keep their hooks in the union. But labor racketeering was a big priority for the FBI. And, unbeknownst to Riggi, he was under investigation for racketeering.

In 1990 Riggi was arrested at his home in Linden and charged with racketeering. The labor power broker was looking at a sizable sentence if convicted. Riggi was indicted with his two sons, Vincent and John J. Riggi. Also brought into the case with Riggi were capo Jimmy Palermo and Salvatore Timpani, a soldier based in Toms River, New Jersey. The racketeering charges included extorting over one million dollars from a Fords, New Jersey, construction company, Akron Construction Company, and infiltration of a number of small construction companies. The trial lasted eight weeks. Riggi was convicted of eight of the thirty-three charges, Timpani convicted of one.

Riggi was sentenced to twelve years in prison, but he did not abdicate the throne. He wanted to run things from behind bars, so a series of acting bosses were put in place. Upon taking over, John D'Amato put Emmanuel Riggi "on the shelf"—a term used to mean forced retirement—at the behest of his son, John. As Anthony Rotondo, a soldier in the family who later turned state's evidence, testified, "It was at the request of John Riggi."[8]

After Riggi began serving his time, the former underboss to Sam the Plumber, Louis "Fat Louie" Larasso, was reported missing by his wife. Police later discovered his car, which had been parked at JFK Airport in a feeble attempt to make it look like Larasso had skipped town. In reality, he had been murdered on October 21, 1991. He'd been lured to a meeting by Vincent "Vinny Oceans" Palermo and killed by Anthony Capo, Greg Rago, and Louis "Louie Eggs" Consalvo, who were all made into the crime family for the hit. Larasso had allegedly been killed on orders from Riggi, who thought him a threat to his leadership. There had been a meeting of DeCavalcante men not loyal to Larasso to vote on whether or not Fat Louie should go. The meeting was held at the childhood home of Anthony Rotondo, who later testified about the decision to kill Larasso.

Q: And the result of the meeting.

(Rotondo) A: He was to be murdered.

Q: In your own mother's house with cold cuts?

A: Cold cuts came later, yes.

Q: The home outside where your own father had been murdered, execution-style, a few years back?

A: Yes.

Q: This vote you mentioned, sir, you alluded to this on direct [that this meeting] basically was a complete charade?

A: Right.

Q: You told us yesterday the outcome was preordained?

A: Yes.

Q: That is the only reason the vote was unanimous?

A: Yes, they left out a couple captains. [9]

The next on the hit list was John D'Amato, acting boss of the crime family. He was murdered on January 6, 1992. Though the popular theory is that D'Amato was murdered because he was gay, in reality he was getting too close to New York for some family members' liking, and there was jealousy that he was chosen to be acting boss over other favored candidates. Once again, Anthony Rotondo was involved with the murder. He recruited Anthony Capo, a young up-and-coming wiseguy in the DeCavalcante family's New York faction.

Q: And you, Anthony Rotondo, directly ordered Capo to shoot D'Amato dead?

A: Yes.

Q: To your knowledge Capo and the other guy then went and assassinated D'Amato right near his girlfriend's home?

A: They shot him in the car.

. . .

Q: Afterwards, sir, you refused to drive upstate with Farone and Palermo to help dispose of the body?

A: That night, yes.

Q: You couldn't bring yourself to do that, could you?

A: No.[10]

The D'Amato killing was done without first consulting other capos in the crime family. So Jake Amari went to some of the captains and laid out the allegations of financial and sexual impropriety, making the case for D'Amato's killing. The captains were unaware that D'Amato had already been slain but went ahead and voted for him to be whacked. This double-crossing and political maneuvering between the factions was destabilizing the organization, slowly weakening it over the next eight years, which would end in the massive takedown of thirty DeCavalcante members and associates in 1999. And from that rubble, high-ranking members, including acting boss, Vinny Oceans Palermo, would decide to turn state's evidence and became federal witnesses against the remaining crime-family members. The DeCavalcantes suffered a serious blow to their family structure. John Riggi was also caught up in that latest assault against the family and hit with additional charges in the early 2000s while still in prison.

One of the crimes that Riggi was charged with was the murder of Fred Weiss. One of those involved in the Weiss murder was Anthony Rotondo, son of Vincent Rotondo. Vincent "Jimmy the Gent" Rotondo, had been murdered on January 4, 1988, in front of his Brooklyn house. He was found with a fish in his lap, echoing the scene in *The Godfather* where Tessio receives Luca Brasi's vest with a fish inside, code that the enforcer "sleeps with the fishes." Jimmy the Gent's alleged miscalculation had been introducing a federal informant to the DeCavalcantes and Gambinos. His murder was ordered by John Gotti, who showed up to his funeral with a posse of twenty

Gambino mobsters, to show their strength over the beleaguered Elizabeth family.

Anthony Rotondo had recruited two other DeCavalcante men to hit Weiss on September 11, 1989. Riggi later admitted in 2003 that he had ordered Weiss's murder. Riggi said matter-of-factly at his plea hearing for the Weiss murder charge that, "Pursuant to the agreement, Fred Weiss was murdered. That's it."[11] In court in 2005, Rotondo also testified about the murder:

Q: Two of your executioners gunned down this total stranger right outside his own home; isn't that a fact?

A: Yes.

Q: Slaughtered him in cold blood, right, sir?

A: He was killed.

. . .

Q: Afterward you brought all the fellows home for some coffee and cake?

A: We went to change cars at my house.

Q: Did you bring them for coffee and cake?

A: We had coffee.[12]

By the mid-1980s and into the 1990s, the Gambino's powerhouse in New Jersey was Robert "Bobby Cabert" Bisaccia. He was promoted to capo after meeting with John Gotti in 1987 at a nightclub in Seaside Heights, New Jersey. Bobby Cabert operated out of Belleville, Bloomfield, and Newark, overseeing Gambino-family concerns in the Garden State, especially their lucrative bookmaking and loan-sharking operations. Bisaccia was also involved in the video-gambling-machine industry, an especially profitable quasi-legitimate racket for the mob across the country, especially in the Chicagoland area.

In New Jersey, Bisaccia controlled accounts and routes, blocking competition from other mobsters and legitimate vendors of the machines. He aligned himself with some of these vendors to expand his territory, offering them his name and protection in exchange for a piece of their profits. An operator later testified to the SCI about threats Bisaccia made should anyone encroach on his territory: "These are my locations, and if anybody goes in there, they are going to have a problem."[13]

The gambling machines were placed in bars and bodegas, mainly in lower-income and blue-collar neighborhoods. "Well, . . . you go to poorer areas of these cities like Elizabeth, Newark, Paterson, Trenton and walk in these stores, and you would see a lot of these— a lot of these games. . . . I mean, just in Down Neck alone, every store I walk in on Ferry Street has got them, and out of the small radius of maybe seven, eight blocks, you're talking— maybe you got a hundred machines there."[14]

One of the mob's biggest suppliers of machines in the New York/New Jersey area was Myron Sugerman, whose father, Barney Sugerman, owned Runyon Sales. Myron Sugerman recounted, "My strength was that I knew the gambling machine business from the fact that I was born and raised in the coin-operated gaming business. I understood it. I understood what makes it work. I understand it backwards and forwards. In the heyday of New Jersey/New York gaming, there were thousands of machines operating in Bodegas, social clubs, barber shops, shoe-shine parlors, bars, restaurants, beauty salons, et cetera."[15]

Myron had known Newark gangster Joey Sodano for years; they'd grown up together at the same time. Sodano was in Tony Bananas Caponigro's crew and had an arrest record for bookmaking and robbery. In 1977, Myron had given some machine to two old coin-machine operators in the Bronx on a revenue-sharing basis. Every Tuesday, Myron went to the Bronx to collect the money. "One Tuesday, they don't show up. I call them, and they say, 'We bought the machines.' I say, 'We had a revenue-sharing deal, and those machines were still mine, and you still owed me the weekly income. That was the deal.' They say, 'Do what you got to do.' So I called Joey Sodano, and he went up to the Bronx with his brother, who I named Jimmy Rogers. Joey and Jimmy were convincing with two pistols, and I got my machines back."[16]

Before long, there was a meeting with Sugerman and some wiseguys from the crews of Tony Bananas and Gambino mobster Frankie Locascio.[17] They put a restrictive covenant on Myron's operations, knowing how essential he was to the slot-machine business. But Angelo Pinball, a guy who worked for the two Bronx men who'd attempted to steal Sugerman's machines, went to Genovese soldier Louis DiNapoli, who was operating in East Harlem. Angelo Pinball told him that they needed to get into the gambling machine business because of all the money to be made, educating them about the opportunity.

Louis DiNapoli, in turn, went to see Louis "Streaky" Gatto, a Genovese capo who ran the Lodi crew in North Jersey. Streaky Gatto was in the Pete LaPlaca crew, and when LaPlaca died, Gatto had taken control. Based on the long-ago partnership between Myron's father, Barney, and Jerry Catena, the Genovese family believed Sugerman should rightfully be under them. "Louis came to see me and told me, 'Welcome home.'"[18]

There was nothing Sodano could do at this point, though by this time he had been made as a member of the Bruno-Scarfo family. Sodano went to tell Tony Bananas that the Genovese had claimed Sugerman and his gambling-machine business. But Bananas knew the rules, and though he had a lot of clout in the Jersey underworld, in terms of sheer size and influence, he was dwarfed by the Genovese family.

The SCI found that "The Sugerman operation was such an important source of revenue to the Genovese family that, according to information picked up in 1983 by federal electronic surveillance, the family boss, two capos, and an associate often made decisions involving the firm's daily operation."[19]

After Gatto moved in and brought Sugerman under the Genovese umbrella in 1982, Sodano set his sights on the Jersey Shore and set up operations with the Storino brothers in a company called SMS Manufacturing, located in Point Pleasant. The Storino brothers were the nephews of Vincent "Jimmy Sinatra" Craparotta. Sodano was officially made into the Bruno-Scarfo family in 1981 and became a consistent source of revenue for Nicky Scarfo, sending the boss four thousand dollars a month from his bookmaking and video-gaming operations.

Myron Sugerman said,

> Once I became liberated, I broke the market wide open. In due time we operated two thousand machines and sold thousands of machines. I had partnerships with every ethnic group imaginable—Israelis, Irish, Italians, Russians, Greeks, Cubans, Puerto Ricans, Dominicans, et cetera. I was an international magnate. I speak seven languages, and so everybody came to me, and we did deals with everybody. We supplied machines. We had good, solid relationships. I didn't know 99 percent of these guys' last names. We knew them by nicknames such as Fat Mikey, Cuban Georgey, Dominican Joe, KGB, Puerto Rican Eddy, Tommy Irish, Spiros the Greek, Miracles, Corsican Eitan, Frenchy Eitan, et cetera. All that we had was their phone numbers and their beeper numbers, but they came religiously. It was a very smooth relationship until the market became saturated.[20]

> In 1981 Sal Miranda worked for me. His father was with Joey Sodano, but Sal was the sales manager and with me. We got in trouble with the feds with our knockoffs of popular video games like Pac-Man, Donkey Kong. We got knockoff boards from Japan, and we used them to make machines. The Storinos manufactured the machines, and we marketed them. We made millions in two months. Then we got raided by the FBI for copyright infringement. I stopped the feds from getting to the Storinos.[21]

After the raid, at a sit-down at the Vesuvius Restaurant, the Lucchese family found out that Jimmy Sinatra was making money off the video-gambling machines but kicking money back up to the leadership. The fallout from the sit-down had repercussions that tore apart the New Jersey Lucchese family. And it started after the sit-down when Tommy Ricciardi went down the Shore to see Jimmy Sinatra and find out why he was keeping the money for himself instead of doing the right thing and sending some of it up the ladder to Lucchese leadership. Ricciardi was planning on giving Jimmy Sinatra a beatdown with golf clubs to show him that the Lucchesi were not happy that he was holding back from them. Unfortunately, things got out of hand, and Jimmy Sinatra died from the beating. It was not the outcome that Ricciardi had wanted. It was described by street sources as one of the more unfortunate killings in Jersey mob history. The beatdown was only supposed to have sent a message, to get a longtime Jersey guy back in the fold, back on track.

Not long after the Jimmy Sinatra killing, the mob's New Jersey video-gambling business was gutted in March of 1985 when more than five hundred police officers confiscated hundreds of machines in New York City and ten New Jersey counties. The effort was called Operation Ocean and was a significant blow to the industry that had been generating tens of millions for organized crime. Operation Ocean resulted in over fifty arrests and severely disrupted, eventually landing a mortal blow to, the video-gambling business in New Jersey.

Close to a decade after the Sinatra killing, the feds indicted Michael Taccetta, Anthony "Tumac" Accetturo Sr., Thomas A. Ricciardi, and an associate, Michael Ryan, on racketeering charges, which included the Jimmy Sinatra murder. Accetturo, of Newark, was the head of the Lucchese family's New Jersey operations in the early 1970s when the SCI subpoenas were coming down. Rather than facing SCI, or spending time in jail for contempt, Accetturo left for Florida. In his place, Michael Taccetta was appointed head of the Lucchese Jersey crew. Taccetta's crew included his younger brother, Martin, and Michael Perna, two younger Lucchese mobsters who rose through the ranks in the 1980s to become heavy players in illegal gambling and other rackets in New Jersey.

In 1986, Tommy Ricciardi, Accetturo, and Taccetta were among nineteen Lucchese mobsters indicted for a host of racketeering charges in one of the largest mob cases in Jersey history. Later the subject of a book and movie, the trial was a massive federal indictment against the Lucchese family as well as against Bruno solider Jackie DiNorscio, who had transferred over to the Lucchese during the bloody Philly mob war. Jackie represented himself at trial (and was played by Vin Diesel in the movie). His crowd-pleasing demeanor, coupled with the massive complexity and length of the case trial, lasting from November of 1986 to August of 1988, resulted in acquittal for all the defendants.

While the 1980s trial was a good outcome for Ricciardi, the Jimmy Sinatra case was not looking like it would result in the same return. The case was against him was strong, there was solid evidence, and Ricciardi was looking at a long prison sentence if convicted. Plus, there were internal issues that had been brewing for years in the Lucchese family between the New York and New Jersey factions, and between Accetturo, Ricciardi, and Taccetta. Whispers of murder contracts, or double-crosses, and of targets on people's backs had everyone on edge.

Another issue was eating away at the Lucchese family: turncoats. In 1991 Fat Pete Chiodo, an overweight capo, decided to become a government informant after he was the victim of an unsuccessful hit attempt—he was shot twelve times—on May 8, 1991. Also that year, acting boss Alphonse D'Arco, fearing he was next to be killed by Lucchese bosses Victor Amuso and Anthony "Gaspipe" Casso, also became a government witness. Then, after a rupture in the alliance between Michael and Martin Taccetta and Tumac Accetturo, Tumac was on the defensive, with the Taccettas gunning for him. There was a contract out on Tumac. He was also arrested while living in North Carolina and sent back to New Jersey to face contempt charges for failing to appear before a state grand jury. With pressure mounting from three sides, Tumac also decided to become a government witness.

So the cards were stacked against Ricciardi, and the old, noble stand-up-guy myth of the Mafia was shattering all around him. The Luccheses had gone from one of the most powerful New Jersey Mafia crews to a crippled mess, hobbling along without knowing from which direction the next problem would appear. With all this in mind, Tommy Ricciardi became a government witness. He decided to testify against the other defendants in the Jimmy Sinatra trial. They were all found guilty. For his cooperation Ricciardi served some time in prison and entered the Witness Protection Program in 2001. Tommy Ricciardi's decision to turn and work for the government affected the course of the Lucchese family's fortune in New Jersey, but it also affected members of his real family.

My brother? Tommy Ricciardi? I'm often asked about him. And I often don't answer at this stage of my life. But, yeah, He cooperated. He was a made guy, eventually a captain. This is the deal, and anyone who is truthful and who understands the life and is honest with themselves who knew him will tell you he was a man's man, a true believer in Cosa Nostra and its rules. No one believed in Cosa Nostra more than Tommy. They had a strong crew, all friends since they were kids, they were young, they had it all, but eventually the greed, the treachery, paranoia, and distrust—basically, the nature of the life ruined it all in the end.

It has been many years since I've spoken with him or have seen him or my other brother, Danny. It really has nothing to do with their defection. There was a significant age gap between us, and we simply never got along. I was also a wild kid, always trying to prove myself, and it usually backfired on me. I have no agenda in defending him. It has been years since we've had contact. And most likely never will again.

When Tommy flipped, I was midway through my five-year bid [in prison]. The FBI came to Otisville [Correctional Facility] and told me part of Tommy's agreement was that I be released. I was in total shock. But I declined the offer. I appreciate my brother trying to help me. I also respect myself for my accountability in refusing the opportunity to "walk." Anyway, when I got out, Petey Black [Pete Campisi] sent for me. He vouched for me and wanted to take me to New York for induction into the Colombo family. He assured me no one held me accountable for my brother's actions. I declined Petey's offer, and having known him from childhood, he graciously understood.

I look back on it and see that my brother saved me and opened a new world for me. I got a job selling cars. I prospered. I wound up in LA working in movies. What John Riggi saw in me was happening. I began to act and write, and that allowed me to see a whole different side of my life and the world around me. I met my wife. I have a son and a legitimate business. Recently I returned to New Jersey to attend the wake of a boyhood friend. Many people were there that I hadn't seen in twenty-odd years. It was great to see them, and they genuinely were glad to see me. One guy, a made Gambino guy, told me he was proud of me. Why? Because I didn't flip? No, because I had created a legitimate life for myself. I don't judge anyone, or tell anyone how to live their lives, but, for me, back then, thinking about it now is so far removed. It was a terrible way to live. [22]

After pleading guilty in the video-gambling racketeering case, Joe Sodano went to prison. When he was released, he returned to the streets of Newark. There was a new boss in town, John Stanfa, who took control of the crime family in the early nineties. Sodano began to complain about having to send money to Philadelphia, and once Ralph Natale replaced the imprisoned Stanfa, Sodano stopped sending money altogether, and though he was called to come down to Philly to make an appearance and pay homage to the new boss, he refused—a tactical mistake on Sodano's part.

Joe Sodano was found slumped over the wheel of his SUV on December 7, 1996, with two bullet shots to the head. The car was parked in front of a senior citizens' center in Newark. Sodano's murder was partially of his own making, if you ask Myron Sugerman. "The reason he got killed is that Philly sent for him twice and he didn't go."[23] Ralph Natale, after he flipped, backed up the story, telling the feds that he and "Skinny Joey" Merlino had ordered the hit on Sodano because Sodano had refused to meet with them and share part of his earnings. "I said he [Sodano] got the message and didn't respond . . . we got to kill him. If we don't, we'll lose the respect of our own family, and we'll lose the respect of the other families. Send the message, he's got to go."[24]

The gunman in the Sodano murder was Philip Casale, who was partners with Peter "Pete the Crumb" Caprio. Casale called up Sodano and told him he wanted to meet, luring Sodano to the location. When Sodano pulled up,

Casale jumped in the passenger seat and immediately shot Sodano in the right side of the head. Then, as the vehicle started to roll backward, "Casale jumped out, dashed around the front, pulled open the driver's door, and shot Sodano again, in the left side of the head."[25] Casale took cash and jewelry off Sodano to make it look like a robbery. In July of 2001, a jury did not find Skinny Joey responsible for the murder of Joey Sodano despite the testimony of Ralph Natale and Pete the Crumb Caprio. He was retried in 2004 and again acquitted of complicity in the Sodano murder.

At a time the other crime families operating in New Jersey were experiencing major shifts in leadership and attention from law enforcement was growing more intense, the Genovese family was not immune. But SCI found that, "Although the Genovese family has been faced with a variety of disruptive incidents within the last few years, it has been able to maintain most of its New Jersey operations."[26] And a good portion of those operations were aimed at the docks at the port, where the mob has maintained a presence for over fifty years.

Chapter Fifteen

On the Docks

The Huck Finn Diner sits on the north side of Morris Avenue in the New Jersey township of Union. Like so many other roadside diners that dot the state, the Huck Finn is open from sun-up to late in the evening, almost twenty-four hours on the weekend. The standard diner fare is served, along with an impressive list of burgers and chicken sandwiches. The back of the parking lot abuts the baseball field for Union High School. Some time in late October 2005, a Silver Acura was parked in the last row of the back lot at the Huck Finn. The owner of the diner thought he knew who the car belonged to, so it didn't arouse too much suspicion when the car sat, undisturbed, until November 30. That day, a patron walking by the car noticed flies gathering around the trunk and a stench emanating from the car and alerted the manager. The manager found that the car was unlocked and retrieved the registration.

When the police were called, they ran the registration and immediately contacted the FBI. The feds had been on the lookout for the car and its driver, the cousin of the car's real owner. And when they popped open the trunk, they found the driver, facedown, shot dead. Though they sent the body to the coroner for an autopsy and official identification, they knew right away they had found Genovese capo Lawrence Ricci, who had last been seen leaving his girlfriend's on October 5.

Earlier that year, in February 2005, Ricci had been indicted, along with Genovese soldier George Barone, International Longshoremen's Association Union president John Bowers, and ILA vice president Arthur Coffey. They had been indicted on extortion and mail fraud in a scheme to keep the top leadership of the union in the hands of the mob, specifically the Genovese and Gambino families. "Over time, the Mafia developed a stranglehold over the ILA and used that control to select ILA officers and used its influence

173

over the officers to steer lucrative contracts to companies controlled by the mob and paying money to the mob."[1] Ricci's part had been to steer a lucrative contracts to a mob-run pharmaceutical company.

At the time of the trial, in the fall of 2005, George Barone had become a witness for the government and testified against the defendants. Maybe fearing Ricci would be next, the old Genovese associate was set up to be killed. The ironic postscript to his murder was that he was acquitted in early November (along with Daggett, Bowers, and Coffey). But it was unclear exactly who had ordered Ricci's killing. Ricci's ties to the Genovese family had been strong for decades. In the late 1970s he had hung around Tino Fiumara's crew and had gotten caught up in the massive Project Alpha investigation. And it was Fiumara, along with Michael Coppola, that investigators figured for prime suspects in the Ricci murder. Authorities theorized that Coppola had killed Ricci under orders from Fiumara. At the time of the Ricci murder, Coppola had already been on the lam for over a decade, hiding out on the Upper West Side of Manhattan. His time on the run had begun after he'd been approached by the FBI in 1996 and asked to give a DNA sample to tie him to the 1977 murder of Johnny Coca-Cola Lardiere.[2]

Fiumara had spent fifteen years in prison. He'd watched from behind bars as the Genovese family's hold on the docks hit some turbulent times. Pressure from the Gambino family and the imprisonment of key Genovese operatives had reduced the footprint of the crime family in the lucrative world of shipping.

Influence over the waterfront has been organized-crime legacy in New Jersey since the early 1900s. From the beginning of the mob's infiltration of the port facilities, "Witnesses testified that payoffs were a part of virtually every aspect of the commercial life of the port. Payoffs insured the award of work contracts and continued contracts already awarded. Payoffs were made to insure labor peace and allow management to avoid future strikes. Payoffs were made to control a racket in workman's compensation claims. Payoffs were made to expand business activity into new ports and enable companies to circumvent ILA work requirements." And it only got more crooked from there. "Corrupt practices were commonplace on the Atlantic and Gulf Coast waterfronts."[3]

Investigations into the International Longshoremen's Association and its practices started back in the mid-1950s, around the time of the movie *On the Waterfront*, which dramatized events that were taking place at docks every day. In 1953, a compact was developed between New York and New Jersey to form the Waterfront Commission of New York Harbor. It was done to address a host of issues but also to reflect the changing geographic nature of where the main waterfront facilities were located. "Shipping firms, unhappy with aging pier facilities in Manhattan, began moving their operations to New Jersey."[4]

During the August 1957 hearings of the Senate Select Committee on Improper Activities in Labor and Management, led by Senator John McClellan of Arkansas, witnesses testified about the unsavory hiring practices and poor working conditions for many of the longshoremen. And it was one of the first times the committee heard about the siphoning of union dues from the coffers of the locals. It was clear that organized crime was exploiting the workers on the docks. To show indignation and promise reform was one thing, but to really accomplish meaningful change was quite another. The money was so great for the mob that they were not about to simply step aside at the whims of a congressional committee. And it wasn't only the stealing of workers' pay that filled the mob's coffers.

In addition to the directly impacting of how labor is allocated, work at the docks provided a veritable cornucopia of hijacking delights. With so much cargo coming and so little oversight, especially in the earlier days before electronic tracking of containers and packages, mob crews tried to steal as much as they could. Those stories of "it fell off a truck" appliances were completely based on fact. Drivers would either be paid to divert their loads, or the loads would simply be stolen. Appliances from television sets to washing machines to all types of household goods would be sold through a fence, traded for other commodities, or, literally sold out of the back of a truck. The theft of goods cost shippers, stevedore companies, and suppliers tens of millions of dollars annually. Dockworkers were also offered a variety of vices to pass their time—from numbers to prostitutes. They drank at mob-owned bars and taverns where loan sharks preyed on the financially challenged. In many ways the docks became mini-empires of vice that were completely mobbed up.

In 1969, "The government believed that organized crime families had divided the Pier of New York into three sections—New Jersey, Manhattan, and Brooklyn. The Gambino family operated on the Brooklyn docks. The Genovese family operated in Manhattan and New Jersey."[5] The main Genovese guys on the docks were John DiGilio and Tino Fiumara.

In the early eighties government oversight of the waterfront unions had turned up some interesting pieces of information regarding Genovese family infiltration. Carol Gardner was an international general organizer for the International Longshoremen's Association, while Thomas Buzzanca was a general organizer and Vincent Colucci an international vice president. According to the McClellan Committee, "Evidence shows that Colucci, Gardner, and Buzzanca took direction from a Genovese crime operative in New Jersey, Tino Fiumara."[6] Fiumara had maintained his close ties with Tieri and had been assigned by the Genovese family to oversee all waterfront activities in northern New Jersey. On May 2, 1980, a jury convicted Fiumara, along with Genovese soldier Michael Clemente, Thomas Buzzanca, Vincent Colucci, Carol Gardner, Michael Coppola, and Gerald Swanton, on 160 counts, including illegal labor payments, tax evasion, and extortion.

Tino Fiumara was behind bars for an important event in the history of the mob on the Jersey waterfront. He was not involved in, though likely aware of, the fate of his once-trusted ally John DiGilio. John DiGilio had fallen out of favor with the Genovese leadership, particularly with Genovese capo Louis "Bobby" Manna, who operated out of Casella's Restaurant in downtown Hoboken, New Jersey. Born in in that city in 1929, Manna had overseen most of the pier thefts on the waterfront for the Genovese family and was considered a powerful capo. During the time of Fiumara's incarceration, Manna became the de facto leader of the Genovese family's Hudson County operations.

While Fiumara was in prison, DiGilio expanded his operations on the waterfront, running a large-scale gambling, loan-sharking, and extortion racket in addition to the labor racketeering and union control. While this was filling the mob's coffers, DiGilio's antics, which drew a lot of attention to the bearded mobster, had been eroding the patience of Genovese leadership for some time. Attention was something that the Genovese family was not fond of, and DiGilio's behavior caused some serious rifts. Things came to a head when DiGilio was indicted along with three associates in a racketeering trial. Rather that retain an attorney, DiGilio, despite warnings from Genovese leaders, chose to represent himself. He was successful in his efforts, drawing an acquittal form the jury. His codefendants, including a union leader, were not so lucky; they were all convicted. To the Genovese family, this was the final straw. The conviction of Donald Carson, who was secretary-treasurer of Local 1587-88 of the International Longshoremen's Association in Bayonne, was a huge blow to the Genovese family. With his removal, they lost a key ally in the union. And, to make matters worse, he was replaced by a Gambino-family associate. This was all too much. The Genovese leadership blamed DiGilio for the convictions. His time was up.

On May 5, 1988, DiGilio drove to a meeting place in Kearny, New Jersey, with Genovese soldier Louis Auricchio and associate George Weingartner. It was the last time anyone would see DiGilio. On May 26, 1988, after he had been missing for three weeks, his body was discovered floating, in a body bag, down the Hackensack River, off the shore of Carlstadt, New Jersey, near the Meadowlands. He had been shot in the back of his head. After DiGilio was taken out, leadership over his rackets was given to Genovese capo Angelo Prisco. Louis Auricchio was convicted at trial in 1994 for the murder of DiGilio and sentenced to thirty years in prison. George Weingartner didn't make it to the end of the trial. He committed suicide, sitting in his running car in the garage of his Ocean County home. Manna also faced a trial based on years of recorded conversation in which he was overheard planning the murder of Gambino boss John Gotti, his brother Gene Gotti, and businessman Irwin Schiff. Manna was convicted of murder conspiracy and racketeering and sentenced to eighty years in prison on September 9, 1989.

Tino Fiumara was released from prison in 1994 and went back to work, not skipping a beat. He once again became the Genovese contact at the waterfront. His time behind bars had done little to diminish his reputation. His time back on the street was relatively low-key. So low-key, in fact, that investigators started wondering how he was communicating with his old mob acquaintances. They followed him, and when they spotted him meeting with convicted felons, a violation of his parole, he was arrested in April of 1999 at his house in the town of Spring Lake, on the Jersey Shore. The parole board determined he had violated parole and was sent him back to prison, where he remained until 2003.

Upon his release in 2003, Tino moved to Long Island and began regularly communicating with a solider in his crew, Stephen "Beach" Depiro. The FBI believed that Depiro had begun handling the day-to-day activities on the Jersey waterfront in Fiumara's stead. It was a sobering revelation to both law enforcement and the public: Despite decades of government crackdown and intense efforts to drive out the mob, organized crime's influence—specifically the Genovese family's influence—permeated the New Jersey waterfront through their control of Local 1235. And the time would never be better for making money off transoceanic shipping.

The rise of mega-ships and a surge in container ships brought unprecedented growth to the Port of New York and New Jersey. By 2014 record traffic meant filling the pockets of union members who worked long hours ensuring the uninterrupted flow of goods coming off the massive ships docking at Port Newark–Elizabeth Marine Terminal. Infrastructure in the area was being upgraded, and bridges, like the Bayonne, were raised to accommodate the massive new post-Panamax ships that were the future of shipping. And the Genovese family was taking their share as well.

Fiumara was back on the FBI's radar, as were his associates. The feds were determined to rid the port of the Genovese family once and for all. An indictment was handed down on September 10, 2010, naming eleven defendants on labor-racketeering charges. In late December 2014 Genovese family soldier Stephen "Beach" Depiro, along with two former ILA Local 1235 officials, pled guilty to taking tribute payments from annual bonuses given to dockworkers at the port. The scheme had been going on for decades, draining money from the paychecks of the hardworking laborers, padding the wallets of the mob and their union accomplices. Tino Fiumara was not part of the verdict. He died of cancer, six days after the indictment was handed down, on September 16, 2010.

The mob may have been pushed back from the docks, but it was by no means out. In January of 2017 the *New York Times* ran an article about the continued presence of organized crime on the Jersey waterfront.[7] There are relatives of mobsters who are appointed to cushy jobs with high salaries and little responsibility. Tribute payments are still extracted from the longshore-men who work the docks. Though their numbers have diminished as technol-ogy has taken over a lot of the grunt work, and containerization of cargo has taken a lot of the stevedore work away, there are still thousands of workers who show up each day at the various facilities along the river between New Jersey and New York. And the mob is still there, the vestiges, some say, of a time long past, but still stubbornly hanging on.

Chapter Sixteen

The Receding Tide

Lenny's Brick Oven Pizzeria is located in a brick-faced strip mall in rural Washington Township, New Jersey. Housed next to a nail salon, and near the usual supermarket/fast-food nexus, Lenny's is noted for good pizza, a rarity in this rural section of western New Jersey, near the Pennsylvania border. It's one of hundreds of small pizza shops dotted across the Garden State landscape, the perfect kind of place for a late dinner or watching the game with a beer and a slice.

But on the night of July 3, 2009, the customers at Lenny's got an up-close-and-personal look at the ugly underside of the state—and a rare sighting of a mob boss. His name was Francesco "Frank" Guarraci, and he was the alleged boss of the DeCavalcante family, having taken over in 2007.

Lenny's had been owned by Lenny Palermo until his death in 2009. Two days after Palermo's death, one of Guarraci's associates approached the manager and told him that Guarraci was now the boss and that he'd be in to make sure everyone knew that, especially the manager. Later that night, while customers were enjoying their pizza, three men burst in to Lenny's. Guarraci told the manager that the pizzeria belonged to him. Customers saw the situation escalating and left without paying their bills.

According to the indictment, Michael "Mikey Red" Nobile, an ex-con with a penchant for utilizing a baseball bat for collecting outstanding debts, attempted to prevent the manager from calling the police. But some of the customers who'd fled the scene were already dialing 911. After Guarraci told the manager, "I run the show," the men left, but police figured out their identities soon enough.

Guarraci and Nobile were indicted on August 2, 2010, on charges of extortion. Guarraci was released on bail, but Nobile was remanded because of his violence-checkered past. That the boss of a Mafia family would be

179

engaging in this kind of 1920s-style extortion indicates the sad state of the Mafia in the twenty-first century.

And then, a few months after the pizzeria fiasco, January 20, 2011, became a watershed day in the history of organized crime. Cobbling together sixteen unrelated indictments, the FBI swept up all the named defendants in a mega-raid of epic proportions. Over 125 suspected crime figures and associates were brought in, from New York to Rhode Island. And, like many of the recent mega-busts designed to let the traditional Mafia know that the FBI has not forgotten about them despite the Justice Department's War on Terrorism–centric priorities, New Jersey–based wiseguys were part of the mix.

One if the indictments centered on the activities of Jerry Balzano and Joseph Collina, both alleged soldiers in the DeCavalcante family. Their crimes were decidedly old-school: extortion, dealing in stolen property and securities, and trafficking in contraband cigarettes. Coming on the heels of the Guarraci indictment, and considering the generally already-disheveled state of the crime family, it was certainly a blow to the small, insular group.

But the blows against the DeCavalcantes only kept coming. In March of 2015, ten members and associates of the DeCavalcante crime family were arrested in New Jersey and Las Vegas. Mob member Charles Stango, consigliere Frank Nigro, and associate Paul Colella were charged with attempting to murder a rival mob member in New Jersey. The remaining defendants were part of a mob-backed cocaine-trafficking operation.

Sources say that a new crew of the DeCavalcantes was operating in Toms River, a fast-growing New Jersey township, directly across Barnegat Bay from Seaside Heights. And it was members of this new crew that were arrested in the March 2015 sweep of DeCavalcante gangsters. Among other crimes, the group was charged with trafficking in cocaine and a prostitution ring in the township. Three Toms River men were arrested.

Then, time came calling for two bosses in less than a year. John Riggi died on August 3, 2015, Frank Guarraci on April 14, 2016. Both men were laid out at the Corsentino Home for Funerals, with a mass at Saint Anthony's Church, back in the old Peterstown neighborhood of Elizabeth. The family had fallen a long way since Sam DeCavalcante had died of a heart attack back on Friday, February 7, 1997, while at a rehab center in Fort Lauderdale, Florida. His funeral services were held in Hamilton Township, and he was buried in the Greenwood Cemetery in Trenton. The arrangements were also handled by the Corsentino Home for Funerals. The funeral home had been owned for many years by DeCavalcante family member Carl Corsentino. It was at the funeral parlor that, according to mob turncoat Anthony Rotondo, the DeCavalcantes utilized the double-decker coffin to dispose of bodies. There would be a false bottom in the casket, and they would stuff a murder victim's body inside for disposal.

Among New Jersey mobsters who turned government informant were a number of gangsters in the DeCavalcante family, including their acting boss Vinnie "Oceans" Palermo, stemming from the December 2, 1999, arrest of over thirty members of the crime family. Others in the crime family turned, including capo Anthony Rotondo and soldier Anthony Capo. By the mid-2000s over forty members of the DeCavalcantes were imprisoned, effectively crippling the family's structure.

The other crime families operating in New Jersey fared about as well. The Genovese family still maintained considerable influence and hold over their remaining rackets in New Jersey. In 2004, New Jersey State Police fanned out across the state and arrested over two dozen members and associates of the Genovese family, including soldier Joe "the Eagle" Gatto, son of the late capo Louis "Streaky" Gatto, a former Genovese power player who died in 2002. Though the Jersey Police's case promised to rip the lid off a massive bookmaking operation that was tied to four other crime families, the Eagle escaped indictment, later dying in 2010. Joe Gatto also died in 2010, leaving his crew leaderless. By 2010 authorities had identified three main captains leading Jersey Genovese crews: Ludwig "Ninni" Bruschi, Angelo Prisco, and Silvio DeVita.

The ranks of mobsters who left the life to start anew as protected witnesses increased, as did those who merely did what they needed to do to extricate themselves from a life that held little regard or loyalty or friendship. "Would I cooperate again?" asks one former Jersey wiseguy, rhetorically.

> I'd like to say no. But the essential self-serving nature of a wiseguy is still there. When you become part of the life, you piss your future away one way or the other. When you "turn," my advice is to be cremated, because you deservedly deserve to have your grave pissed on. I was this "nothing" in the big picture. My legacy is, "That guy? Yeah, I remember that rat." Unfortunate, because once it was, "That guy? Good kid." No excuses, yet in a very self-serving, nonhypocritical way, I can live with it. You want to be a mob guy, leave your conscience at the door. Because in actuality it is a rat's life. Brothers kill brothers, friends lug each other to get clipped when ordered. One day you get a call. "Did you hear so-and-so got clipped??" And you answer, "No shit! I just had lunch with him yesterday. Fucking shame. Okay, forget that, how did we do last night? We had a lot of action on the Knicks?" . . . Mob Life 101.[1]

In 2016, the New Jersey State Commission of Investigation initiated a series of hearings into the lax regulation and oversight of the state's waste-disposal industry—specifically, the disposal of contaminated soil and construction debris and the construction-recycling industry. The hearings stemmed from the SCI's 2011 report, *Industrious Subversion*, which detailed "evidence that convicted felons, including organized members and associates, profit heavily from commercial recycling, which, through a lucrative adjunct to solid waste, has remained largely unregulated."[2]

It was a story that had been repeated over some forty-odd years. Despite the efforts of the SCI, organized crime was still finding ways to infiltrate the industry, albeit at a lower level than they had in the past when the unregulated nature of the industry had left things wide open. One of the examples the SCI cited as an example of a mob figure still in the industry despite SCI's best efforts to keep him out was Joseph Lemmo Jr., described as a Genovese associate whom the SCI had cited as far back as 1989. With records for racketeering, tax evasion, firearms, and drug distribution, Lemmo kept his involvement in the industry with a South Plainfield, New Jersey, trucking company. Only after additional work by the SCI did the state finally bring the law down on Lemmo, and he sold his company in 2009.

The report went on to detail other Genovese and Gambino crime figures and even the alleged one-time acting boss of the Philadelphia mob, Joseph "Uncle Joe" Ligambi, who were deeply involved in New Jersey waste-disposal, trucking, and recycling companies.

In late 2016, a large-scale mob bust netted dozens of wiseguys from the Bonanno, Lucchese, Gambino, and Genovese crime families, as well as Skinny Joey Merlino, whom the feds believe is really the boss of the Philadelphia mob, even as he maintains he is retired in Boca Raton. Among those arrested were New Jersey–based guys Marco "the Old Man" Minuto, long-time Lucchese guy from Upper Saddle River, Anthony "Tony the Cripple" Cassetta from Belmar, and Daniel Marino Jr., son of a longtime powerful capo in the Gambino family. Daniel Jr. lives in Short Hills.

The current director of the SCI was asked about the arrest, showing that, despite decades of law-enforcement action against traditional organized crime, the mob, though significantly depleted, is still around in New Jersey. "Tony Soprano may have gone off the air, but the mob never did. In the real world these guys are still active, and, as this indictment shows, they haven't faded away—because there's a lot of money to be made."[3]

As of the writing of this book, some of the mobsters arrested in the August 2016 sweep have pled out for reduced sentences, with only a few, including Joey Merlino, opting to go to trial. But it was only one of a number of mob arrests and indictment in the mid-2000s. With the redirection of federal agencies' priorities shifting to terrorism in the post–9/11 world, there have been discussion about how the fight against organized crime has been affected and whether the Mafia would find a way with the decreased scrutiny to make a comeback. In some ways assimilation into greater society has lessened the recruiting pool for the Mafia, as it did for Irish- and Jewish-American gangsters in years prior. But as with any power vacuum, when there is one in the underworld, there are always groups quick to move in.

In 2004, the SCI came out with a comprehensive overview of the chang-ing nature of organized crime in New Jersey. And while that report is over a decade old, its conclusions are still valid in the current underworld scene. The report talked of the rise of "heavily armed drug-trafficking gangs"[4] and the rise of transnational organized-crime syndicates best exemplified but Russian and Eurasian criminal syndicates and the Mexican cartels. Many of these groups concentrate on individual criminal activities here in the United States, making it less likely they'll succeed in infiltrating so many aspects of American life from legitimate businesses to politics as the mob did. And law-enforcement agencies are shifting their priorities and strategies to keep apace with new crime groups and the ways they do business. "Any time you have a demand for illicit goods and services you'll have a group or groups to pro-vide services."[5]

But for all the talk of the mob being dead, a vestige of the past, "elements of la Cosa Nostra are assiduously engaged in efforts to reclaim at least a share of the underworld empire they dominated until its dismantling by pros-ecutions and infighting during the 1980s and 1990s."[6] The traditional mob is still operating out there. There is a ton of money to be made off illegal sports betting alone.[7]

A former New Jersey wiseguy takes a little different view on things. "The mob isn't going away. The talent pool has thinned, and that enhanced thin-ness will eventually seep into the cracks of law enforcement. The best guys ever in the mob were the guys from the greatest generation. Despite their proclivity for violence and criminal enterprise, they reflected the dedication of an entire generation."[8]

The Mafia in the United States might be a shadow of its former self, but in the New York/New Jersey metro area, there are still wiseguys and wan-nabes working scams, extorting businesses, running gambling, selling drugs, and branching out into white-collar crime. And they are continuing a tradi-tion that's over one hundred years old. But even with the dissolution of many of the crime-family crews in New Jersey, competition from emerging ethnic criminal enterprises and street gangs, and the relentless pursuit of law en-forcement, the mob remains a presence in the New Jersey–underworld land-scape.

Notes

1. THE NEWARK FAMILY

1. James A. Edgerton, "Black Hand Murder Trust," *Asbury Park (NJ) Press*, April 16, 1909, 11.

2. Joseph Ricciardi, personal interview with the author about the New Jersey Mafia, e-mail, February 20, 2007.

3. *(Bridgewater, NJ) Courier News*, "In Terror of Black Hand," January 16, 1905.

4. The heart of the neighborhood, Seventh Avenue, still exists today, though much of the old buildings and businesses were felled by urban renewal in the 1950s.

5. Edgerton, "Black Hand Murder Trust."

6. *(New Jersey) Courier News*, "Italy and America Both Warring on the Italian Criminal," January 28, 1911.

7. Michael Immerso, *Newark's Little Italy: The Vanished First Ward* (New Brunswick, NJ: Rutgers University Press, 1999).

8. G. V. Straus, "The Newark, NJ Police," *The Police Journal* 7 (March 1921), 78.

9. Ibid.

10. Adubato's family was recognized at a Police Unity ceremony at the Newark fallen-officers memorial in 2016.

11. John P. Wilgus, *La Cosa Nostra—Newark Division.* Newark Field Office, Federal Bureau of Investigation, 1963.

12. *New York Times*, "2 Slain, 3 Wounded by Jersey Gunmen; Score of Revolver Shots Rake Candy Store in the Italian Section of Newark," August 23, 1935, 5.

13. *Trenton Evening News*, "Lottery Gunfire Kills Two," August 22, 1935.

14. *Asbury Park (NJ) Press*, "Shooting Witness Held," August 27, 1935.

15. *Plainfield (NJ) Courier-News*, "Former Boxer Slain, Brother Is Wounded," February 23, 1937.

16. D'Amico ended up in Puerto Rico, where he died on October 1, 1975.

17. *Philadelphia Inquirer*, "2 Gangsters Slain, Drowned in Jersey," September 14, 1931.

18. Milk's identity is not revealed but likely is Frank Majuri.

19. Criminal complaint, United States v. Charles Stango et al., (D.N.J. 2015, Mag. no. 15-3528), available online at http://bitterqueen.typepad.com/files/decavalcante-complaint.pdf.

20. Limited, "Anthony Rotondo 2005 Cross Examination," *The Black Hand Forum*, posted by B., May 7, 2016, http://theblackhand.club/forum/viewtopic.php?f=29&t=1824&hilit=rotondo+cross+examination (registration required).

21. John P. Wilgus, *La Cosa Nostra—Newark Division*, Newark Field Office, Federal Bureau of Investigation, 1963.

22. John Patrick Devlin, *La Cosa Nostra*, Newark, Federal Bureau of Investigation, 1967.

2. DRY YEARS IN JERSEY

1. William G. Hosie, "An Honest Bootlegger Can Make Money; They're Mostly Crooks; Says 'King' McCoy," *Brooklyn Daily Eagle*, December 16, 1923, 61.

2. Ibid.

3. Harlan S. Miller, "'Rum Row' Produces Volsteadian Hero in Mccoy, Skipper Chief," *Pittsburgh Post*, November 28, 1923.

4. Don Linsky, *Atlantic City and Gaming*, e-book, 1st ed. (N.p.: Eagleton Institute of Politics, 2014).

5. Michael Clark and Dan Good, "Nucky Johnson: The Man Who Ran Atlantic City for 30 Years," *Press of Atlantic City*, August 15, 2010, http://www.pressofatlanticcity.com/blogs/ boardwalk_empire/nucky-johnson-the-man-who-ran-atlantic-city-for-years/article_4277415c-a815-11df-be3f-001cc4c002e0.html.

6. *Asbury Park (NJ) Press*, "Says Booze Flows in Atlantic City," March 10, 1924.

7. George Anastasia, author and journalist, personal interview with the author regarding the Bruno-Scarfo family, email, March 18, 2017.

8. Linsky, *Atlantic City and Gaming*.

9. *Asbury Park (NJ) Press*, "Enoch Johnson 'Real Governor,'" April 2, 1929.

10. *MonopolyCity.com* (blog), "Early Hotels—From Atlantic City's Nostalgic Past," 2008, http://www.monopolycity.com/ac_earlyhotels.html.

11. Bill Tonelli, *Mob Fest '29: The True Story behind the Birth of Organized Crime* (San Francisco: Byliner, 2012).

12. *Baltimore Sun*, "Atlantic City Police Don't Want Capone Around," May 16, 1929.

13. United Press, "Capone Made Peace with Moran Gang," *Mount Carmel (PA) Item*, May 17, 1929.

14. *Albany (OR) Democrat-Herald*, "Feud at End," May 17, 1929, 1.

15. J. Anne Funderburg, *Bootleggers and Beer Barons of the Prohibition Era*, 1st ed. (Jefferson, NC: McFarland, 2014).

16. *Red Bank (NJ) Register*. "Killed in Street Fight." October 24, 1923.

17. *Asbury Park (NJ) Press*, "Rum Runners Boast of Busy Christmas Trade," December 26, 1923.

3. ZWILLMAN

1. Though some sources spell it *Longie*, for consistency's sake this book references Zwillman's nickname as Longy, throughout.

2. Mark A. Stuart, *Gangster No. 2: Longy Zwillman, the Man Who Invented Organized Crime* (Washington, DC: Lyle Stuart, 1985).

3. Myron Sugerman, personal interview with the author regarding New Jersey organized crime, Newark, New Jersey, February 7, 2017.

4. Ibid.

5. Stuart, *Gangster No. 2*.

6. Warren Grover, *Nazis in Newark* (New Brunswick, NJ: Transaction Publishers, 2003), 42.

7. Federal Bureau of Investigation. "Abner Zwillman, Part 1 of 3." May 21, 1935–October 25, 1955. BUFILE 62-36085. https://vault.fbi.gov/Abner%20Zwillman/ Abner%20Zwillman%20Part%201%20of%207.

8. Stuart, *Gangster No. 2.*

9. US Congress, *Hearings Before the Select Committee to Investigate Organized Crime in Interstate Commerce*, Washington, DC, 1951.

10. Irina Reyn, ed., *Living on the Edge of the World: New Jersey Writers Take On the Garden State* (New York: Touchstone, 2007), 166.

11. Myron Sugerman, personal interview with the author regarding New Jersey organized crime, Newark, New Jersey, February 7, 2017.

12. Federal Bureau of Investigation, "Abner 'Longie' Zwillman FBI Files."

13. *Asbury Park (NJ) Press*, "State Ready to Aid Vote Probe," November 19, 1932, 3.

14. Today Waverly is Muhammad Ali Avenue, and Jesse Allen Park is the lot where the Third Ward Political Club used to stand.

15. Stuart, *Gangster No. 2.*

16. US Congress, *Hearings Before the Select Committee To Investigate Organized Crime In Interstate Commerce* (1951).

17. Reyn, *Living on the Edge of the World*, 166.

18. Grover, *Nazis in Newark*, 45.

19. Martha Glaser, *The German-American Bund in New Jersey*, 1st ed. (Ann Arbor: University of Michigan Press, 1974), 33.

20. Rising Sun Brewing Co. v. United States, 55 F.2d 827 (1932).

21. Gerald Tomlinson, *Murdered in Jersey* (New Brunswick, NJ: Rutgers University Press, 1994), 35.

22. *Pittsburgh Post-Gazette*, "Dry Agent Is Slain in Raid on Brewery," September 20, 1930, 1.

23. *Philadelphia Inquirer*, "Suspect Seized Here in Murder of Dry Agent," September 22, 1930, 4.

24. Federal Bureau of Investigation, Special Agent in Charge, Newark Field Office, *Top Hoodlum Program Weekly Summary, Anthony "Ham" Dolasco Herman 'Red Cohen*, 1960.

25. *(Wilmington, DE) Morning News*, "Fugitive in Slaying of Dry Agent Caught," October 20, 1933.

26. *Brooklyn Daily Eagle*, "Waxey Gordon Is a Coward Just like the Rest, Says Sullivan," May 23, 1933, 3.

27. Tona Frank v. Metropolitan Life Insurance Company (Supreme Court Appellate Division- First Department 1934), available online at https://books.google.com/books.

4. DUTCH, LONGY, JERRY, AND THE BOOT

1. United Press. "Billion Annual Tribute at Stake in New York's Vice and Racket Inquiry." *(Hammond, IN) Times*, July 24, 1935, 68.

2. Paul Sann, *Kill The Dutchman! The Story Of Dutch Schultz*, 1st ed. (N.p.: Birdye's Books LLC, 2015).

3. Ibid.

4. Ibid.

5. Ibid.

6. The Disposable Heroes of Hiphopricy, "The Last Words of Dutch Schultz (This Is Insane)," *Spare Ass Annie and Other Tales*, Island Red Label PRCD 5003-2, 1993, CD.

7. Richard Stratton, "The Man Who Killed Dutch Schultz," *GQ*, September 2001.

8. *(Bridgewater, NJ) Courier-News*, "Zwillman Balks in Crime Quiz; Faces Recall by Jury Today," August 16, 1939, 1.

9. E. A. Tamm, *Re: Crime Situation in Newark*, memo to the director, Federal Bureau of Investigation, Newark, 1935.

10. Federal Bureau of Investigation, "Abner Zwillman, Part 1 of 3," May 21, 1935–October 25, 1955, BUFILE 62-36085, https://vault.fbi.gov/Abner%20Zwillman/Abner%20Zwillman%20Part%201%20of%207.

11. Special Agent M. B. Parker, *Nevada Gambling Industry*, Federal Bureau of Investigation, Las Vegas, 1964.

12. Myron Sugerman, personal interview on New Jersey organized crime, Newark, New Jersey, February 7, 2017.

13. US Congress, *Hearings Before The Select Committee . . . Commerce* (1951).

14. Ibid.

15. Ibid.

16. Ibid.

17. Ibid.

18. Ibid.

19. Richard Linnett, *In the Godfather Garden: The Long Life and Times of Richie "the Boot" Boiardo* (New Brunswick, NJ: Rutgers University Press, 2013).

20. *(Wilmington, DE) Evening Journal*, "Men, Ablaze, Flee as Still Explodes," October 25, 1927.

21. *Asbury Park (NJ) Press*, "Bassone Put on Year Probation," May 24, 1930.

22. Stuart, *Gangster No. 2*.

23. *(Wilmington, DE) Morning News*, "Newark Gangster Is 'Put On Spot,'" November 27, 1930.

24. John Lipari, "Vittorio Castle 1937–1952," *Newark's Attic* (blog), March 27, 2016, https://newarksattic.blog/2016/03/27/vittorio-castle-1937-1952/. The site where Vittorio's Castle used to stand is now the Winona Lippman Gardens apartment complex.

25. Linnett, *In the Godfather Garden*, 58.

26. Victor Carelli, *Benjamin Kutlow*, Federal Bureau of Investigation, New York, 1959.

27. *"They had now the hopper . . ."* Mickey Wichinsky of Las Vegas, associate of Catena and Green, was the one who came up with the hopper unit that revolutionized the slot-machine business. Myron Sugerman, personal interview on New Jersey organized crime, Newark, New Jersey, February 7, 2017.

28. Ibid.

29. Katz was convicted of bribery and sentenced to seven years in prison. He was paroled on March 27, 1964.

30. Stuart, *Gangster No. 2*.

31. Ibid.

32. Dorothy Kilgallen, "Some Question Suicide of 'Longie' Zwillman," syndicated, March 5, 1959.

33. Stuart, *Gangster No. 2*.

34. Myron Sugerman, personal interview on New Jersey organized crime, Newark, New Jersey, February 7, 2017.

5. THE MORETTI HIT

1. Some sources say the full name was Duke's Bar and Grill.

2. Drew Pearson, "Washington Merry Go Round," syndicated column, 1957, archived at http://auislandora.wrlc.org/islandora/object/pearson%3A1?page=761.

3. Ed Scarpo [pseud.], "The Mafia Hit the Jackpot with the Slot-Machine," *Cosa Nostra News* (website), June 9, 2015, http://www.cosanostranews.com/2015/06/the-mafia-hit-jackpot-with-slot-machine.html.

4. Joe Adonis's real name was Giuseppe Doto.

5. Moretti was born June 4, 1894, in New York City.

6. US Congress, *Hearings Before the Select Committee to Investigate Organized Crime in Interstate Commerce*, Washington, DC, 1951.

7. Ibid.

8. Ibid.

9. Ibid.

10. Ibid.

11. US Congress, *Senate Resolution 202, 81st Congress*, 1950.

12. US Congress, *Hearings Before the Select Committee . . . Commerce*, 1951.

13. Ibid.

14. US Congress, *Brief on Federal Intervention in Organized Gambling*, 1951.

15. The Elbow Room was located at 793 Palisade Avenue and now houses an Italian restaurant, Villa Amalfi.

16. One version has Moretti being driven up in the Packard by a chauffeur, possibly Genovese mobster Peter LaPlaca.

17. Thom L. Jones, "Whack Out on Willie Moretti." *Gangsters Inc* (website), November 18, 2008. http://gangstersinc.ning.com/profiles/blogs/whack-out-on-willie-moretti.

18. "A Gangster Is Buried in the Old-Time Style, October 22, 1951, 36–37, archived at https://books.google.com/books?id=rFQEAAAAMBAJ&pg=PA36&lpg=PA36 -v=onepage& q&f=false.

19. Federal Bureau of Investigation, *La Cosa Nostra*, 1963.

20. Volz and Bridge, *The Mafia Talks*, 29.

21. Senate Permanent Subcommittee on Investigations, United States of America, *Organized Crime and Illicit Traffic in Narcotics: Hearing Before the U.S. Senate Permanent Subcommittee on Investigations, Part 1, Part 2, Part 3, Part 4, Part 5, and Index, September 25, 27, October 1, 2, 8, and 9, 1963; October 10, 11, 15, and 16, 1963; October 29, 1963, July 28, 29, and 30, 1964* ([Washington, DC]: US Congress, 1964), archived at https://www.ncjrs.gov/pdffiles1/Digitization/119303NCJRS.pdf.

22. The unnamed informant was likely California mobster Frank Bompensiero.

23. *St. Petersburg (FL) Times*, "New Jersey Police Chief, Awaiting Trial, Ends Life," October 7, 1951, archived at https://news.google.com/newspapers?id=yR0LAAAAIBAJ&sjid=GE8DAAAAIBAJ&pg=2035,2095540&dq=fort+lee+police.

24. Senate Permanent Subcommittee on Investigations, *Organized Crime and Illicit Traffic in Narcotics*.

6. THE DECAVALCANTES

1. William Sherman and Matt Sullivan, "Bidder End for Mob House," *New York Daily News*, August 4, 2002, http://www.nydailynews.com/archives/news/bidder-mob-house-article-1.493826.

2. Various sources give numbers between fifty-eight and sixty-two detained. The official 1958 State of New York report gives the number at sixty-two (or more) attendees, sixty detained, fifty-eight identified from out of town, and fifty-eight questioned. Later, twenty of the men were hit with federal conspiracy charges.

3. United States v. Bufalino, 285 F.2d 408, (2d cir. 1960).

4. Gary Hafer, "Mafia in Apalachin," *GreaterOwego.com*, accessed November 12, 2016, http://www.greaterowego.com/apalachin/apalachin01.htm.

5. Some sources have it as LaRasso.

6. *(Bridgewater, NJ) Courier-News*. "Attend Outing," May 14, 1928.

7. John McCullough, "NJ Beer Baron Is Named Chief Suspect in Slayings," *Philadelphia Inquirer*, September 23, 1930.

8. Federal Bureau of Investigation, "Angelo De Carlo, Aka. AR," memorandum from Special Agent in Charge, Newark Field Office, to Director, in *Frank Sinatra FBI Files*, November 7, 1962, https://archive.org/stream/SinatraFBI/sinatra09c_djvu.txt.

9. Volz and Bridge, *The Mafia Talks*, 24.

10. C. A. Evans, *Criminal Intelligence Digest*, US Department of Justice, government memorandum, 1964.

11. The earliest records available indicate DeCavalcante grew up in Westfield, New Jersey, a town in Union County.

12. Volz and Bridge, *The Mafia Talks*, 21.

13. US Treasury Department, Bureau of Narcotics, *Mafia: The Government's Secret File on Organized Crime*, 1st ed. (New York: HarperCollins, 2007), 284.

14. National Commission for the Review of Federal and State Laws Relating to Wiretapping and Electronic Surveillance, *Commission Hearings, Volume 2* (Washington, DC: 1976), text available at https://archive.org/stream/commissionhearin02unit/commissionhearin02unit_djvu. txt.

15. Pennsylvania: Pennsylvania Crime Commission, *1975–76 Report* (St. Davids: Pennsylvania Crime Commission, 1977), archived at https://www.ncjrs.gov/pdffiles1/Digitization/ 49097NCJRS.pdf.

16. Raymond Tuers, "The Mob and Ocean County: FBI Takes Show Penetration," *Asbury Park (NJ) Press*, February 2, 1970.

17. The tapes were made public on June 10, 1969.

18. Mike Sabella was a New York–based capo in the Bonanno family at that time; ziginette is a popular Sicilian card game. Volz and Bridge, *The Mafia Talks*, 98.

19. National Commission . . . Surveillance, *Commission Hearings*.

20. Volz and Bridge, *The Mafia Talks*, 165.

21. Ibid., 174.

22. Gaspar DiGregorio's family is the Bonanno family. National Commission . . . Surveillance, *Commission Hearings*.

23. The widows are the wives of Phil Amari and Nick Delmore. Volz and Bridge, *The Mafia Talks*, 97.

24. National Commission . . . Surveillance, *Commission Hearings*.

25. Ibid.

26. Ibid.

7. ON THE WIRE

1. SAGE Publishing, *CQ Almanac Online Edition: 1963*, 2017, https://library.cqpress.com/ cqalmanac/document.php?id=cqal63-1315434 (registration required).

2. Federal Bureau of Investigation, *The Decarlo Tape Transcripts (Original Full Set)*, n.d.

3. Indiviglio was killed in 1965.

4. Federal Bureau of Investigation, "Angelo De Carlo, Aka. AR."

5. John P. Wilgus, *The Criminal Commission*, Federal Bureau of Investigation, Newark Division, 1963.

6. Robert Wells, *Anti Racketeering Conspiracy*, New York, Federal Bureau of Investigation, 1968.

7. Polidori was a Genovese soldier from East Paterson, in Gene Catena's crew. He was originally under Willie Moretti but switched over to Catena after Moretti's murder.

8. Federal Bureau of Investigation, *The Decarlo Tape Transcripts*.

9. Frederick T. Martens, *We'll Make You an Offer You Can't Refuse: A Primer on the Investigation of Public Corruption*, 1st ed. (N.p.: Mint Associates, 2015), 1.

10. Federal Bureau of Investigation, *The Decarlo Tape Transcripts*.

11. Paul Hoffman, "The Unmaking of Mayor Addonizio," *Tiger in the Court: Herbert J. Stern* (Chicago: Playboy Press), full text available at http://mafianj.com/addonizio/addonizio8. shtml.

12. National Commission . . . Surveillance. *Commission Hearings*.

13. Ibid.

14. Federal Bureau of Investigation, *The Decarlo Tape Transcripts*.

15. Ibid.

16. Fred Cook, "The People v. The Mob; Or, Who Rules New Jersey?" *New York Times*, February 1, 1970, http://www.nytimes.com/1970/02/01/archives/the-people-v-the-mob-or-who-rules-new-jersey-the-people-v-the-mob.html.

17. United States v. Angelo Decarlo et al. Appellant in No. 18705. Appeal of Daniel Cecere, 458 F.2d 358 (3d Cir. 1972).

18. Ibid.

19. Cook, "The People v. The Mob."

20. Murray Illson, "DeCarlo of Mafia Dead of Cancer," *New York Times*, October 21, 1973, http://www.nytimes.com/1973/10/21/archives/decarlo-of-mafia-dead-of-cancer-impropriety-denied-mobster.html.

8. BAYONNE JOE

1. *Lebanon (PA) Daily News*, "Retired Gambling Czar Is Burned, Beaten," May 28, 1971, 21.

2. Joan Cook, "Joseph (Newsboy) Moriarty, 68, Longtime Jersey Gambler, Dies," *New York Times*, February 26, 1979, http://www.nytimes.com/1979/02/26/archives/joseph-newsboy-moriarty-68-longtime-jersey-gambler-dies-money-found.html.

3. *Lebanon (PA) Daily News*, "Retired Gambling Czar."

4. US Senate, Special Committee to Investigate Organized Crime in Interstate Commerce, "(b) Northern New Jersey," *Kefauver Committee: Final Report, Aug. 31, 1951*, 82nd Cong. (1951), 65–72, archived at http://www.onewal.com/kef/kef4.html#northern.

5. Lincoln J. Stokes, *Joseph Arthur Zicarelli*, Newark, Federal Bureau of Investigation, 1959.

6. Paul G. Durkin, *Harold Konigsberg*, New York, Federal Bureau of Investigation, 1965.

7. Stokes, *Joseph Arthur Zicarelli*.

8. *Life*, "The Congressman and the Hoodlum," August 9, 1968, 22, archived at https://books.google.com/books?id=RT8EAAAAMBAJ&pg=PA22&lpg=PA22&dq.

9. *Delaware County Daily Times*, "Wiretaps Records Involve Officials," July 11, 1969.

10. Vito DeFillippo was the New York underboss.

11. Federal Bureau of Investigation, Special Agent in Charge, *La Cosa Nostra, Memorandum*, Newark, 1969.

9. BRUNO AND THE DOWN NECK MOB

1. Former New Jersey wiseguy, personal interview with the author regarding Newark and the Down Neck mob, in person, January 2017.

2. Volz and Bridge, *The Mafia Talks*, 22.

3. George Anastasia, e-mail interview with the author, regarding Bruno-Scarfo family, March 18, 2017.

4. Jim Barry, "Trouble with a Capital N," *Philadelphia City Paper*, April 19–26, 2001, text available at https://mycitypaper.com/articles/041901/news.mob.shtml.

5. Anastasia, *Blood And Honor*, 95.

6. Myron Sugerman, personal interview with the author regarding New Jersey organized crime, Newark, New Jersey, February 7, 2017.

7. National Commission . . . Surveillance, *Commission Hearings*.

8. Former New Jersey wiseguy, personal interview with the author regarding Newark and the Down Neck mob, in person, January 2017.

9. He was also arrested in 1977 as part of a stolen-property ring that included Bruno guy Joe Sodano and Genovese soldier Joseph Gatto.

10. *Lansing (MI) State Journal*, "Six Men Nabbed in Armed Robbery," November 10, 1947.

11. This information appeared on a wanted poster for Gerardo Fusella, issued October 19, 1944, by the US Department of Justice.

12. Paul G. Durkin, *Harold Konigsberg, Bureau Airtel 8/16/65*, Newark, Federal Bureau of Investigation, 1965.

13. George Fresolone and Robert J. Wagman, *Blood Oath: The Heroic Story of a Gangster Turned Government Agent Who Brought Down One of America's Most Powerful Mob Families* (New York: Simon and Schuster, 1995), 44.

14. Former New Jersey wiseguy, personal interview with the author regarding Newark and the Down Neck mob, in person, January 2017.

15. Fresolone and Wagman, *Blood Oath*, 46.

16. John Patrick Devlin, *La Cosa Nostra—Newark Division*, Newark, Federal Bureau of Investigation, 1967.

17. Federal Bureau of Investigation, *The Decarlo Tape Transcripts (Original Full Set)*, 1962.

18. J. Robert Pearce, Special Agent, *Angelo Bruno, Special Summary Report*, Philadelphia, Federal Bureau of Investigation, 1962).

19. Devlin, *La Cosa Nostra*.

20. Francis Patrick, "Killer Who Squealed on 9 Mobsters Faces Death Each Day," *San Antonio Star*, June 6, 1976.

21. Paul Hoffman, *To Drop A Dime* (New York: Putnam, 1976), 104.

10. THE GENOVESE FAMILY

1. Eric Pace, "Eboli Chauffeur Being Questioned," *New York Times*, July 18, 1972, http://www.nytimes.com/1972/07/18/archives/eboli-chauffeur-being-questioned-tells-police-he-didnt-see-killer.html.

2. Former New Jersey wiseguy, personal interview with the author regarding the Genovese family in New Jersey, e-mail, November 2016.

3. Myron Sugerman, personal interview with the author regarding New Jersey organized crime, Newark, New Jersey, February 7, 2017.

4. William Eastmond, "Indictment of Byrne's Ex Law Partner Part of Wider Probe," *Asbury Park (NJ) Press*, December 6, 1977.

5. Today West Paterson is known as Woodland Park. Louis DiVita, *Mob in New Jersey—Interview*, phone interview, 2016.

6. Ralph Blumenthal, "Illegal Dumping of Toxins Laid to Organized Crime," June 5, 1983, http://www.nytimes.com/1983/06/05/nyregion/illegal-dumping-of-toxins-laid-to-organized-crime.html?pagewanted=all.

7. Bob Delaney, *Covert: My Years Infiltrating the Mob*, with Dave Scheiber, 1st ed. (New York: Union Square Press, 2008), 95.

8. Delaney, *Covert*, 95.

9. Ibid, 82.

10. Robert Rudolph, *The Boys from New Jersey: How the Mob Beat the Feds*, 1st ed. (New Brunswick, NJ: Rutgers University Press, 1995), 69.

11. THE STATE COMMISSION OF INVESTIGATION

1. Lee Seglem, SCI acting director, and Mike Hoey, former SCI agent, personal interview with the author on the creation of the SCI, telephone, September 29, 2016.

2. Chris Baud, "'Entirely Too Comfortable' with the Jersey Mafia," *Trentonian*, December 2, 2001, text available at http://www.capitalcentury.com/1970.html.

3. State of New Jersey Commission of Investigation, *Industrious Subversion: Circumvention of Oversight in Solid Waste and Recycling in New Jersey* (Trenton: State of New Jersey Commission of Investigation, 2011), http://www.state.nj.us/sci/pdf/Solid Waste Report.pdf.

4. New Jersey State Commission of Investigation, *Report to the Special Committee to Review the State Commission of Investigation* (Trenton: New Jersey State Commission of Investigation, 1995.

5. Sinatra v. New Jersey State Commission of Investigation, 311 F.Supp. 678 (D.N.J. 1970).

6. *Charleston (WV) Daily Mail,* "Frank Sinatra to Spurn N.J. Crime Inquiry," October 22, 1969, 12.

7. Catena v. Seidl, 66 N.J. 32, 327 A.2d 658 (1974).

8. Myron Sugerman, personal interview with the author regarding New Jersey organized crime, Newark, New Jersey, February 7, 2017.

9. Philip Leonetti, Scott M. Burnstein, and Christopher Graziano, *Mafia Prince: Inside America's Most Violent Crime Family and the Bloody Fall of la Cosa Nostra* (San Diego: Running Press, 2014), 39.

10. In Re Ippolito, 75 N.J. 435 (1978).

11. New Jersey State Commission of Investigation, *Report to the Special Committee.*

12. Volz and Bridge, *The Mafia Talks,* 116.

13. Walter H. Waggoner, "Accused Mobsters Still Silent," *New York Times,* November 24, 1974, http://www.nytimes.com/1974/11/24/archives/accused-mobsters-still-silent-catena-practices-golf-the-silent-nine.html.

14. Guy Sterling, "Arrest Ends Long Search for Suspect in Mob Killing," *(Newark, NJ) Star-Ledger,* March 13, 2007, text available online at http://johnnieupahts1.proboards.com/thread/36. The gunman then pulled out a .38 and shot Lardiere three times, in the head, neck, and stomach. The sixty-eight-year-old Lardiere was dead.

15. Press State House Bureau, "Russo Is Freed after Agreeing to Talk with SCI," *Asbury Park (NJ) Press,* April 12, 1974.

12. THE BIG BETS

1. The building is now the Bonanza Gift Shop.

2. Oscar Goodman, personal interview with author, Las Vegas, Nevada, December 3, 2016.

3. Lane Bonner and Terrence Doughterty, *ELSUR Logs, 1/15/63–1/18/63,* electronic surveillance logs, Federal Bureau of Investigation, Miami Field Division, 1963.

4. Commission of Investigation of the State of New Jersey, *Report for the Year 1972 of the Commission of Investigation of the State of New Jersey to the Governor and the Legislature of the State of New Jersey* (Trenton: State of New Jersey Commission of Investigation, 1973), http://www.state.nj.us/sci/pdf/annual3-1972.pdf.

5. State of New Jersey Commission of Investigation, *Report for the Year 1974 of the Commission of Investigation of the State of New Jersey to the Governor and the Legislature of the State of New Jersey* (Trenton: State of New Jersey Commission of Investigation, 1975), available online at https://dspace.njstatelib.org/xmlui/bitstream/handle/10929/17136/5annual1974.pdf?sequence=1&isAllowed=y.

6. *Asbury Park (NJ) Press,* "Las Vegas a Roller Coaster to Late Shore Rackets Boss." January 13, 1980, 90.

7. Ibid.

8. Anthony Russo's collection of cats was a nod to his past as a cat burglar—where he allegedly got the nickname, Little Pussy.

9. *Asbury Park (NJ) Press,* "Juror Ousted after Talk with Defendant," May 3, 1980, 12.

10. US Senate, "(b) Northern New Jersey."

11. Jonathan Van Meter, *The Last Good Time: Skinny D'Amato, the Notorious 500 Club, and the Rise and Fall of Atlantic City,* 1st ed. (New York: Three Rivers Press, 2003), 136.

12. Special Agent in Charge, Philadelphia, *Angelo Bruno, FBI Airtel 6/22/62,* Federal Bureau of Investigation, 1962.

13. Richard C. Ross, *Nicodemo Dominick Scarfo*, Newark, Federal Bureau of Investigation, 1973.

14. J. Robert Pearce, *Angelo Bruno, Aka Angelo Bruno, Analore (True Name), Ange, Russo*, special summary report, Philadelphia, Federal Bureau of Investigation, 1961.

15. *(Newark, OH) Advocate*, "Boardwalk Possible Center of Crime," December 9, 1976, 30.

16. "Casino Policing Questions Unanswered," *Asbury Park (NJ) Press*, December 12, 1976.

17. Sherry Conohan, "Russo Tapes Tell of Mob's Atlantic City Casino Tie-Ins," *Asbury Park (NJ) Press*, February 11, 1980, 2.

18. Martorano was shot on January 17, 2002, by two gunmen outside his home in Philadelphia. He drove to his doctor's office with shots to the arms and chest. He died of his injuries on February 5, 2002.

19. State of New Jersey Commission of Investigation, *Ninth Annual Report of the Commission of Investigation of the State of New Jersey to the Governor and the Legislature of the State of New Jersey*. Trenton: The Commission of Investigation of the State of New Jersey, 1978. http://www.state.nj.us/sci/pdf/annual9.pdf.

13. SOUTH JERSEY WAR

1. Lyrics from Bruce Springsteen, "Atlantic City," *Nebraska*, Columbia Records CBS 2794, 1982, LP.

2. *Philly.com*, "Mob Scene: 'Tony Bananas,'" YouTube video, 4:12, posted June 2, 2009, https://www.youtube.com/watch?v=qPnCotgE9GM.

3. Anastasia, *Blood and Honor*, 91.

4. Ibid, 92.

5. Dennis M. Culnan, "2 Bruno Associates Found Executed in New York," *(New Jersey) Courier-Post*, April 30, 1980.

6. Fresolone and Wagman, *Blood Oath*, 60.

7. Myron Sugerman, in personal interview with the author regarding New Jersey organized crime, Newark, New Jersey, February 7, 2017.

8. Maria Gallagher, "Boom Times for the Mob?" *Philadelphia Daily News*, January 20, 1984.

9. Ibid.

10. J. Robert Pearce, *Angelo Bruno, aka, Special Summary Report*, Philadelphia, FBI, 1962.

11. Pennsylvania Crime Commission, *Organized Crime in Pennsylvania: A Decade of Change; 1990 Report* (Conshohocken: Pennsylvania Crime Commission, 1991), archived at https://www.ncjrs.gov/pdffiles1/Digitization/133208NCJRS.pdf.

12. George Anastasia, personal interview with the author regarding the Bruno-Scarfo family, e-mail, March 6, 2017.

13. Pennsylvania Crime Commission, *Organized Crime in Pennsylvania*.

14. Fresolone and Wagman, *Blood Oath*, 159.

15. George Fresolone died at age forty-eight of a heart attack on March 17, 2002.

16. Former New Jersey wiseguy, personal interview with the author regarding Newark and the Down Neck mob, email, January 2017.

14. THE EAGLE AND VIDEO GAMBLING

1. Volz and Bridge, *The Mafia Talks*, 65.

2. *Around About Peterstown* (Elizabeth, NJ), "John Riggi Passes at Age 90," no. 101 (August/September 2015): 15, archived at http://peterstownnewjersey.com/wp-content/uploads/2013/10/AAPAug15.pdf.

3. Former DeCavalcante associate, personal interview with the author regarding the DeCavalcante family, telephone, July 2016.

4. Ibid.

5. Sherry Conohan, "Riggi Described as Mob Boss at Racketeering Trial." *Asbury Park (NJ) Press*, May 25, 1990, 31.

6. Joseph Ricciardi, personal interview with the author about the New Jersey Mafia, e-mail, February 20, 2017.

7. Former DeCavalcante associate, personal interview with the author regarding the DeCavalcante family, telephone, July 2016.

8. Limited, "Anthony Rotondo 2005 Cross Examination," *The Black Hand Forum*, posted by B., May 7, 2016, http://theblackhand.club/forum/viewtopic.php?f=29&t=1824&hilit=rotondo+cross+examination (registration required).

9. Ibid.

10. Ibid.

11. Ted Sherman, "John Riggi, Jersey Mob Boss Who Inspired 'The Sporanos,'" Dead at 90," *NJ Advance Media*, August 4, 2015.

12. Limited, "Anthony Rotondo 2005 Cross Examination," *The Black Hand Forum*, posted by B., May 7, 2016, http://theblackhand.club/forum/viewtopic.php?f=29&t=1824&hilit=rotondo+cross+examination (registration required).

13. New Jersey State Commission of Investigation, *Video Gambling* (Trenton: New Jersey State Commission of Investigation, 2001), http://www.state.nj.us/sci/pdf/video.pdf.

14. Ibid.

15. Myron Sugerman, personal interview with the author regarding New Jersey organized crime, Newark, New Jersey, February 7, 2017.

16. Ibid.

17. Frank "Frankie Loc" Locascio became consigliere to John Gotti.

18. Myron Sugerman, personal interview with the author regarding New Jersey organized crime, Newark, New Jersey, February 7, 2017.

19. New Jersey State Commission of Investigation, *Video Gambling*.

20. Myron Sugerman, personal interview with the author regarding New Jersey organized crime, Newark, New Jersey, February 7, 2017.

21. Ibid.

22. Joseph Ricciardi, personal interview with the author about the New Jersey Mafia, e-mail, March 2, 2017.

23. Myron Sugerman, personal interview with the author regarding New Jersey organized crime, Newark, New Jersey, February 7, 2017.

24. Guy Sterling, "A Mob Chief's Desire for Respect and Murder," *Newark Star-Ledger*, February 21, 2004.

25. Jim Barry, "Trouble with a Capital N," *Philadelphia City Paper*, April 19–26, 2001, text available at https://mycitypaper.com/articles/041901/news.mob.shtml.

26. State of New Jersey Commission of Investigation, *21st Annual Report: 1989* (Trenton: State of New Jersey Commission of Investigation, 1990), http://www.state.nj.us/sci/pdf/annual21.pdf.

15. ON THE DOCKS

1. John Marzulli, "Dock Union Bigs Go on Trial Accused of Plotting with Mob," *New York Daily News*, September 21, 2005, http://www.nydailynews.com/archives/boroughs/dock-union-bigs-trial-accused-plotting-mob-article-1.566257.

2. Coppola was tracked down by the FBI and arrested in March of 2007.

3. Permanent Subcommittee on Investigations of the Committee on Governmental Affairs United States Senate, *Waterfront Corruption* (Washington, DC: US Senate, 1984).

4. Ibid.

5. Ibid.

6. Ibid.

7. Joseph Goldstein, "Along New York Harbor, 'On the Waterfront' Endures," *New York Times*, January 6, 2017, https://www.nytimes.com/2017/01/06/nyregion/new-york-harbor-on-the-waterfront.html.

16. THE RECEDING TIDE

1. Former New Jersey wiseguy, personal interview with the author regarding the mob in New Jersey, in person, November 2016.

2. State of New Jersey Commission of Investigation, *Industrious Subversion*.

3. Ted Sherman, "Mob Arrests Show Wiseguys Still at Work in N.J., Feds Say," *NJ Advance Media*, August 6, 2016, http://www.nj.com/crime/index.ssf/2016/08/another_big_mob_hit_this_one_b.html.

4. State of New Jersey Commission of Investigation, *The Changing Face of Organized Crime in New Jersey: A Status Report* (Trenton: State of New Jersey Commission of Investigation, 2004), http://www.state.nj.us/sci/pdf/ocreport.pdf.

5. Lee Seglem, acting executive director of SCI, and Mike Hoey, former SCI agent, personal interview with the author on the creation of the SCI, telephone, September 29, 2016.

6. State of New Jersey Commission of Investigation, *The Changing Face of Organized Crime*.

7. Lee Seglem, acting executive director of SCI, and Mike Hoey, former SCI agent, personal interview with the author on the creation of the SCI, telephone, September 29, 2016.

8. Former New Jersey wiseguy, personal interview with the author regarding the current state of mob in New Jersey, e-mail, January 2017.

Bibliography

Abner 'Longy' Zwillman-Kefauver Hearings. Video clip. 1951. Posted at http://www.efootage. com/stock-footage/43939/Abner_Longy_Zwillman-_Kefauver_Hearings/.

Addonizio v. United States, 573 F.2d 147 (3d Cir. 1978).

Albany (OR) Democrat-Herald. "Feud at End," May 17, 1929.

Anastasia, George. *Blood and Honor*. 1st ed. New York: W. Morrow, 1991.

———. *Mob Father*. 1st ed. New York: Zebra, 1993.

Around About Peterstown (Elizabeth, NJ). "John Riggi Passes at Age 90," no. 101 (August/ September 2015): 15. Archived at http://peterstownnewjersey.com/wp-content/uploads/ 2013/10/AAPAug15.pdf.

Asbury Park (NJ) Press. "All Newark Bills Quashed by Porter," January 28, 1940.

———. "Bassone Put on Year Probation." May 24, 1930.

———. "Casino Policing Questions Unanswered." December 12, 1976.

———. "Delmore Farms, Doesn't Worry." August 7, 1953, 1.

———. "Enoch Johnson 'Real Governor.'" April 2, 1929.

———. "Fear Bombs and Guns Will Pick Capone's Successors." May 18, 1929, 5.

———. "Government Trying to Stop Helping to Making Crime Pay." April 8, 1973.

———. "Indict Mayor, 20 Ocean City Police." March 22, 1929.

———. "Juror Ousted after Talk with Defendant." May 3, 1980, 12.

———. "Jury in State Mob Case to Hear Opening Views." March 31, 1980, 6.

———. "Las Vegas a Roller Coaster to Late Shore Rackets Boss." January 13, 1980, 90.

———. "'Longie' Zwillman Gets Six Month Term." December 12, 1930.

———. "9 Arrested Unloading Stolen TVs," June 29, 1977, 57.

———. "Rum Runners Boast of Busy Christmas Trade," December 26, 1923, 1.

———. "Says Booze Flows in Atlantic City," March 10, 1924.

———. "Sinatra Wins Round, Gets Writ against NJ," December 2, 1969.

———. "State Ready to Aid Vote Probe," November 19, 1932, 3.

———. "The Mob and Ocean County: FBI Tapes Show Penetration." February 2, 1970.

———. "Two Men Slain in Jersey Gang War," September 14, 1929.

———. "Shooting Witness Held." August 27, 1935.

———. "Witness Killed, Cop Shot in Rising Sun Outgrowth," November 7, 1932, 1.

Associated Press. "Jury Acquits Mob Figure of Murder, Conspiracy." *Los Angeles Times*, March 9, 2004. http://articles.latimes.com/2004/mar/09/nation/na-mob9.

———. "Police Make Slot Machine Raids." *New York Times*, March 26, 1985. http://www. nytimes.com/1985/03/26/nyregion/police-make-slot-machine-raids.html.

———. "The Region; 3 Guilty of Aiding Mobsters at Casino." *New York Times*, October 23, 1981. http://www.nytimes.com/1981/10/23/nyregion/the-region-3-guilty-of-aiding-mobsters-at-casino.html.

———. "Reputed Crime Figure Is Cleared of Charges." *New York Times*, October 10, 1981. http://www.nytimes.com/1981/10/10/nyregion/reputed-crime-figure-is-cleared-of-charges.html.

Atlanta Constitution. "Liquor Schooner Seized Despite British Registry." September 27, 1921.

Baltimore Sun. "Atlantic City Police Don't Want Capone Around." May 16, 1929.

———. "Zwillman, Ex-Bootlegger Cited in Probe Hangs Self." February 27, 1959.

Barry, Jim. "Trouble with a Capital N." *Philadelphia City Paper*, April 19–26, 2001. Text available at https://mycitypaper.com/articles/041901/news.mob.shtml.

Baud, Chris. "'Entirely Too Comfortable' with the Jersey Mafia." *Trentonian*, December 2, 2001. Text available at http://www.capitalcentury.com/1970.html.

Beckerman, Jim. "Marking the End of an Era for Fort Lee's Riviera Nightclub." *(North Jersey) Record*, December 31, 2013. http://archive.northjersey.com/news/marking-the-end-of-an-era-for-fort-lee-s-riviera-nightclub-1.658834?page=all.

Benenati, J. J. Dossier of subjects attending the November 14, 1957, Apalachin Meeting. Bureau of Criminal Investigation, Criminal Intelligence Unit. Report CIU-C137. [1957?]. Archived in two parts at http://afnyst.org/uploads/3/4/3/6/34369069/apalachin_benenati__comb_pgs_1-10.pdf and http://afnyst.org/uploads/3/4/3/6/34369069/apalachin_benenati__comb_pgs_11-20.pdf.

Berger, Meyer. "City Gambling Mob a Power in Jersey; As Gambling Flourished in Bergen County." *New York Times*, December 4, 1951, 36.

Billboard. "N.Y. Coinmen Entertain Brooklyn Youngsters." January 4, 1960, 71. Archived at https://books.google.com/books?id=Ch8EAAAAMBAJ&pg=PA70&lpg=PA70&dq="Coinmen+Entertain+Brooklyn+Youngsters"&source=bl&ots=1Vn37BJzYH&sig=W5SqDtqu3zayuys-Y_D0DVslg0M&hl=en&sa=X&ved=0ahUKEwiv5uiv5dTTAhViVWMKHbS1AH8Q6AEIIzAA   -v=onepage&q="Coinmen Enter.

Block, Alan A. *East Side, West Side: Organizing Crime in New York, 1930–1950*. 3rd ed. New Brunswick, NJ: Transaction Publishers, 1983.

Blumenthal, Ralph. "Illegal Dumping of Toxins Laid to Organized Crime." June 5, 1983. http://www.nytimes.com/1983/06/05/nyregion/illegal-dumping-of-toxins-laid-to-organized-crime.html?pagewanted=all.

Bonner, Lane, and Terrence Dougherty. *ELSUR Logs, 1/15/63–1/18/63*. Electronic surveillance logs. Miami Field Division. Federal Bureau of Investigation, 1963.

(Bridgewater, NJ) Courier-News. "Attend Outing." May 14, 1928.

———. "Berkeley Notes." August 24, 1928.

———. "Cosa Nostrans Summoned." October 20, 1964.

———. "Extradition Hearing Being Resumed." November 14, 1947.

———. "FBI Seizes Suspect." January 4, 1946.

———. "Gangster Slain in Hospital by Pair Who Flee." November 4, 1930.

———. "In Terror of Black Hand." January 16, 1905.

———. "Italy and America Both Warring on the Italian Criminal." January 28, 1911.

———. "Jersey's Youngest Sheriff." November 12, 1908.

———. "Louis Luciano Assassinated." February 13, 1971.

———. "Nick Delmore Deportation Ruling Due." September 3, 1953.

———. "Request Township to Erect Building." October 18, 1928.

———. "Several Court Cases Heard in Westfield." December 30, 1938.

———. "Slain Detective Was Known Here." September 16, 1918.

———. "3 Dockworkers Denied Licenses." January 2, 1954.

———. "Two Held in Robbery of Berkeley Heights Store." August 3, 1926.

———."Zwillman Balks in Crime Quiz; Faces Recall by Jury Today," August 16, 1939, 1.

Brooklyn Daily Eagle. "Son Born to Schultz during US Tax Trial." August 4, 1935, 1.

———. "Weighted, Bound Bodies of 2 Found in Jersey Waters." September 14, 1931, 19.

Brudereck, Jason. "Colorful Pair Team Up to Solve 1933 Mob Hit." *Reading (PA) Eagle*, April 16, 2007. http://www2.readingeagle.com/article.aspx?id=30419.

Bryk, William. "The Jesus de Galindez Case." *New York Press*, August 21, 2001. http://www.nypress.com/the-jesus-de-galindez-case/.

Buccino, Bob. *New Jersey Mob: Memoirs of a Top Cop*. 1st ed. Pittsburgh: Dorrance Publishing Co., 2016.

Byrne, Brendan Carney. "What Do You Call an Irishman from Atlantic City?" *Lapham's Quarterly*, November 19, 2012. http://www.laphamsquarterly.org/roundtable/what-do-you-call-irishman-atlantic-city.

Camden (NJ) Courier-Post. "Camden Man Quizzed On Gang Parley," December 3, 1957, 3.

Caparella, Kitty. "Merlino Lawyer Files Appeal on New Raps." *Philadelphia Daily News*, October 27, 2001, 9.

Carelli, Victor. *Benjamin Kutlow*. New York. Federal Bureau of Investigation. 1959.

Catena v. Seidl, 66 N.J. 32, 327 A.2d 658 (1974).

Cawley, Maureen. "Prohibition: When the Wildwoods Were 'Wet.'" *Wildwood Properties*. Accessed 3 August 2016. Available online at http://wildwoodhistory.org/prohibition-when-wildwoods-were-wet.html.

Charleston (WV) Daily Mail. "Frank Sinatra to Spurn N.J. Crime Inquiry." October 22, 1969, 12.

Chicago Tribune. "Crime Board Finds Sinatra Cooperative." February 18, 1970. http://archives.chicagotribune.com/1970/02/18/page/14/article/crime-board-finds-sinatra-cooperative/.

———. "Tax Men Win 2.4 Million of N.J. Gambler." July 13, 1965. Archived at http://archives.chicagotribune.com/1965/07/13/page/36/article/tax-men-win-2-4-million-of-n-j-gambler.

Clark, Michael, and Dan Good. "Nucky Johnson: The Man Who Ran Atlantic City for 30 Years." *Press of Atlantic City*, August 15, 2010. http://www.pressofatlanticcity.com/blogs/boardwalk_empire/nucky-johnson-the-man-who-ran-atlantic-city-for-years/article_4277415c-a815-11df-be3f-001cc4c002e0.html.

Cohen, Noah. "Newark Hosts Police Unity Tour, Officers to Pedal 320 Miles for Fallen Cops." *NJ.com*, May 9, 2016. http://www.nj.com/essex/index.ssf/2016/05/newark_hosts_police_unity_tour_as_officers_pedal_3.html.

Cohen, Rich. *Tough Jews: Fathers, Sons and Gangster Dreams*. New York: Simon and Schuster, 1998.

Commission of Investigation of the State of New Jersey. *Report for the Year 1971 of the Commission of Investigation of the State of New Jersey to the Governor and the Legislature of the State of New Jersey*. Trenton: State of New Jersey Commission of Investigation, 1972. http://www.state.nj.us/sci/pdf/annual2-1971.pdf.

———. *Report for the Year 1972 of the Commission of Investigation of the State of New Jersey to the Governor and the Legislature of the State of New Jersey*. Trenton: State of New Jersey Commission of Investigation, 1973. http://www.state.nj.us/sci/pdf/annual3-1972.pdf.

Connors, John H. *Gerardo V. Catena*. Newark. Federal Bureau of Investigation. 1964.

Conohan, Sherry. "Riggi Described as Mob Boss at Racketeering Trial." *Asbury Park (NJ) Press*, May 25, 1990, 31.

———. "Russo Tapes Tell of Mob's Atlantic City Casino Tie-Ins." *Asbury Park (NJ) Press*, February 11, 1980, 2.

Cook, Fred J. *Mafia!* 1st ed. Greenwich, CT: Fawcett, 1973.

———. "The People v. The Mob; Or, Who Rules New Jersey?" *New York Times*, February 1, 1970. http://www.nytimes.com/1970/02/01/archives/the-people-v-the-mob-or-who-rules-new-jersey-the-people-v-the-mob.html.

Cook, Joan. "Joseph (Newsboy) Moriarty, 68, Longtime Jersey Gambler, Dies." *New York Times*, February 26, 1979. http://www.nytimes.com/1979/02/26/archives/joseph-newsboy-moriarty-68-longtime-jersey-gambler-dies-money-found.html.

Criminal complaint, United States v. Charles Stango et al., (D.N.J. 2015, Mag. no. 15-3528). Available online at http://bitterqueen.typepad.com/files/decavalcante-complaint.pdf.

Culnan, Dennis M. "2 Bruno Associates Found Executed in New York." *(New Jersey) Courier-Post*, April 30, 1980.

Daniszewski, John. "Bruno Death Blamed on Power Struggle." *(New Jersey) Courier-Post*, September 11, 1980.

Dark Past of Long Branch (blog). "05. The Death of Anthony Russo." Accessed 12 April 2016. Archived at https://web.archive.org/web/20101229073940/http://darkpastoflongbranch. wikispaces.com:80/05.+The+Death+of+Anthony+Russo.

Dash, Mike. *The First Family: Terror, Extortion, Revenge, Murder and the Birth of the American Mafia.* New York: Ballantine Books, 2010.

Delaney, Bob. *Covert: My Years Infiltrating the Mob.* With Dave Scheiber. 1st ed. New York: Union Square Press, 2008.

Delaware County Daily Times. "Wiretaps Records Involve Officials," July 11, 1969.

Delmore v. Brownell, 236 F.2d 598, 600 (3rd Cir. 1956).

Detroit Free Press. "Union Leader Shot Dead," January 5, 1988, 5.

Devlin, John Patrick. *La Cosa Nostra.* Newark. Federal Bureau of Investigation. 1967.

The Disposable Heroes of Hiphopricy. "The Last Words of Dutch Schultz (This Is Insane)." *Spare Ass Annie and Other Tales.* Island Red Label PRCD 5003-2. 1993. CD.

Dowell, Ken. "Beer Barons of New Jersey: Gottfried Krueger and Max Hassel." *Off the Leash* (blog). October 25, 2015. https://offtheleash.net/2015/10/25/nj-beer-barons-2/.

Durkin, Paul G. *Harold Konigsberg.* New York. Federal Bureau of Investigation. 1965.

———. *Harold Konigsberg, Bureau Airtel 8/16/65.* Newark. Federal Bureau of Investigation. 1965.

Eastmond, William. "Indictment of Byrne's Ex Law Partner Part of Wider Probe," *Asbury Park (NJ) Press*, December 6, 1977, A7.

Edgerton, James A. "Black Hand Murder Trust." *Asbury Park (NJ) Press*, April 16, 1909, 11.

Elias v. Catena, 404 U.S. 807 (1971).

English, T. J. "The Numbers King." *New York Daily News*, June 12, 2005.

———. *Paddy Whacked: The Untold Story of the Irish American Gangster.* New York: HarperCollins Publishers, 2006.

Erik2020. "History of a Shopping Center Casino, 1963–1981," 2188. *Vegas - Now and Then* (blog). May 11, 2010. http://vegasnowandthen.blogspot.com/2010/05/history-of-shopping-center-casino.html.

Evans, C. A. *Criminal Intelligence Digest.* US Department of Justice, government memorandum. 1964.

Ex Parte Zwillman 48 F.2d 76 (3d Cir. 1931).

Federal Bureau of Investigation. "Abner Zwillman, Part 1 of 3." May 21, 1935–October 25, 1955. BUFILE 62-36085. https://vault.fbi.gov/Abner%20Zwillman/ Abner%20Zwillman%20Part%201%20of%207.

———. "Abner 'Longie' Zwillman." Full FBI Files. 1958– . Archived at https://vault.fbi.gov/ Abner%20Zwillman/Abner%20Zwillman%20Part%201%20of%207.

———."Angelo De Carlo, Aka. AR." Memorandum from Special Agent in Charge, Newark Field Office, to Director. In *Frank Sinatra FBI Files.* November 7, 1962. https://archive.org/ stream/SinatraFBI/sinatra09c_djvu.txt.

———. *Anthony Boiardo, 12/24/64. Anti-Racketeering.* Newark. 1964.

———. *Bureau Airtels Dated 10/22, 23/59.* Newark. 1959.

———. *Criminal Intelligence Program, Newark Division.* Newark. 1962.

———. *La Cosa Nostra.* 1963.

———. *La Cosa Nostra, Bureau Letter Dated 4/1/164, Miami Letter Dated 6/8/64.* Washington, DC. 1964.

———. *La Cosa Nostra, Memorandum.* Newark. 1969.

———. *La Cosa Nostra—Newark Division.* Newark Field Office. 1963.

———. *La Cosa Nostra, Re: San Diego Airtel to Bureau 10/18/67.* San Diego. 1967.

———. *The DeCarlo Tape Transcripts (Original Full Set).* 1962.

———. "General Crime Survey—Outline." In *Purple Gang (AKA Sugar House Gang)*, dossier. Newark Field Division. October 15, 1948. Text available at https://archive.org/stream/

PurpleGangAKASugarHouseGang/Pur-
ple%20Gang%20(aka%20Sugar%20House%20Gang)%2004_djvu.txt.
———. Special Agent in Charge. *Angelo Bruno, FBI Airtel 6/22/62*. Philadelphia. 1962.
———. Special Agent in Charge. *Anthony Boiardo, Aka. Ar, Bureau Airtel 11/24/64*. Newark.
    1964.
———. Special Agent in Charge. *Top Hoodlum Program Weekly Summary, Anthony "Ham"
    Dolasco Herman 'Red Cohen*. Newark Field Office. 1960.
Fishman, Joanne A. "Pappy Seaman, Now 92, Still Active in Designing." *New York Times*,
    April 6, 1975. http://www.nytimes.com/1975/04/06/archives/pappy-seaman-now-92-still-
    active-in-designing.html.
Fitchburg (MA) Sentinel. "Defendant Missing in Gem Case Trial," February 2, 1937, 1.
———. "Jury Charged in Gem Case," February 10, 1937, 10.
Flynn, James P. *La Cosa Nostra, File 92-6054*. New York Field Office. Federal Bureau of
    Investigation. 1963.
Flood, John J. Document regarding *US v. Palmieri*. IPSN.org (blog) http://www.ipsn.org/
    court_cases/us_vs_palmeri_et_al-appeal-1980-09-03.htm.
Foderaro, T. J. "When the Jersey Shore Was Rum Row." *Inside Jersey*, April 27, 2012. http://
    www.nj.com/inside-jersey/index.ssf/2012/04/when_the_jersey_shore_was_rum_row.html.
Fresolone, George and Robert J. Wagman. *Blood Oath: The Heroic Story of a Gangster Turned
    Government Agent Who Brought Down One of America's Most Powerful Mob Families*.
    New York: Simon and Schuster, 1995.
Funderburg, J. Anne. *Bootleggers and Beer Barons of the Prohibition Era*. 1st ed. Jefferson,
    NC: McFarland, 2014.
Gallagher, Maria. "Boom Times for the Mob?" *Philadelphia Daily News*, January 20, 1984.
Glaser, Martha. *The German-American Bund in New Jersey*. 1st ed. Ann Arbor: University of
    Michigan Press, 1974.
Gold, Jeffrey. "Witnesses Blasted in 'Skinny Joey' Trial." *(Bridgewater, NJ) Courier-News*,
    February 3, 2004, 3.
Goldstein, Joseph. "Along New York Harbor, 'On the Waterfront' Endures." *New York Times*,
    January 6, 2017. https://www.nytimes.com/2017/01/06/nyregion/new-york-harbor-on-the-
    waterfront.html.
Greenhouse, Linda. "The Ellis Island Verdict: The Ruling; High Court Gives New Jersey Most
    of Ellis Island." *New York Times*, May 27, 1998. http://www.nytimes.com/1998/05/27/
    nyregion/ellis-island-verdict-ruling-high-court-gives-new-jersey-most-ellis-island.html.
Grover, Warren. *Nazis in Newark*. New Brunswick, NJ: Transaction Publishers, 2003.
Hafer, Gary. "Mafia in Apalachin." *GreaterOwego.com*. Accessed November 12, 2016. http://
    www.greaterowego.com/apalachin/apalachin01.htm.
Haller, Mark H. "Philadelphia Bootlegging and the Report of the Special August Grand Jury."
    Pennsylvania Magazine of History and Biography, April 1, 1985, 215–33. https://journals.
    psu.edu/pmhb/article/view/44049/43770.
Heine, William. "Witnesses Say Mob Money Started Joker Poker Firm." *Asbury Park (NJ)
    Press*, June 25, 1993.
Hendley, Nate. *Dutch Schultz: The Brazen Beer Baron of New York*. 1st ed. Neustadt, Ont.:
    Five Rivers Chapmanry, 2011.
Hoffman, Paul. "The Unmaking of Mayor Addonizio." *Tiger in the Court: Herbert J. Stern*.
    Chicago: Playboy Press. Text available at http://mafianj.com/addonizio/addonizio8.shtml.
Hosie, William G. "An Honest Bootlegger Can Make Money; They're Mostly Crooks; Says
    'King' McCoy." *Brooklyn Daily Eagle*, December 16, 1923, 61.
Illson, Murray. "DeCarlo of Mafia Dead of Cancer." *New York Times*, October 21, 1973. http://
    www.nytimes.com/1973/10/21/archives/decarlo-of-mafia-dead-of-cancer-impropriety-
    denied-mobster.html.
Immerso, Michael. *Newark's Little Italy: The Vanished First Ward*. New Brunswick, NJ:
    Rutgers University Press, 1999.
In Re Robilotto, 24 N.J. Super. 209 (1953).
Jackson, Chanta L. "Iconic 'Goodfella' Robert Bisaccia Dies in Prison." *NJ.com*, December 4,
    2008. http://www.nj.com/newark/index.ssf/2008/12/iconic_goodfella_robert_bisacc.html.

Johnson, Nelson. *Boardwalk Empire: The Birth, High Times, and Corruption of Atlantic City.* 1st ed. Medford, NJ: Plexus Publishing, 2010.

Jones, Thom L. "Whack Out on Willie Moretti." *Gangsters Inc* (website), November 18, 2008. http://gangstersinc.ning.com/profiles/blogs/whack-out-on-willie-moretti.

Kaplan, James. *Sinatra: The Chairman.* 1st ed. New York: Knopf Doubleday Publishing Group, 2016.

Kentucky New Era. "Gambler Shot Dead by 4 Men." October 5, 1951.

Kilgallen, Dorothy. "Some Question Suicide of 'Longie' Zwillman." Syndicated. March 5, 1959.

Knoedelseder, William. K. Jr. *Los Angeles Times.* "Growing Force of Investigators Probes Mob Ties to Record Industry." October 19, 1986. http://articles.latimes.com/1986-10-19/business/fi-6153_1_record-industry.

Kramer, Michael. "Is Something Rotten in the State of New Jersey?" *New York Magazine*, October 1973, 75–83.

Lansing (MI) State Journal. "Six Men Nabbed in Armed Robbery." November 10, 1947.

Lebanon (PA) Daily News. "Retired Gambling Czar Is Burned, Beaten." May 28, 1971, 21.

Leggett, Ben. "Smuggling with the 'Real McCoy.'" *Drinking Cup.* Accessed September 3, 2016. http://www.drinkingcup.net/1920-smuggling-with-the-real-mccoy/.

Leonetti, Philip, Scott M. Burnstein, and Christopher Graziano. *Mafia Prince: Inside America's Most Violent Crime Family and the Bloody Fall of la Cosa Nostra.* San Diego: Running Press, 2014.

Life. "The Congressman and the Hoodlum." August 9, 1968, 21–26. Archived at https://books.google.com/books?id=RT8EAAAAMBAJ&pg=PA22&lpg=PA22&dq.

———. "A Gangster Is Buried in the Old-Time Style." October 22, 1951, 36–37. Archived at https://books.google.com/books?id=rFQEAAAAMBAJ&pg=PA36&lpg=PA36   -v= onepage&q&f=false.

———. "From Shadows, Hoodlums: A Searching Look at Big Crime." February 23, 1959, 19–28. Archived at https://books.google.com/books?id=L0gEAAAAMBAJ&pg=PA19& source=gbs_toc_r&cad=2 -v=onepage&q&f=false.

Limited. "Anthony Rotondo 2005 Cross Examination." *The Black Hand Forum.* Posted by B. May 7, 2016. http://theblackhand.club/forum/viewtopic.php?f=29&t=1824&hilit=rotondo+cross+examination (registration required).

Lincoln J. Stokes. *Joseph Arthur Zicarelli.* Newark. Federal Bureau of Investigation. 1959.

Linnett, Richard. *In the Godfather Garden: The Long Life and Times of Richie "the Boot" Boiardo.* 1st ed. New Brunswick, NJ: Rutgers University Press, 2013.

Linsky, Don. *Atlantic City and Gaming.* E-book. 1st ed. N.p.: Eagleton Institute of Politics, 2014.

Lipari, John. "Vittorio Castle 1937–1952," *Newark's Attic* (blog), March 27, 2016. https://newarksattic.blog/2016/03/27/vittorio-castle-1937-1952/.

Lumbard, J. Edward. "The Administration of Criminal Justice: Some Problems and Their Resolution." *American Bar Association Journal* 49, no. 9 (1963): 840–47. Text archived at https://books.google.com/books?id=Nm9bGkl8pMwC&pg=PA840&lpg=PA840&dq= Lumbard,+J.+Edward.+"The+Administration+of+Criminal+Justice:+Some+Problems+ and+Their+Resolution."&source=bl&ots=3hT_r0ERV2&sig=elrRT1ulWZqbgSd3NR-H18U-lH8&hl=en&sa=X&ved=0ahUKEwix6q_ 3ndfTAhUK3mMKHQhIALoQ6AEIKDAB#v=onepage&q=Lumbard%2C%20J. %20Edward. %20"The%20Administration%20of%20Criminal%20Justice%3A%20Some%20Problems %20and%20Their%20Resolution."&f=false.

Maas, Peter. *The Valachi Papers.* 1st ed. London: Panther Books, 1970.

Manahan, Kevin. "The King Of Cool and His 500 Club." *NJ Advance Media*, September 26, 2011. http://www.nj.com/inside-jersey/index.ssf/2011/09/the_king_of_cool_and_his_500_ club.html.

Martens, Frederick T. *We'll Make You an Offer You Can't Refuse: A Primer on the Investigation of Public Corruption.* 1st ed. N.p.: Mint Associates, 2015.

Marzulli, John. "Dock Union Bigs Go on Trial Accused of Plotting with Mob." *New York Daily News*, September 21, 2005, http://www.nydailynews.com/archives/boroughs/dock-union-bigs-trial-accused-plotting-mob-article-1.566257.

McCullough, John. "NJ Beer Baron Is Named Chief Suspect in Slayings." *Philadelphia Inquirer*, September 23, 1930.

Miller, Harlan S. "'Rum Row' Produces Volsteadian Hero in Mccoy, Skipper Chief." *Pittsburgh Post*, November 28, 1923.

Mintz, John. "A Mob Seen." *Washington Post*, January 9, 1980. https://www.washingtonpost.com/archive/politics/1980/01/09/a-mob-seen/42a1e174-0255-4092-8121-d3170c45cbeb/.

Monmouth County Archives. *The Bootlegger Era: Prohibition in New Jersey*. Exhibit at the Monmouth County Library Headquarters. Manalapan, NJ: Monmouth County Archives, 2013. Text archived at https://archive.org/stream/TheBootleggerEraProhibitioninNewJersey/Prohibition_exhibition_ FINAL_djvu.txt.

MonopolyCity.com (blog). "Early Hotels—From Atlantic City's Nostalgic Past." 2008. http://www.monopolycity.com/ac_earlyhotels.html.

Moore, Bob, and Bill John. "History: Jersey Speed Skiffs." *Vintage Race Boat Shop*. Accessed 27 January 2016. http://www.vintageraceboatshop.com/JerseySpeedSkiffs.htm.

Mosier, Anne. "Police Trace Mobster's Last Day." *(Bridgewater, NJ) Courier-News*, April 11, 1977.

Musleah, Rahel. "The Jewish Traveler: Atlantic City," *Hadassah Magazine*, June 2011. http://www.hadassahmagazine.org/2011/06/13/atlantic-city/.

National Commission for the Review of Federal and State Laws Relating to Wiretapping and Electronic Surveillance. *Commission Hearings, Volume 2*. Washington, DC: 1976. Text available at https://archive.org/stream/commissionhearin02unit/commissionhearin02unit_djvu.txt.

(Newark, OH) Advocate. "Boardwalk Possible Center of Crime." December 9, 1976, 30.

Newark Star-Eagle. "Another Faces Quiz in Lottery Deaths." September 14, 1935.

———. "Release Due in Gang Killings." September 15, 1935.

(New Jersey) Courier-Post. "Few Mourn Zwillman at Newark Vigil." February 27, 1959.

———. "Jury Finds 'Gyp' DeCarlo Guilty on All 3 Counts in Loansharking Case," January 29, 1970.

New Jersey State Commission of Investigation. *Report to the Special Committee to Review the State Commission of Investigation*. Trenton: New Jersey State Commission of Investigation, 1995.

———. *Video Gambling*. Trenton: New Jersey State Commission of Investigation, 2001. http://www.state.nj.us/sci/pdf/video.pdf.

New Jersey State Police. *Analysis of DeCavalcante Tapes*. Handwritten notes. 1970.

———. *Analysis of DeCavalcante Tapes*. Handwritten notes. 1968.

Newton, Michael. *The Mafia at Apalachin, 1957*. 1st ed. Jefferson, NC: McFarland, 2012.

New York Times. "Boxer Is Shot Dead in Newark Tavern." February 23, 1937, 24.

———. "Enoch L. Johnson, Ex-Boss in Jersey; Prohibition-Era Ruler of Atlantic City, 85, Dies." December 10, 1968, 47.

———. "Rum Runner Caught; See 'Startling' Plot; Schooner Under British Flag Taken Beyond Three-Mile Limit Without Legal Precedent. MASTER AND MATE ESCAPE Vessel Brought Here and Her Crew Detained as Officials Seek Heads of Conspiracy." August 3, 1921.

———. "Sleuth Kills Saloon Keeper," March 6, 1909.

———. "Third Shooting Victim Dies." August 24, 1935.

———. "2 Slain, 3 Wounded by Jersey Gunmen; Score of Revolver Shots Rake Candy Store in the Italian Section of Newark." August 23, 1935, 5.

North Adams (MA) Transcript. "Mrs. Kennedy Goes on Stand." February 3, 1937, 1.

Pace, Eric. "Eboli Chauffeur Being Questioned." *New York Times*, July 18, 1972. http://www.nytimes.com/1972/07/18/archives/eboli-chauffeur-being-questioned-tells-police-he-didnt-see-killer.html.

———. "Police, Seeking Crime Figures Named by His Chauffeur, Film Eboli Cortege." *New York Times*, July 20, 1972. http://www.nytimes.com/1972/07/20/archives/police-seeking-crime-figures-named-by-his-chauffeur-film-eboli.html.

Palisades Interstate Park Commission, New Jersey. "Remembering 'America's Showplace.'" *Cliff Notes*, January 2006. http://www.njpalisades.org/rememberingAmericasShowplace.html.

Parker, M. B., Special Agent. *Nevada Gambling Industry*. Las Vegas. Federal Bureau of Investigation. 1964.

Patrick, Francis. "Killer Who Squealed on 9 Mobsters Faces Death Each Day." *San Antonio Star*, June 6, 1976.

Pearce, J. Robert. *Angelo Bruno, Aka Angelo Bruno, Analore (True Name), Ange, Russo*. Special summary report. Philadelphia. Federal Bureau of Investigation. 1961.

———. *Angelo Bruno Aka, 1/16/59*. Anti-Racketeering. Philadelphia. Federal Bureau of Investigation. 1959.

———. Drew Pearson, "Washington Merry Go Round," syndicated column, 1957, archived at http://auislandora.wrlc.org/islandora/object/pearson%3A1?page=761.

———. *Angelo Bruno, Special Summary Report*. Philadelphia. FBI. 1962.

Pennsylvania Crime Commission. *1981 Annual Report*. St. Davids: Pennsylvania Crime Commission, 1982. Archived at https://www.ncjrs.gov/pdffiles1/Digitization/83697NCJRS.pdf.

———. *1975–76 Report*. St. Davids: Pennsylvania Crime Commission, 1977. Archived at https://www.ncjrs.gov/pdffiles1/Digitization/49097NCJRS.pdf.

———. *Organized Crime in Pennsylvania: A Decade of Change; 1990 Report*. Conshohocken: Pennsylvania Crime Commission, 1991. Archived at https://www.ncjrs.gov/pdffiles1/Digitization/133208NCJRS.pdf.

Pensacola News Journal. "Sinatra Wins Extension on Testifying." January 14, 1970.

Perlmutter, Emanuel. "A Key Gang Figure Slain in Brooklyn." *New York Times*, July 17, 1972. http://www.nytimes.com/1972/07/17/archives/a-key-gang-figure-slain-in-brooklyn-eboli-is-felled-by-5-bullets-in.html.

Permanent Subcommittee on Investigations of the Committee on Governmental Affairs United States Senate. *Waterfront Corruption*. Washington, DC: US Senate, 1984.

Philadelphia Inquirer. "Five Men Rounded Up in $100,00 Pay Holdup." November 10, 1947.

———. "Suspect Seized Here in Murder of Dry Agent," September 22, 1930, 4.

———. "2 Gangsters Slain, Drowned in Jersey." September 14, 1931.

Philly.com. "Mob Scene: 'Tony Bananas.'" YouTube video, 4:12. Posted June 2, 2009. https://www.youtube.com/watch?v=qPnCotgE9GM.

Pittsburgh Post-Gazette. "Dry Agent Is Slain in Raid on Brewery." September 20, 1930, 1.

Pittsburgh Press. "'Longy' Zwillman Hangs Self in Home." February 26, 1959.

Plainfield (NJ) Courier-News. "30 Indicted in Newark Investigation." December 3, 1937, 18.

———. "'Farmer' Delmore Buys 200 Acres Near Freehold." February 20, 1943, 2.

———. "Former Boxer Slain, Brother Is Wounded." February 23, 1937.

(Pottstown, PA) Mercury. "Reputed Mobster, on Prison Furlough, Is Shot to Death." April 11, 1977, 8.

Powers, Thomas. *John Lardiere*. Newark: FBI, 1965.

Press State House Bureau. "Russo Is Freed after Agreeing to Talk with SCI." *Asbury Park (NJ) Press*, April 12, 1974.

Red Bank (NJ) Register. "Killed in Street Fight." October 24, 1923.

Reno Evening Gazette. "Plea Bargaining Sought in Casino Profit-Skimming Case." July 1, 1981.

Reuter, Arthur L. *Report on the Activities and Associations of Persons Identified as Present at the Residence of Joseph Barbara, Sr., at Apalachin, New York, on November 14, 1957, and the Reasons for Their Presence*. State of New York Executive Department, Office of the Commission of Investigation. [New York]: Commissioner of Investigation, 1958.

Reyn, Irina, ed. *Living on the Edge of the World: New Jersey Writers Take On the Garden State*. New York: Touchstone, 2007.

Rising Sun Brewing Co. v. United States, 55 F.2d 827 (1932).

Rockford (IL) Morning Star. "Truce Declared by Gangsters." August 20, 1930.

Ross, Richard C. *Nicodemo Dominick Scarfo*. Newark. Federal Bureau of Investigation. 1973.

Rudolph, Robert. *The Boys from New Jersey: How the Mob Beat the Feds*. 1st ed. New Brunswick, NJ: Rutgers University Press, 1995.

———. "Solving a Two-Decade-Old Mafia Hit." *(New Jersey) Star Ledger*, February 9, 1998. Text archived at http://www.oocities.org/stevenlenehan/19980209.html.

Russell, Michael. *Undercover Cop: How I Brought Down the Real-Life Sopranos*. With Patrick Picciarelli. 1st ed. New York: Thomas Dunne Books, 2013.

SAGE Publishing. *CQ Almanac Online Edition: 1963*. 2017. https://library.cqpress.com/cqalmanac/document.php?id=cqal63-1315434 (registration required).

St. Petersburg (FL) Times. "New Jersey Police Chief, Awaiting Trial, Ends Life." October 7, 1951. Archived at https://news.google.com/newspapers?id=yR0LAAAAIBAJ&sjid=GE8DAAAAIBAJ&pg=2035,2095540&dq=fort+lee+police.

Sann, Paul. *Kill the Dutchman! The Story of Dutch Schultz*. 1st ed. N.p.: Birdye's Books LLC, 2015.

Sarasota Herald-Tribune. "Big Rum Ring Did Business of Huge Size." October 20, 1929.

Scarpo, Ed [pseud.]. "The Mafia Hit the Jackpot with the Slot-Machine." *Cosa Nostra News* (website), June 9, 2015. http://www.cosanostranews.com/2015/06/the-mafia-hit-jackpot-with-slot-machine.html.

Senate Permanent Subcommittee on Investigations, United States of America. *Organized Crime and Illicit Traffic in Narcotics: Hearing Before the U.S. Senate Permanent Subcommittee on Investigations, Part 1, Part 2, Part 3, Part 4, Part 5, and Index, September 25, 27, October 1, 2, 8, and 9, 1963; October 10, 11, 15, and 16, 1963; October 29, 1963, July 28, 29, and 30, 1964*. [Washington, DC]: US Congress, 1964. Archived at https://www.ncjrs.gov/pdffiles1/Digitization/119303NCJRS.pdf.

Shamokin (PA) News-Dispatch. "Hunt Beer Runners in Connection with Slaying." September 22, 1930.

Sherman, Ted. "Mob Arrests Show Wiseguys Still at Work in N.J., Feds Say." *NJ Advance Media*, August 6, 2016. http://www.nj.com/crime/index.ssf/2016/08/another_big_mob_hit_this_one_b.html.

Sherman, William, and Matt Sullivan. "Bidder End for Mob House." *New York Daily News*, August 4, 2002. http://www.nydailynews.com/archives/news/bidder-mob-house-article-1.493826.

Shore News Today (Marmora, NJ). "In Another Time > Prohibition Came to the Boardwalk, Several Times." October 18, 2011. http://www.shorenewstoday.com/wildwood/history/in-another-time-prohibition-came-to-the-boardwalk-several-times/article_7ea3c062-4535-508c-89e9-63cb5465959a.html.

Sinatra v. New Jersey State Commission of Investigation, 311 F.Supp. 678 (D.N.J. 1970).

Smigelski, Fred W. "Addonizio Is Guilty of Extortion." *Philadelphia Inquirer*, July 23, 1970.

Smith, Kati Cornell. "Gotti Whacked My Dad: Canary." *New York Post*, August 17, 2005. http://nypost.com/2005/08/17/gotti-whacked-my-dad-canary/.

Smith, Sandy. "Power Struggle after a Death in the Family." *Life*, February 28, 1969.

Springsteen, Bruce. "Atlantic City." *Nebraska*. Columbia Records CBS 2794, 1982, LP.

Sullivan, Ronald. "Jersey Lawmaker Is Facing Inquiry." *New York Times*, February 6, 1971. http://www.nytimes.com/1971/02/06/archives/jersey-lawmaker-is-facing-inquiry-court-disciplinary-hearing.html.

———. "A Jersey Legislator Cited on Bar Ethics; 2d Guilty in U.S. Suit." *New York Times*, February 24, 1971. http://www.nytimes.com/1971/02/24/archives/a-jersey-legislator-cited-on-bar-ethics-2d-guilty-in-us-suit-a.html.

State of Florida Organized Crime Control Council. *1976 Annual Report*. Tallahassee: State of Florida, 1977. https://www.ncjrs.gov/pdffiles1/Digitization/44576NCJRS.pdf.

State of New Jersey Commission of Investigation. *The Changing Face of Organized Crime in New Jersey: A Status Report*. Trenton: State of New Jersey Commission of Investigation, 2004. http://www.state.nj.us/sci/pdf/ocreport.pdf.

———. *Industrious Subversion: Circumvention of Oversight in Solid Waste and Recycling in New Jersey*. Trenton: State of New Jersey Commission of Investigation, 2011. http://www.state.nj.us/sci/pdf/Solid Waste Report.pdf.

————. *Ninth Annual Report of the Commission of Investigation of the State of New Jersey to the Governor and the Legislature of the State of New Jersey*. Trenton: The Commission of Investigation of the State of New Jersey, 1978. http://www.state.nj.us/sci/pdf/annual9.pdf.

————. *Report and Recommendations of the State of New Jersey Commission of Investigation on the Incursion by Organized Crime into Certain Legitimate Businesses in Atlantic City*. Trenton: The Commission of Investigation of the State of New Jersey, 1977.

————.*Report for the Year 1974 of the Commission of Investigation of the State of New Jersey to the Governor and the Legislature of the State of New Jersey*. Trenton: State of New Jersey Commission of Investigation, 1975. Available online at https://dspace.njstatelib.org/xmlui/bitstream/handle/10929/17136/5annual1974.pdf?sequence=1&isAllowed=y.

————. *21st Annual Report: 1989*. Trenton: State of New Jersey Commission of Investigation, 1990. Archived at http://www.state.nj.us/sci/pdf/annual21.pdf.

State of New Jersey Department of Law and Public Safety, Division of Gaming Enforcement. "Attorney General Harvey Announces Filing of Complaint to Revoke License of Company Tied to Mob." Press release. November 15, 2005.

State v. Zicarelli, 300 A.2d 154 (N.J. Supr. 1973).

State v. Zicarelli, 381 A.2d 398 (N.J. Supr. 1977).

Sterling, Guy. "Arrest Ends Long Search for Suspect in Mob Killing." *(Newark, NJ) Star-Ledger*, March 13, 2007. Text available online at http://johnnieupahts1.proboards.com/thread/36.

————. "A Mob Chief's Desire for Respect and Murder." *Newark Star-Ledger*, February 21, 2004.

Stratton, Richard. "The Man Who Killed Dutch Schultz." *GQ*, September 2001.

Straus, G. V. "The Newark, NJ Police." *The Police Journal* 7 (March 1921): 78.

Strunsky, Steve. "3 Plead Guilty to Extorting Christmas 'Tributes' from Longshoremen." *NJ Advance Media*, December 19, 2014. http://www.nj.com/news/index.ssf/2014/12/3_plead_guilty_extorting_longshoremen.html.

Stuart, Mark A. *Gangster No. 2: Longy Zwillman, the Man Who Invented Organized Crime*. Washington, DC: Lyle Stuart, 1985.

Swiggum, Sue, and Marj Kohli. "Ship Descriptions - R." *TheShipsList* (website). Last updated June 6, 2008. http://www.theshipslist.com/ships/descriptions/ShipsR.shtml.

Taggert, Edward A. *Bootlegger: Max Hassel, the Millionaire Newsboy*. 1st ed. New York: Writer's Showcase, 2003.

Talburtt, Orville R. *La Cosa Nostra- New Haven Division*. New Haven: FBI, 1963.

Tamm, E. A. *Re: Crime Situation in Newark*. Memo to the director. Newark. Federal Bureau of Investigation. 1935.

Tomlinson, Gerald. *Murdered in Jersey*. New Brunswick, NJ: Rutgers University Press, 1994.

Tona Frank v. Metropolitan Life Insurance Company (Supreme Court Appellate Division- First Department 1934).

Trento, Joe, and Jacquie Powers. "Not Guilty Plea Is Entered by Jock." *(Wilmington, DE) Morning News*, April 13, 1978, 3.

Trenton Evening News. "Lottery Gunfire Kills Two." August 22, 1935.

Trenton Evening Times. "Finger Man Held in Dual Slaying." August 23, 1935.

Tuttle, Brad R. *How Newark Became Newark*. New Brunswick, NJ: Rivergate Books, 2009.

United Press. "Billion Annual Tribute at Stake in New York's Vice and Racket Inquiry." *(Hammond, IN) Times*, July 24, 1935, 68.

————. "Capone Made Peace with Moran Gang." *Mount Carmel (PA) Item*. May 17, 1929.

US Bureau of the Census. *Fourteenth Census of the United States: 1920; 11th District–Newark*. [Washington, DC]: Department of Commerce, 1922.

US Congress. *Brief on Federal Intervention in Organized Gambling*, 1951.

————. *Hearings Before the Select Committee to Investigate Organized Crime in Interstate Commerce, Part 12*. Washington, DC, 1951.

————. *Senate Resolution 202, 81st Congress*. 1950.

United States Russo v. State of New Jersey, 438 F.2d 1343 (3d cir. 1971).

US Treasury Department, Bureau of Narcotics. *Mafia: The Government's Secret File on Organized Crime*. 1st ed. New York: HarperCollins, 2007.

US Senate. *Departments of State, Justice, and Commerce, the Judiciary, and Related Appropriations for Fiscal Year 1968: Hearings Before a Subcommittee of the Committee on Appropriations.* 90th Cong. 1967. Archived at https://babel.hathitrust.org/cgi/pt?id=uc1.$b642655;view=1up;seq=9.

US Senate, Special Committee to Investigate Organized Crime in Interstate Commerce. "(b) Northern New Jersey." *Kefauver Committee: Final Report, Aug. 31, 1951.* 82nd Cong. (1951), 65–72. Archived at http://www.onewal.com/kef/kef4.html#northern.

United States v. Alberti, 568 F.2d 617 (CA2 1977).

United States v. Angelo Decarlo et al. Appellant in No. 18705. Appeal of Daniel Cecere, 458 F.2d 358 (3d Cir. 1972).

United States v. Bendetti, 498 F.Supp. 450 (D.N.J. 1980).

United States v. Bonanno Organized Crime Family, 695 F. Supp. 1426, (E.D.N.Y. 1988).

United States v. Bufalino, 285 F.2d 408, (2d cir. 1960).

United States v. Joseph Merlino, 310 F.3d 137 (3d Cir. 2002).

United States v. Merlino, 204 F.Supp 2d 83, 92 (2002).

United States v. Palmieri, 630 F.2d 192 (3d Cir. 1980).

United States v. Riggi, 951 F.2d 1368 (3rd cir. 1991).

United States v. Stephen Depiro et al., 2011.

Van Meter, Jonathan. *The Last Good Time: Skinny D'Amato, the Notorious 500 Club, and the Rise and Fall of Atlantic City.* 1st ed. New York: Three Rivers Press, 2003.

Vincent Aloi And Others. Washington, DC: Justice Department, 1972.

Volz, Joseph, and Peter J. Bridge. *The Mafia Talks.* Greenwich, CT: Fawcett Gold Medal, 1969.

Waggoner, Walter H. "Accused Mobsters Still Silent." *New York Times*, November 24, 1974. http://www.nytimes.com/1974/11/24/archives/accused-mobsters-still-silent-catena-practices-golf-the-silent-nine.html.

Wells, Robert. *Anti Racketeering Conspiracy.* New York: FBI, 1968.

Wilgus, John P. *The Criminal Commission, Newark Division.* Newark: FBI, 1963.]

(Wilmington, DE) Evening Journal. "Men, Ablaze, Flee as Still Explodes." October 25, 1927.

(Wilmington, DE) Morning News. "Fugitive in Slaying of Dry Agent Caught," October 20, 1933.

———. "Newark Gangster Is 'Put On Spot,'" November 27, 1930.

(York, PA) Gazette and Daily. "Jewel Robbers Get Term in Prison," February 11, 1937.

Zecker, Robert M. *Metropolis: The American City in Popular Culture.* Westport, CT: Praeger Publishers, 2007.

Index

About the Author

Scott M. Deitche is author of seven books on organized crime. He has also written dozens of articles on organized crime for local and national magazines and newspapers. Scott has been featured on the Discovery Channel, the History Channel, A&E, C-SPAN, Oxygen, and American Heroes channel, as well as on dozens of national and local news and radio shows. Scott lives in St. Petersburg, Florida.

2019